# UNBREAKABLE SPIRIT

## Rising Above All Odds

RAINER ZITELMANN

# UNBREAKABLE SPIRIT

## Rising Above All Odds

ISBN: 978-1-962825-04-7

ATLAS ELITE
PUBLISHING
PARTNERS

# Contents

# Foreword - Saliya Kahawatte

"You'll never make the grade!" I remember sitting there in front of my high school principal as he gravely uttered those words. He put his glasses back on and leaned over the table to examine the certificate from the eye clinic in front of him for the umpteenth time. "You are almost blind. Let's face it, you won't get anywhere here. You need to transfer to a school for the blind and learn braille." Somewhat shaken, I slid around on my chair in the drab, unimaginatively furnished principal's office, sadly shifted my gaze to the floor, and felt my mother somewhat tentatively reach for my right hand. "Saliya, don't be sad. You're going to have to learn to live with your disability. Your life is going to be very different from now on."

Even though so much time has passed, I still vividly remember this dramatic turn of events. I had always been a carefree and happy-go-lucky kid. In late summer 1985, I was 15 years old. I had just transferred to high school, into the tenth grade. A few weeks before the long summer vacation, I was diagnosed with a severe retinal detachment, which left me with a 100% disability. Most of my vision was irretrievably lost. I see the world as if through a thick pane of frosted glass, everything is gray and very blurry.

I didn't follow the ophthalmologist's advice or the school board's recommendations—I made my decision very quickly: "I want to stay in the world of the sighted and pursue a career, whatever it takes!" After only a few days, I put my plans into action and feverishly searched for a new way to somehow follow the lessons at school. "If you can't do it with your eyes," I told myself, "Why not try it with your ears?" as I focused my attention entirely on my teacher's words.

After just a few weeks, I had trained myself to effortlessly memorize six hours of spoken material at a stretch. In the afternoons, I went back over the lessons that I had stored in my long-term memory's "mailbox." That was how I did my homework. And because I couldn't check what I had written, my mother or sister read it all back to me in the evening so that I could make sure I had written everything down correctly.

Perhaps surprisingly, my grades didn't really suffer. By the end of the first semester, my teachers were convinced I had what it would take to make it through regular high school. Even as a teenager, I quickly realized that the only way to compensate for my disability and keep up with the lessons was through hard work and self-discipline. It was clear to me that I couldn't afford to use my time like my classmates did. While they went to the disco, got their driver's licenses, or went on dates, I sat alone at my desk and struggled through the increasingly demanding subject matter.

In 1989, I graduated from high school. To put it mildly, I was overjoyed. I had achieved my first goal. Unfortunately, my moment of success was short-lived. Not long after, my parents separated, and I needed to grow up quickly. I wanted to be able to stand on my own two feet, so I applied for an apprenticeship in the hotel industry. I was totally honest about my disability in every application I sent. Although my grades were good, I wasn't invited to a single interview. It was clear that Germany's strict regulations on hiring and firing disabled people scared most employers. So, I decided to take a risk. In my next few applications, I didn't mention my disability at all. Suddenly, potential employers wanted to meet me. At the end of my very first interview, I was offered a training position as a hotel manager in a five-star hotel.

Just like at high school, I was left almost entirely to my own devices. My only ally was the will to make it somehow. The first day of my apprenticeship was the start of my "Mission Impossible." With clouded vision, I set out in search of the secret, hidden paths that would lead me to my goal in the world of the sighted.

I memorized hundreds of item numbers so that I could enter orders into the cash register "blind," and I trained my sense of touch so that I could place cutlery and glasses correctly on guests' tables. With my finely attuned sense of hearing, I could tell by the sound of a glass whether I had polished it to a shine, and I mixed exotic cocktails at the bar, following recipes I knew by heart and pouring the drinks into glasses by feel. Fortunately, I secretly had someone in my corner; one of the other apprentices knew about my handicap, kept it to himself, and helped me as much as he could when it looked like someone might discover my secret. After passing my final exams, I moved to Hamburg. Again, I concealed my disability and continued my career in the luxury hotel business as a waiter captain.

In the summer of 1994, I opened my own restaurant with my then girlfriend. We felt like we had the world at our feet and were spending money like there was no tomorrow. It was a great time and I remember it fondly. But again, life had another painful twist up its sleeve: I was diagnosed with cancer. A year of exhausting chemotherapy and radiation followed.

It was a close shave. Once I was back on my feet, I slowly fought my way back to work. Unfortunately, the next challenge was already waiting for me. Our restaurant was about to go under. While I was unable to work, my debts to suppliers and the tax authorities had become unmanageable. There was no way we could get the business back on an even keel. The restaurant went bankrupt, and I broke up with my girlfriend in an argument about money.

I was destitute. My life had fallen apart. I was kicked out of my apartment and forced to live on the street. I became severely depressed. On a cool, gloomy fall day, I was standing in front of a homeless shelter, my head tilted to the sky, when the bright yellow beams of the sun broke through the clouds. The pleasantly warm sensation of the sun's rays on my skin inspired a flash of inspiration. I chided myself. "Hey, remember your plan. It's high time to get a move on!" Again, I concealed my disability and returned to the luxury hotel business. I became a bartender, a sommelier, and even a head waiter.

I was pushing myself to the limit every single day. My job was a house of cards built on a foundation of lies. I played the role of a sighted person without realizing that I had bitten off more than I could chew. With every new responsibility at work, my anxiety increased. Again and again, I was overcome by violent pangs of self-doubt, which sawed with a sharp, jagged blade at the very core of my being.

At some point, I couldn't take it anymore. I turned to alcohol and medication to numb the pain, and at work I fueled myself with cheap drugs so that I could get through the day unscathed.

When I became a restaurant manager, I had to write duty rosters, program the computerized cash registers and check the trainees' logbooks. This time, the stakes were too high, the foundation of lies crumbled under my feet, and I completely fell apart. I lost my job. All I could do was mope around at home, feeling useless and lost. I started drinking even more. I reached rock bottom, a total addict. I had completely given up on myself.

After numerous suicide attempts, I was admitted to a closed psychiatric ward, where I spent several months, followed by long-term therapy. I realized that I needed to reassess everything I had ever done before I could start planning a new life.

One cold, rainy March evening, I trudged through the park behind the clinic where I was having therapy, talking incessantly to myself. Although the rain was getting heavier, I just kept walking until, at some point, I stopped, completely soaked, raised my fists to the dark sky and screamed, "You have to accept your disability!" Sobbing, I slumped on a wooden bench under a streetlight and stared into a puddle. I made my decision: "Your lies led you to this point. From this moment on, you need to be honest about your disability!"

After therapy, I started in a workshop for the disabled and attended the Hamburg school for the blind, where I learned to use special software, which let me write emails and surf the net on my own. I wanted to get out of the workshop and was ready to look for my next challenge.

In the summer of 2003, I enrolled in an international management degree program and, after successfully completing it, made a point of being totally honest about my severe disability in every job application I sent. My disability cast an impenetrable shadow over the brilliant grades of my bachelor's degree. I wrote more than 250 applications. Not a single employer responded. HR managers simply couldn't look past my disability. They clearly didn't appreciate my positive self-image, willpower, and self-discipline. "Giving up is not an option, you have to try a different approach," I thought to myself one day. Then I had an epiphany: "Turn your flaw into a brand and build your own business on your disability!"

Although I was living on unemployment benefits, had no start-up capital and the economy was about to tank as the financial crisis hit, I confidently went into the market with my "vendor's tray." I was determined to try my luck as a writer, coach, and consultant. My first year of self-employment was a disaster. I tried cold calling but didn't manage to acquire a single client. In every business meeting I always heard the same thing: "Where are your client testimonials, where are your offices, and where is your homepage?" I had nothing, absolutely nothing. I got depressed from time to time, but I never thought of giving up.

Despite the innumerable setbacks, I began to write about my experiences in life and contacted countless publishers—but all I got were rejection slips. After rewriting my story for the sixth time, my persistence was finally rewarded. In fall 2009, I presented my autobiography *Mein Blind Date mit dem Leben* (*My Blind Date with Life*) at the Frankfurt Book Fair, followed by countless media appearances. My newfound fame boosted my business, and I was soon in a position to rent a small office and hire my first employees. Over and over again, I was approached by companies who wanted me to tell my story in front of an audience. I dusted off one of my old learning techniques. Since I can't simply read a text straight off the page, I used my computer's text-to-speech software to help me learn my speeches by heart.

In 2017, my autobiography was adapted for the screen and released in cinemas across Germany. From there, my extraordinary story quickly became a global sensation. Even Hollywood knocked on the door and secured the rights to my story. Today, I am an author, coach, and keynote speaker. I am also working on a novel and the sequel to the first feature film. Together with my team, I now get to travel all around the world. I can honestly say: "With the strength of my willpower, I have made a career for myself in the world of the sighted—my teenage plan has come to fruition!" When I look back on my life from a bird's eye perspective, one thing becomes clear: It was my supposed shortcomings that enabled me to develop into the person I am today!

In summer 2020, I received an email from a fellow author I greatly admire, Dr. Rainer Zitelmann. Of course, I know many of his 27 books, which are also very successful abroad, and I almost couldn't believe that he wanted to write a book about people with disabilities—and he even wanted me to write the foreword. On a lovely warm September day, I was visited in my Hamburg office by a very dynamic man, who greeted me with a resolute voice and an equally resolute handshake. It was immediately clear to me who I was dealing with. A clear image formed in my mind's eye: "This is an upstanding man who knows exactly what he wants!"

Rainer Zitelmann enthusiastically outlined his book project and all the famous people with disabilities he was going to portray in his work. I felt more than a little flattered and asked him why, of all people, I should be the one to write the foreword. The amiable, professional author immediately explained: "Just like everyone else in my new book, you are an authentic example of real-life resilience, you should definitely be the one." Without hesitation, I looked in his direction and nodded. "Dr. Zitelmann, it is a great honor for me to accept your request. You can count on me."

As the deadline approached, I had doubts about whether I would be ready with the promised foreword on time, especially as almost every minute of every day was taken up with my other projects. Cautiously, I asked Zitelmann what his Plan B was if I couldn't make the deadline. He wrote back a minute later, "There is no Plan B, I know I can count on you as a man of your word."

In the weeks that followed our meeting, we stayed in constant email contact. In quick succession, I received one freshly written chapter of his book after another. I listened attentively as my computer's text-to-speech software read each chapter to me. It wasn't long until I came to an astonishing realization: Yes, each of the people portrayed in this book was or is severely disabled. And yet they have all been able to apply their tremendous willpower to reach their full potential and transcend their physical limitations. Whether Frida Kahlo, Thomas Quasthoff, Margarete Steiff or Stevie Wonder, all 20 fighters impressively depicted by Rainer Zitelmann on the following pages have one thing in common: they have all achieved things that most people without disabilities would never dare to do, even though each accomplishment would be so much easier without a disability.

As I was preparing to write this foreword, I went through a process of identifying myself with each protagonist in turn and spent a significant amount of time reflecting on my own life. If you will allow me, I would also like to count myself a member of the family of successful people with disabilities. Regardless of the severity of our disabilities, none of us has ever allowed ourselves to be deflected from our chosen paths. We transformed our self-perceptions, determined not to allow our disabilities to define us and devoted all of our energy to enhancing our strengths. Whenever something doesn't work out, we take a hard look at ourselves, don't get caught up in the blame game, and devote ourselves with maximum discipline to what is called "conscious practice." With a level of commitment that people without disabilities cannot even comprehend, we work, sometimes over years, to achieve our goals and develop an extraordinary tolerance for frustration.

Even if this process isn't always smooth or free of obstacles, and sometimes takes decades, we stick with it. People with disabilities do not regard setbacks as mistakes, they are simply a natural part of the process when you invest time and work hard to learn something new and increase the quality of our acquired skills. As you read each of Rainer Zitelmann's detailed, unvarnished and masterful portraits, you will gain insights into the power of learnable resilience, the importance of developing your own strategies for success, the benefits of self-determination, and much more.

If you like, you can consider this book a treasure trove of human diamonds. We all know that every rare gem was once an ordinary piece of coal that withstood tremendous pressure over a long period of time, becoming ever harder and purer, and only achieving its unique brilliance through precise cutting and polishing.

It's time to go diamond prospecting!

# Preface

Just take a second or two to think about successful people with disabilities. How many names from the fields of politics, sports, music, business, science, or cinema—dead or alive—come to mind? It's an interesting question and I was curious to find out what would happen when the American public is asked whether they can name any successful people with disabilities, so I commissioned Ipsos MORI to conduct a representative survey in February 2021. The survey's respondents were asked to name up to three people.

The survey found that 51 percent of Americans could not name a single successful person with a disability, 21 percent could think of only one person, and just 28 percent were able to come up with two or more names. Stephen Hawking was mentioned most frequently, followed by Michael J. Fox, Stevie Wonder, Franklin D. Roosevelt, and Helen Keller.

I was inspired to write this book for very personal reasons. Shortly after my 61st birthday, during a routine ophthalmic examination, I was caught entirely unaware when my doctor told me that I had epiretinal gliosis. In other words, a membrane or thin sheet of fibrous tissue had formed on the sharp focusing area at the back of my eye (the macula). In my right eye, my ophthalmologist told me, the condition was advanced. My left eye was also affected, but at that point only a little. In the worst case, the condition would leave me unable to read, even with the strongest glasses in the world. I didn't need an operation immediately, he said, but would probably require surgery at some point. When I asked him about the chances of success, he replied: "There is a one-in-three chance that your condition will stay the same and not improve; a one-in-three chance that an operation will improve things; and a one-in-three chance that the surgery will make things worse."

I consulted other specialists and finally decided to see a professor at the Charité Hospital in Berlin. Over the next two years, I went for regular check-ups. I noticed that even with my glasses, I could only read with my left eye. If I closed my left eye, the words I was trying to read looked like indecipherable squiggles rather than intelligible text. So, I decided to have the operation, which took place two years after the initial diagnosis. The professor told me that the first ophthalmologist I had seen had been overly negative. But she was reluctant to put the operation's chances of success in percentage terms. All she would say is that it can often take half a year or more before the benefits of the surgery become apparent, and usually a second, smaller operation is necessary.

Half a year later, on Christmas Eve, I was standing directly under a lamp at a table laden with gifts, holding a Christmas card from my girlfriend. I had forgotten my reading glasses and was surprised to find that in the bright light I could read with my operated eye even without glasses. What an incredible Christmas surprise! I had developed what is called "monovision": one of my eyes is better at seeing things in the distance and the other eye is more attuned to nearby objects, so the two complement each other.

In life, whenever I face a problem, I start with the worst-case scenario. Then I try to focus on the positives. In this case, one major positive is the book you are now holding in your hands, which I wouldn't have written if it weren't for my eye condition. I started reading books about people with visual impairments and vision loss—including the great book by Saliya Kahawatte *Mein Blind Date mit dem Leben.* Again, if it weren't for the epiretinal gliosis, I would never have met this extraordinary man and he would never have written the foreword to this book.

Inspired by his book, I started to read about other successful people with disabilities. I read tens of thousands of pages of books, reports, and interviews about and with people with disabilities. I wanted to know what it was that gave them the strength to achieve the extraordinary despite their disabilities. I was even able to talk to some of these incredible people personally. Among the people featured in this book, you can read about

- a blind mountaineer who conquered the Seven Summits, the loftiest peaks on all seven continents, including Mount Everest, the highest mountain in the world.
- a successful and world-renowned gallerist who was almost blind when he opened his first gallery.
- the "Blind Traveler," a blind Englishman who, roughly 200 years ago, traveled far and wide with only a little money, experienced 200 cultures and whose journeys took him further than the distance between the Earth and the Moon.
- Ludwig van Beethoven, who was almost completely deaf when he composed his Ninth Symphony.
- Vincent van Gogh, who painted his most famous pictures while in a psychiatric hospital.
- Margarete Steiff, founder of the Steiff stuffed toy company and producer of the world's first 'Teddy Bears,' who, after a bout of childhood polio, was confined to a wheelchair.
- Stephen Hawking, the explorer of black holes and the most famous scientist of our time.
- Nick Vujicic, the motivational speaker and author, who was born without arms and legs and has encouraged millions of people in 63 countries with his inspirational speeches.

- Helen Keller, who lost her sight and hearing at the age of one and a half and later became an internationally successful writer.
- Ray Charles, the "High Priest of Soul," who lost his sight at the age of seven and went on to become one of the most successful singers of all time.

This book contains the life stories of 20 famous and lesser-known people who, despite their many differences, all achieved incredible things in their own, very unique ways. I have deliberately chosen to write about both famous figures, such as Beethoven and Van Gogh, and individuals most of the readers will not be familiar with, such as the American historian William Hickling Prescott and the track and field athlete Marla Runyan. What these people have achieved varies greatly: some made history with their works, others had a far more limited impact. But even for those to whom the latter applies—Christy Brown, for example—it is true that they achieved far more with the opportunities they were given than most of their contemporaries would ever have believed possible.

Of course, I hope that this book becomes a source of encouragement to people with disabilities and the parents of children with disabilities. But it is especially aimed at people without disabilities. I want to show everyone that adverse external circumstances need not shape our lives if we can only fully appreciate the power of our minds, set ourselves ambitious goals and...

No, I'll stop there. I don't want to reveal all the secrets yet. You will discover them for yourself in each chapter! This book is a treasure trove full of hidden insights, and I would only be depriving you of the joy of discovering them for yourself if I revealed them before you even get to the main body of the book. I can promise you now that every profile is far more than just a recounting of the major events and incidents in the lives of each of the figures portrayed.

Each chapter also explores what we can learn from these people. It would be a good idea if, as you are reading, you write out these lessons for yourself so that you can reflect on them—and use these insights to think your way to success!

If you think of a successful life as a 'beautiful' life, then you will need to qualify your definition of 'success' for a number of the people portrayed in this book. This is especially true for those who suffered from mental illnesses (Van Gogh and Nash), and also applies to someone like the writer Christy Brown, who eventually ruined his writing career and life through alcohol.

One of the qualities that all of the people in this book share is that they never gave up, even in the face of the greatest possible challenges. This is as true, for example, of the actor Michael J. Fox, who suffers from Parkinson's disease, as it is of the renowned American historian William Hickling Prescott, who battled against a severe eye condition for almost his entire life.

When you analyze the lives of successful people, you will find that most successful people—just like everyone else—experienced setbacks and difficulties that they could have offered up as excuses if they had failed. One person might have grown up in poverty, another is overshadowed by their successful father, one is from an immigrant family, and another was deprived of a high-quality education. Some might have felt too young to embark on a great career, others may have felt too old to start something new. In the decades that I have been involved with successful people, I have noticed that none of them has ever cited such real or perceived shortcomings as excuses. And this is exactly the same for the people with disabilities I portray in this book.

Today, many people have a victim mentality—they see themselves as victims of society, disadvantage or discrimination, victims of adverse circumstances. The people in this book never saw themselves as victims. Nor did they seek pity. They saw themselves as creators of their own destinies and believed that they could achieve things that even most people without disabilities would never achieve. What do you think you would achieve if you could tap into the same astonishing strength that enabled each of these individuals to do such incredible things?

People often say that health is the most important thing in life. It's a phrase I myself have sometimes thoughtlessly said and believed. At least until I started to immerse myself in the lives of the people you will read about in this book. When I read the biography of Ray Charles, for example, it gave me comfort: even if I were to lose my sight—which is extremely unlikely in my case—or were left unable to read, I realized that I could still live a happy and creative life. Yes, health is important. But it's not as important as our inner attitude. And most important of all is that we come to understand the hidden powers that lie within us all.

I would like to thank Erik Weihenmayer, Felix Klieser and Johann König in particular for answering my questions about their lives.

*Rainer Zitelmann, October 2023*

Ludwig van Beethoven (portrait by Joseph Karl Stieler, 1820): "Strength is the morality of the man who stands out from the rest, and it is mine."
Credits: GL Archive / Alamy Stock Photo

# 1. Ludwig van Beethoven
## "I shall take fate by the throat."

Over the course of 45 years, Beethoven wrote 138 works with opus numbers and around 240 works without opus numbers[1], and even people with little interest in classical music will most likely have heard at least one of them, whether Beethoven's wonderful *Symphony of Fate* (his fifth) or his *Eroica* symphony (his third), or perhaps one of his many piano sonatas, such as the *Moonlight Sonata*, or his piano composition, *Für Elise*. Even if someone is unfamiliar with these masterpieces, almost everybody will have heard Beethoven's Ninth Symphony—or at least the main theme of its final movement, which was adopted as the official anthem of the European Union in 1985.

Beethoven's Ninth Symphony premiered in Vienna on May 7, 1824. The performance was officially conducted by Michael Umlauf, although Beethoven shared the stage with him. It is reported that the great composer tried to enrich the musical expression with his own sweeping gestures.[2] He raced "back and forth like a madman. One moment he was stretching himself up to the heavens, the next he was crouching low to the ground, he flailed about with his hands and his feet as if he wanted to play all of the instruments and sing the chorus all by himself."[3] The musicians, however, concentrated solely on Umlauf and paid no attention to the almost totally deaf Beethoven, who could no longer hear his own music and certainly could not conduct it.

"That evening," writes Jan Caeyers in his biography *Beethoven. A Life*, "Beethoven experienced one of the greatest triumphs of his career."[4] No sooner had the orchestra finished the second movement than the audience erupted in loud and enthusiastic applause.

Apparently, Beethoven, his back to the auditorium, was completely unaware until the singer, Caroline Unger, pulled him around to face the public to accept their adulation and standing ovation. The final crescendo was met with rapturous applause as the auditorium exploded in ecstasy and a sea of waving hats and handkerchiefs. Beethoven was summoned back to the stage for five curtain calls— even members of the imperial family normally made do with three.[5]

Beethoven committed his Ninth Symphony to paper in a little over nine months between May 1823 and February 1824, although he had already spent years gathering ideas and materials for his great work.[6]

Beethoven was born in Bonn, Germany on December 16, 1770, to a family with a rich musical heritage. His grandfather, who bore the same first name, was court conductor in Bonn. Despite the fact that the younger Ludwig van Beethoven was only three years old when his grandfather died, he retained a life-long and great admiration for the older Beethoven. Beethoven's father, Johann van Beethoven, a tenor in the court orchestra, was also a musician, although he was not particularly talented and increasingly fell into alcoholism. Johann retired early in 1789 and his eldest son Ludwig was appointed legal guardian over his younger brothers. Nevertheless, Beethoven's strict father had given him his first music lessons and, at the age of eight, the son performed as a pianist for the first time in public in Cologne.

Beethoven's father realized that there was only so much he could teach his incredibly talented son, which is why, at the age of eleven, he enrolled his son for piano and composition lessons with Christian Gottlob Neefe, who became his first significant mentor. In 1783, Neefe published an oft quoted article in the Hamburg-based journal *Magazin der Musik* effusively praising his student's "very promising talent": "This young genius deserves support, so that he might travel. He will undoubtedly become a second Wolfgang Amadeus Mozart, if he continues as he has begun."[7]

Four years later, Beethoven traveled to Vienna with the aim of introducing himself to Mozart, although they didn't actually meet. In 1792, Beethoven met Joseph Haydn in Bonn and hoped to take composition lessons from him. Beethoven did manage to complete an internship of sorts with Haydn, who, after Mozart's death, had become the most influential composer of his time. Beethoven studied under Haydn from his arrival in Vienna in November 1792 until shortly before Haydn's departure for England in January 1794. "The significance of this latter period of study cannot be underestimated," writes Caeyers. "In Bonn, Beethoven had already demonstrated his command of the fundamentals of composition. He could write a beautiful and coherent melody, knew the principles of classical structure, had mastered every stock-standard harmonic device, and had a thorough grounding in orchestration." Beethoven had learned and mastered the basics of his profession, but he knew that Haydn and Mozart had "an edge" that set them apart from their contemporaries, above all "more complex thematic material."[8] Beethoven also wanted to learn to compose this way. He systematically experimented throughout his career and wanted to make a name for himself in Vienna, which he adopted as his new home, and beyond.

Thus, in February 1796, he set out on a concert tour to Prague, Dresden, Leipzig, and Berlin. His audiences in Prague were enthusiastic; in reviews, Beethoven was celebrated as a "genius" and a "God."[9] In Berlin, he played before King Frederick William II, who is said to have even considered taking Beethoven into his service. However, concrete negotiations never took place, partly due to the king's unexpected death in 1797.[10]

Beethoven became increasingly settled in Vienna, where he found excellent teachers, aristocratic sponsors who supported him financially, and an audience that adored him. His first decade in Vienna was a period of unrelenting success. Celebrated by the masses and courted by music publishers, his self-confidence grew, as he confided to his friend Nikolaus Zmeskall: "Strength is the morality of the man who stands out from the rest, and it is mine."[11]

Beethoven's working day was disciplined. He got up very early and then worked, interrupted only by one or two short breaks, until lunch at two or three o'clock. After lunch, he went for a walk. When he did so, he paid little attention to his surroundings, his mind being entirely occupied by his music. Now and again, he would stop to jot down useful ideas, which he explored more fully the next day at his desk or piano. Beethoven was constantly composing, "no matter where he was." His compositions went through a series of processes: "starting from a vague idea, which took shape very slowly and ultimately—after a great deal of effort, and not always following a logical sequence—crystallized into a fully developed and coherent musical work."[12]

Beethoven had started out as a pianist and his original goal had been to become a conductor. Then, a problem with his hearing progressively worsened and his life took an unexpected turn. Initially, the problems with his hearing seemed quite innocuous: at first, only the hearing in his left ear was impaired, but it didn't take long until his right ear was affected too. Fortunately, his hearing loss didn't have too much of a negative impact on his piano playing, although he did have problems with conversations. He found it increasingly difficult to understand what other people were saying. He went from one doctor to another, and they all suggested different treatments but none managed to improve his hearing. But Beethoven refused to resign himself to his illness and, in November 1801, he wrote a stubborn letter to his friend, Franz Gerhard Wegeler: "I shall take fate by the throat and will not be brought to my knees. For to lead such a life—a still life—no, it cannot be that I was made for this."[13]

In early May 1802, acting on the advice of his doctor, he moved to Heiligenstadt, at the time a small village with only 400 inhabitants. All his life, Beethoven had suffered from abdominal complaints and his doctors suspected that this was the root of his hearing problem. A bathing cure and distance from the hustle and bustle of Vienna were, they said, bound to provide relief.[14]

Beethoven had tried to hide his hearing loss from his friends and the public at large, fearing that it would damage his career as a musician if anyone found out. However, on a walk through the countryside with his student Ferdinand Ries, his secret was exposed and Ries reports calling Beethoven's attention "to a shepherd in the forest who was playing most pleasantly on a flute cut from lilac wood. For half an hour Beethoven could not hear anything at all and became extremely quiet and gloomy, even though I repeatedly assured him that I did not hear anything any longer either (which was, however, not the case)."[15]

Towards the end of his time in Heiligenstadt, it seems that Beethoven suffered a physical breakdown. Although he recovered quickly, this was probably what drove him to draw up a document in early October 1802, a letter to his brothers, that later became famous as his "Heiligenstadt Testament." Beethoven kept the document hidden among his private papers, where it remained until after his death. In all likelihood, he never showed it to anyone. It was not so much a will in the conventional sense as it was not really intended to settle his estate. Far more, it contained Beethoven's vehement rejections of accusations about his behavior. At this point, it probably helps to know that Beethoven was famously difficult to get along with and frequently got into heated arguments with friends, patrons, publishers—with everyone. Helene von Breuning, who was something of a substitute mother to Beethoven, gave a name to these outbursts: "He has his raptus again today," she would remark, using the medical term for a fit of rage.[16] One very well-known and oft quoted statement comes from Goethe, who met Beethoven in 1812: "I met Beethoven in Teplitz. His talent astounded me; but unfortunately his natural temperament is completely uncontrolled, and although, indeed, not at all wrong in thinking the world detestable, still, in doing so, he does not make it more pleasant, either for himself or for others."[17] And Beethoven's friend, the surgeon and man of letters Aloys Weißenbach, once wrote: "The intense irritability of his mind and the forceful stubbornness of his artistic genius constitute both his happiness and his unhappiness. His happiness, in so far as they always lead him back to his inner self; his unhappiness, in so far as they keep him in a constant state of tension with the world."[18]

In a letter to Ferdinand Ries, who at times served as his secretary, Beethoven explained that he possessed the power of "concealing and suppressing" his "sensitiveness," but if someone irritated him at an inopportune moment when he was "susceptible to anger" and would "speak straight out, more so than any other person."[19] There are countless reports of his irritability and flashes of temper, which sometimes went as far as physical attacks. He was reported to have thrown books and chairs at servants and on one occasion he even poured a bowl of hot soup over a clumsy waiter.[20]

Apparently, criticism of Beethoven's behavior had become so widespread that he sought to present his version of events in his "Heiligenstadt Testament." The importance of the document lies primarily in the fact that it provides us with a unique insight into his psychological state and into the growing despair he was experiencing as a result of his worsening deafness. The text, which is somewhat difficult to read because Beethoven wrote long passages without punctuation or paragraphing, begins: "Oh you men who think or say that I am malevolent, stubborn, or misanthropic, how greatly do you wrong me. You do not know the secret cause which makes me seem that way to you. From childhood on my heart and soul have been full of the tender feeling of goodwill, and I was ever inclined to accomplish great things. But think that for 6 years now I have been hopelessly afflicted, made worse by senseless physicians, from year to year deceived with hopes of improvement, finally compelled to face the prospect of *a lasting malady* (whose cure will take years, or perhaps be impossible). Though born with a fiery, active temperament, even susceptible to the diversions of society, I was soon compelled to withdraw myself, to live life alone. If at times I tried to forget all this, oh how harshly was I flung back by the doubly sad experience of my bad hearing. Yet it was impossible for me to say to people, 'Speak louder, shout, for I am deaf.' Ah, how could I possibly admit an infirmity in the *one sense* which ought to be more perfect in me than in others, a sense which I once possessed in the highest perfection, a perfection such as few in my profession enjoy or ever have enjoyed..."[21]

Beethoven goes on to say that he was forced to live "like one who has been banished" because he was afraid that his deafness might be noticed by those around him. In such situations, he confesses that "a hot terror" seized him and he feared being exposed to the danger that his condition might be noticed, he was driven "almost to despair," and came close to ending his life. It was, he adds, "only *my art* that held me back. Ah, it seemed to me impossible to leave the world until I had brought forth all that I feel was within me." Despite all the burdens placed on him by nature, Beethoven still did everything in his power "to become accepted among worthy artists and men." It was only thanks to virtue and to his art, he writes, that "I did not end my life by suicide."[22]

In seeking to explain his outbursts, these remarks were not convincing because his flashes of rage preceded the onset of his illness and continued even after he was no longer under pressure—as described in his "Heiligenstadt Testament"—to hide his deafness. It should be added that such outbursts, temper tantrums and fits of rage are not unusual among geniuses. Much more recently, we have heard many reports of extreme behavior from extraordinary individuals such as Steve Jobs and Bill Gates.[23]

The value of the "Heiligenstadt Testament" has been aptly described by Beethoven's biographer Jan Caeyers: This was a "solemn creed set out by Beethoven with great stylistic and calligraphic care in order to convince himself that the path he had chosen was the right one." And he adds, "Modern-day psychologists and counselors frequently apply the same technique and would certainly have urged Beethoven to do the same."[24]

Beethoven's hearing continued to deteriorate. Various ear trumpets that he had made did nothing to alleviate his condition. He even asked his piano builder to construct louder instruments for him.[25] Conducting also became increasingly difficult, as he could no longer hear anything. At a rehearsal for one of his compositions, the opera *Fidelio*, he created such chaos and confusion that he had to be removed from the conductor's podium.[26] As his hearing continued to deteriorate, he found he could only communicate if other people shouted directly into his ear. When even this approach failed, he resorted to communicating in writing, in what he called "conversation books," which have today become a unique historical record. The people he was 'speaking' with wrote words, sentences and sentence fragments in his books and he responded.

But, like all great and successful people, Beethoven succeeded in turning this disadvantage into an advantage. Successful people, just like everyone else, are constantly confronted by crises and challenges, but what makes them different is that they are able to seize opportunities as they emerge, because they understand—as Napoleon Hill repeatedly stressed—"that every failure brings with it the seed of an equivalent success."[27]

Although he fell into a temporary despair and contemplated suicide, in one respect Beethoven's deafness actually proved to be a blessing rather than a curse. "Fate," writes Caeyers, "thus spared him an agonizing decision by forcing him to give up a promising career as a concert pianist and leaving no other option than to concentrate fully on composition."[28] In addition, increasingly withdrawing from society and retreating into his own mental bubble because of his illness had proved to be advantageous, not only for Beethoven himself, but also for his music: "Beethoven became progressively less concerned with existing rules and conventions, and his involuntary auditors abstinence allowed him to develop a new musical language, one that he had already codified as 'the new way.' In this manner, Beethoven's personal, social and emotional tragedy transformed into a quality that would push him into unexplored and unsuspected musical territory."[29]

We know that other brilliant people have often tried to avoid distractions and external influences in their lives. The genius investor Warren Buffett, for example, has spent his entire life in Omaha, not New York, partly because he doesn't want to get distracted by the hustle, bustle and influences of Wall Street. For Beethoven it was probably also an advantage that, as his hearing deteriorated, he was increasingly forced to fall back on his own imagination, which allowed him to concentrate on his compositions without being buffeted by shifting fashions and external influences. Perhaps this is the reason his music was so unusual to contemporary ears—and, for some tastes, took more than a little getting used to.

Financially, Beethoven often struggled, although he did earn handsomely in certain periods of his career. He had also bought some shares, but he would only sell or borrow against them when his needs were greatest. When the Italian composer Rossini visited him, Rossini was amazed at the discrepancy between his own luxurious lifestyle and the modest conditions in which Beethoven lived: "When I mounted the stairs leading to the poor lodgings of the great man, I barely mastered my emotions. When the door opened, I found myself in a sort of attic terribly disordered and dirty. I remember particularly the ceiling. It was under the roof and showed crevices through which the rain could not help pouring down in streams."[30]

Beethoven didn't care at all whether his rooms were tidy or not; he was equally indifferent to what visitors thought of his home. And it didn't matter to him whether people complained about his scruffy attire, his unshaven jawline or his unkempt hair. Beethoven, who as a youth had identified with the heroes of Greek antiquity and felt called to achieve great things, was not bothered by such trifling matters because he knew that at the end of his life, he would not be judged by whether his apartment and hairstyle were neat, but by his work.

Beethoven increasingly devoted all of his energies to his compositions. This unwavering focus, combined with his habit of delegating as many tasks as he could to other people, is one of the major secrets of his success. His income was not insignificant, but he spent considerable sums employing other people to perform tasks for him so that he could focus entirely on his compositions. He had staff to manage his household, but he clashed with them so often that they didn't tend to stay in his service for very long. And he employed a fairly large circle of copyists, which also cost money. He delegated everything he could, and also used the copyists as secretaries and messengers, as well as getting them to run all manner of errands. He was also forced to hire a team of lawyers to manage his frequent legal disputes. In addition, doctors were a significant expense, because Beethoven not only suffered from hearing loss, but had so many different medical conditions that their description and analysis fills an entire, 271-page book.[31]

"In view of the financial burdens he bore, Beethoven's increasing fear of old-age poverty in the 1820s seems understandable," writes his biographer Matthias Henke. "Unlike most of his colleagues, he hardly did anything to earn money besides composing."[32] He had abandoned his career as a pianist as his hearing deteriorated. Other composers earned extra money as teachers, but Beethoven did not want to be distracted in any way. It was only for extraordinarily talented students that he gladly made an exception. And, of course, when the opportunity arose, he gave lessons to young, attractive women; not infrequently, he developed feelings for his students in the process.

Matthias Henke writes that Beethoven's reluctance to pursue part-time employment opportunities may have simply corresponded to an inclination or "desire to concentrate on the essential, on his 'new way.'"[33] At the same time, his restraint in such matters forced him to be all the more emphatic and forceful in his negotiations with publishers. After his return from Heiligenstadt, Beethoven decided to ask his brother Kaspar Karl to manage his financial affairs and negotiations.[34] After Beethoven had turned his back on other matters and restricted himself entirely to composing, a publisher contacted Kaspar Karl to request some smaller compositions. Kaspar Karl replied that his brother only wrote longer works, such as oratorios or operas. If the publisher wanted smaller-scale works, Kaspar Karl insisted, he would have to make an unusually generous offer.[35] Having his brother organize his affairs in this way was a great relief for Beethoven. However, the arrangement lasted just four years until it ended in 1806 when Kaspar Karl got married.[36]

Beethoven never married. He fell in love on a fairly regular basis, but most of his affairs lasted no more than a few months. He was passionate about women who were unattainable—noble women, for example, or married women, or women who only wanted a husband with better financial prospects. One of his most famous letters is called "Letter to the Immortal Beauty," which he wrote in July 1812. Scholars have remained divided on the intended recipient ever since the letter was discovered following the composer's death. No one can say for sure who the letter was intended for, whether it was Josephine Brunsvik, as some researchers claim, or Antonie Brentano as others insist.[37] It is, of course, possible that, rather than writing to a specific woman, Beethoven was in fact addressing an eternal "ideal of womanhood."[38] In any case, the letter is an expression of love for a woman who was already married, which is why a formal relationship seemed impossible.[39]

As with his music, Beethoven was probably a perfectionist, including with regard to women—a man who placed the highest demands on himself and others in pursuit of a perhaps unattainable ideal. We know that he rewrote his musical pieces over and over again, never achieving complete satisfaction with any of his works. This productive dissatisfaction is a characteristic of lots of incredibly successful people, but in his search for the perfect woman, it meant that he remained alone and without a family. On the one hand, being single made it easier for him to focus entirely on his work. On the other hand, he obviously missed having a family, because he fought obsessively (incurring substantial legal fees in the process) for the guardianship of his nephew Karl, the son of his brother Kaspar, after Kaspar's death in 1815. The years of legal disputes certainly consumed as much of his energy as his later concern for the development of his nephew. Beethoven's perfectionism, which benefited him so much in music but harmed him so much in his personal relationships, was equally evident in his relationship with Karl, who was born in 1806, and whom Beethoven treated as a son. Beethoven literally had his beloved nephew shadowed, always consumed by the fear that Karl might make an irredeemable mistake of one kind or another. The nephew, who eventually attempted suicide (but survived), said that he had "become worse" because his uncle "wanted him to be better."[40]

Beethoven's final public appearance as a concert pianist was on December 22, 1808, in Vienna.[41] He had waited a long time for this and assailed the audience with a host of his own compositions. The audience was put to a hard test: the hall was almost as cold as a Siberian winter and the concert lasted four hours. Beethoven played poorly in his last public appearance as a pianist. Unfortunately, the orchestra that accompanied him did not play well either. During rehearsals, Beethoven had such fiery arguments with the orchestra that he had to be removed from the hall. During the concert itself, there was so much chaos and confusion that they had to stop and start all over again.[42]

For a while, it looked as if this concert would mark Beethoven's final goodbye to Vienna. A few weeks earlier, he had been offered the position of court conductor in Kassel. At the time, Kassel was the capital of the new kingdom of Westphalia and was ruled by Napoleon's youngest brother, Jérôme, from 1807 to 1813. Beethoven did seriously consider Jérôme's offer. In January 1809, he wrote that he felt forced to leave so that he "could escape the constant plotting, scheming and fighting" in Vienna.[43] His secretary negotiated a contract, and a sense of alarm spread through Vienna. Several aristocrats banded together to make Beethoven an offer of 4,000 guilders per year for the rest of his life if he stayed in Vienna. The agreement placed only vague obligations on Beethoven and the noblemen demonstrated their understanding of his needs when they stated: "Since it has been demonstrated, however, that only a person living entirely free from care can dedicate himself fully to a single pursuit [...] and produce sublime works of such grandeur that they pay tribute to art itself, the undersigned thus undertake to put Herr Beethoven in a position such that his most basic needs will no longer be of concern to him, leaving his powerful genius unfettered."[44]

However, the contract, despite being intended to solve Beethoven's financial problems, was actually the source of additional headaches and the subject of numerous legal disputes over the years. First of all, not all of his sponsors paid him regularly, partly because they could not. Second, inflation devalued the amount Beethoven was due to be paid. Beethoven was not only desperate because of his financial situation, but above all because the repeated legal disputes distracted him from his music. After all, the whole point of the contract had been to allow him to focus entirely on his art. "What an awful business for an artist, to whom nothing is so dear as his art," Beethoven complained on the occasion of an impending legal dispute over the contract.[45]

There are artists whose importance was not recognized by their contemporaries and who only attained fame in posterity. There are others who were famous during their own lifetimes. Beethoven managed both. He was not one of those unknowns who were underappreciated by his contemporaries and only discovered after his death. At times he was celebrated as a genius, although towards the end of his career, there were other musicians that were far more popular. Caeyers sees a certain tragedy in the fact that Beethoven's fame, among broad sections of the population, peaked with compositions such as the battle symphony "Wellington's Victory." Composed in 1813, the piece sent Viennese audiences into raptures. Of course, Beethoven was delighted to see audiences embrace his work. At the same time, this was not the type of music that was closest to his heart.

"We might wonder," writes the biographer, "why he never reached such dizzying heights with the nearly one hundred works written over the preceding ten years, into which he had poured his very heart and soul. Some consolation can be derived, however, from meditating on a hypothetical and potentially far greater injustice: the possibility that Beethoven might have pursued fame exclusively through popular kitsch, never producing his other, better works."[46] It is true for many artists that they make compromises throughout their careers. On the one hand, they produce art of great personal import that they hope will be adequately appreciated by later generations, and on the other, they cater to prevailing tastes in order to earn money.

Ideally, composers hope to attract three types of recognition: from contemporary audiences; from music experts; and from generations to come. Beethoven's Ninth Symphony is a prime example of how these three can combine. His iconic symphony is loved by music aficionados and casual listeners and concertgoers alike, was greeted by enthusiastic applause at its first performance, and continues to captivate people to this day. It can even be argued that, in this case at least, the general public demonstrated a surer taste than some experts at the time. The composer and violinist Louis Spohr, for example, wrote: "I [...] freely confess that I have never been able to acquire a taste for Beethoven's later works. Yes, the much admired Ninth Symphony must be counted among them [...],

and whose fourth movement seems to me [...] monstrous and taste-
less and in its conception of Schiller's ode so trivial that I still cannot understand how a genius like Beethoven could have written it.
I find in it a new proof of what I previously noticed in Vienna, that
Beethoven lacks aesthetic imagination and a sense of beauty."[47] Of
course, there were other opinions at the time. One prestigious journal, the *Allgemeine musikalische Zeitung*, celebrated the symphony
in three consecutive issues; it was the longest critique in the magazine's history. For Beethoven's fans, the magazine even commissioned an engraved portrait of the composer, which was published
as a free supplement.[48]

The review eulogized: "The finale announces itself like a
crashing thunderclap. When finally, after a call from the solo bass,
the full choir launches into the 'Ode to Joy' in majestic splendor,
the joyful heart opens wide to an ecstatic sensation of heavenly
bliss, and a thousand voices rejoice [...] Art and truth celebrate their
most brilliant triumph, and one could justifiably say: non-plus ul-
tra! Who could possibly surpass this incomparable passage?"[49]

As he was working on the symphony, Beethoven was not only
almost completely deaf, but also—as is less well known—suffering
from a serious eye disease. Indeed, he was half blind.[50] His health
deteriorated over the next few years, and his considerable alcohol
consumption aggravated his numerous ailments, including cirrho-
sis of the liver. He died on March 26, 1827, and was buried a few
days later. Tens of thousands paid their final respects. The actor
Heinrich Anschütz delivered the eulogy written by the playwright
Franz Grillparzer: "For he was an artist, and all that was his, was his
through art alone. The thorns of life had wounded him deeply, and
as the cast-away clings to the shore, so did he seek refuge in thine
arms, O thou glorious sister and peer of the Good and True, thou
balm of wounded hearts, heaven-born Art!"[51]

James Holman with his Noctograph: "If my undertakings...be productive of no other benefit than that of proving to the world how much may be done by a cheerful perseverance under a heavy affliction...I shall be content to think that my labours have not been altogether destitute of utility."

# 2. James Holman
## The man who travelled 250,000 miles, blind

"For my own part, I have been conscious from my earliest youth of the existence of this desire to explore distant regions, to trace the varieties exhibited by mankind under the different influences of different climates, customs, and laws," James Holman recalled in the first volume of his travels, published in 1834.[52] From an early age, the British adventurer set himself ambitious goals: "... I felt an irresistible impulse to become acquainted with as many parts of the world as my professional avocations would permit, and I was determined not to rest satisfied until I had completed the circumnavigation of the globe."[53]

And he turned his dreams into reality! By the time the internal combustion engine was invented, Holman was the most widely traveled man in the world. He almost always traveled alone, "without counsel, and without attendance. I was not sustained by advice of assistance from anybody, and performed my journeys, which were often arduous, and which, on the whole, embrace a vast surface, upon extremely limited pecuniary means."[54] He used mail coaches, farm carts, horses, sailed and often walked; but never traveled by train. In 1866, the eminent journalist, William Jerdan, noted: "... he traversed the great globe itself more thoroughly than any other traveler that ever existed."[55] Holman had traveled no less than a quarter of a million miles,[56] ten times the circumference of the Earth and farther than from the Earth to the Moon. "He could claim a thorough acquaintance with every inhabited continent, and direct contact with at least two hundred distinctly separate cultures."[57]

But he never saw any of these countries with his own eyes—when he started traveling, he was already blind.

James Holman was born in Exeter, a port city in southwest England, on October 15, 1786. he was the son of an apothecary and joined the British Royal Navy at the age of 12, quickly progressing up the ranks. At the age of sixteen, Midshipman Holman was promoted to captain of not one, but a whole string of ships.[58] He probably would have had a successful career in the Navy had he not fallen seriously ill. Exactly what he was suffering from we don't know, but he experienced severe pain in his limbs and could hardly walk. The diagnosis was "Diseas'd ancle joint and flying Gout,"[59] but it is unlikely that it was actually gout.

For as long as he could, he tried not to make a fuss and continued to do his job. But that only made the disease worse. Eventually, he was unable to move for weeks on end and was confined to his bed. The therapies at the time were brutal. One consisted of 'burning' the patient with a heated poker, boiling water, or acids— the resulting pain was supposed to help fight the disease. Briefly, his condition improved—whether because of or in spite of this therapy is unclear. Nevertheless, the pain soon returned, and with increased intensity. Again, the doctors tried their burning treatments, supplemented by leeches and bleeding. The pain not only returned, but from one day to the next, he also suffered a serious— and completely unexpected—affliction of the eye.

Until this moment in time, Holman had always had perfect eyesight—had never even required spectacles. Now, "on an otherwise ordinary day he found himself cupping his face in his hands, struggling to maintain his composure. Something was wrong with his eyes."[60] He was in severe pain and soon had to confine himself to a darkened room, his face wrapped in cold compresses. Soon after, he went completely blind. He later recalled, referring to himself in the third person: "It is sufficient to say, that at the age of twenty-five ... his prospects were irrecoverably blighted by the effects of an illness, resulting from his professional duties, and which left him deprived of all the advantages of 'heaven's prime decree.'"[61]

The worst part was the uncertainty. His doctors seemed unable to diagnose his condition or even say whether his blindness would be permanent or temporary. "The suspense which I suffered, during the period when my medical friends were uncertain of the issue, appeared to me a greater misery than the final knowledge of the calamity itself."[62] He begged his doctors to tell him the truth. He would rather hear the worst, that his sight would never return, than continue to endure the agonies of doubt.

When he was finally certain that his blindness was permanent, he writes that this "determined me to seek, in some pursuit adapted to my new state of existence, a congenial field of employment and consolation."[63] First, however, like all blind people, he had to learn to rely more on his senses of hearing and touch. The blind man, he wrote, "can detect the slightest variations, the finest fractional point of tone ... they tell minutely all the alteration of welcome, of regard, of coldness, pleasure, pain, joy, reproof."[64]

Like other blind people portrayed in this book, Holman refused to use a typical blind man's cane or to identify himself as blind in any other way. He used a normal walking stick. Holman did not want to stand out in any way.

Unlike most blind people at the time, he also learned to write. Braille had not yet been invented and typewriters did not yet exist. At that time, most people wrote with a quill and ink, but blind people could not use quills because it was impossible to judge the right amount of ink and they produced indecipherable scrawls. Just a few years before Holman went blind, however, a new device had been invented, and he was probably one of the first blind people to use it for writing. The device was called a Noctograph, and it worked as follows: a sheet of paper is blackened on one side with dried print-er's ink and fixed in a frame with a sheet of normal paper under-neath. The writer uses a solid stylus to 'write' (or press) on the up-per sheet and this pressure transfers the dried ink onto the normal paper to form legible text. Since he was blind, he could not read his own writing, but compared to dictating what he wanted to write, as was the standard approach at the time, it had the advantage that he was not dependent on other people. He took his Noctograph with him on all his journeys. In any case, while he was traveling, he would have been unable to dictate his words, since, for example, in the jungles of Brazil, isolated regions of Africa or Siberia, there was no one around who knew English anyway.

But before he could even think of traveling, he had some fundamental problems to solve. Discharged from the Navy, he was faced with the question of how to earn a living. Since 1803, an order of knights called the Naval Knights of Windsor had been paying modest salaries to former lieutenants who had served on warships. The order was limited to only seven members, and they were sub-jected to strict obligations. They were required to attend services twice a day in a chapel, were not permitted to leave their homes for more than ten days a year without permission, spend the night outside their respective apartments, or "haunt the towns and tav-erns."[65] They were also not allowed to marry. Moreover, they had to swear a solemn oath that they would obey all of these rules. Their attendance at church services was monitored and recorded in a so-called "Knight's Check Book," as was their attendance at the order's evening meal.

There was only one opening in the order at the time, and thou-sands of applicants met the criteria for membership. A minister and two wardens of Holman's baptismal church certified in writing that Holman was among "single men without children" and ready to "lead a virtuous, studious and devout life."[66] This assurance was important as an indication that his blindness was not the result of venereal disease—a common suspicion leveled at blind men at the time. Holman was accepted, which meant that he was entitled to half the pay of a reserve officer for the rest of his life. That was a modest income, but at least he didn't have to go begging and he had a place to stay. That was the positive side. The negative side was that he, a 26-year-old man full of energy, was required to do nothing all day except attend church services twice a day. This, of course, was not the kind of life Holman had imagined.

So, he did something that was very unusual at the time, especially for a blind man: He declared that he wanted to study at the University of Edinburgh. He even received permission to do so, perhaps because the so-called Visitors, who adjudicated applications for academic leave from Naval Knights of Windsor, suspected that he would abandon his studies after one or two semesters anyway.

Unlike today, there were no formal admission requirements to enroll at Edinburgh University at that time. Theoretically, anyone who paid the enrollment fee, and the lecture hall tickets could attend the lectures. The cost of lectures consumed a third of Holman's income. There were no textbooks, and even if there had been, he would not have been able to read them anyway. Students attended lectures and took notes. Holman studied literature and medicine, although the main focus of medical studies at the time was chemistry.

Unfortunately, his health had seriously deteriorated. The old ailments that had already forced him to leave the navy had returned. He was so weakened that he had already given up hope of making a voyage, although this had been his boyhood dream. So, it seemed like a lucky twist of fate that this was precisely what his doctors proposed: a "restful, sun-soaked residence in the more favoured clime of the southern parts of Europe."[67] A year on the coasts of the Mediterranean, was, in his doctors' opinion, his last hope for recovery, and he was granted the necessary leave of absence from both the Royal Navy and the Naval Knights.

Travel had always been Holman's dream. And now that he was blind, he felt that urge even more strongly than ever before. In one of his later travelogues, he explained: "Where the mind is properly constituted, the diminution of one faculty naturally calls others into more extensive action. In my case, the deprivation of sight has been succeeded by an increased desire of locomotion."[68] The mere prospect of the trip sent him into a state of euphoria and led to an improvement in his health.

On October 15, 1819, the then 32-year-old embarked on the first of three great journeys. And it was to last not one year, but two. The journey took him from Calais to Paris, on to Bordeaux and Toulouse, finally via the French Mediterranean coast of Marseilles and Nice to Genoa, Florence, and Naples. The return leg led him via Milan, Geneva, and Bern, to Strasbourg, Cologne, and Amsterdam and from there back to England.

Holman, having studied medicine, began to treat himself on the trip—and his therapy involved healthy eating and plenty of exercise. When others started the day with bread, he ate a breakfast of fresh fruit. Once, when a headache struck during a coach journey, he asked the coachman to stop and let him walk for a while—the coach was not much faster than he was on foot anyway. When the coachman refused, Holman threatened to jump out of the moving carriage. The coachman stopped, and Holman knotted a rope at one end of the carriage and held on to the other. "I then followed in this way, on foot for several miles, to the no small amusement of the villagers, who laughed heartily, and even shouted after me.

I had, however, the satisfaction of getting rid of my headache, and succeeded in completely tiring myself."[69] Along the way, he earned some money, for example, helping with the grape harvest. Most of the time he traveled alone, but he did make friends with a fellow, disabled Englishman, who was deaf. They decided to travel together for a time, their disabilities complementing each other. His travel companion, who was deaf but not mute, would describe the landscapes to him or tell him if a girl they met was pretty.

Holman, who had actually been granted only one year's leave, had been on the road for a total of more than 700 days, but he was not punished, even though he had violated the rules of the order. Back in the monastery, he began to write an account of his travels—or rather, to dictate it to scribes. It was to become his first book. He was able to draw on countless notes because he had had the Noctograph with him every step of the way. The book became a success, but for Holman it was only a prolog to an even more ambitious journey. On July 19, 1822, the day his book was delivered to the bookstores, he set off on a second journey, which would make the first seem like a walk in the park.

He had not given up his childhood dream of traveling round the world. Holman was determined not to let his blindness prevent him from achieving his dreams. On the contrary, for him it was an added motivation to prove to himself and others the full scale of his capabilities. In his travel report he wrote: "I was farther stimulated by a desire to prove to the world, that notwithstanding my personal defects, I was capable of overcoming difficulties which to them might appear impossible."[70]

Many people entertain big dreams as children, but most forget or give up on them. One reason is that people tell them to be 'realistic' and stop dreaming. If you talk to other people about your dreams, there is a good chance that they will amplify any doubts you might already have. That is why the successful author Napoleon Hill advised his readers to keep their dreams to themselves and not to talk about them with others.

Holman also kept his dream from those around him, even from his best friends. "To talk openly of setting out to circle the globe—particularly alone, as was now his preference—was to invite an uproar, if not a diagnosis of insanity,"[71] writes his biographer Roberts, who also quotes a journalist who wrote of Holman: "We do think that the formation of such a scheme would have argued great boldness in the clearest-sighted mortal that ever lived; in one buried in a 'total eclipse' it was altogether marvelous; yet it was formed, arranged, entered upon, and completed in a manner which has already earned for Mr. Holman the respect of his contemporaries, and will command for him the admiration of future ages."[72]

Holman had an idea that most people would probably have called crazy: in order to save money for a long sea voyage on the one hand, and to deceive people about his actual intentions (namely a trip round the world), he had planned to start his journey by heading east, rather than the direction he really wanted to go, namely west. He did not tell his friends about his plans to circle the world but pretended that he was going to St. Petersburg to visit a friend he had met during his first trip around Europe. "My motives for concealing so important a part of these views, it will not be difficult to explain: they are attributable to the opposition my kind friends have always been inclined to make against what, under my peculiar deprivation, they are disposed to regard as Quixotic feelings; a feeling on their parts which I am desirous to suppress, since, on various occasions, I have to charge it with the disappointment of my most anxious wishes."[73]

To reach the Pacific by land, he needed to cross the vast steppes of Siberia, which even then were home to the dreaded penal colonies of the Russian empire. Had he announced his intention, he would indeed have been declared insane. He wanted to travel first to St. Petersburg, then on to Moscow, and finally to Siberia. And all this without a traveling companion, without a guide and without an interpreter, although he did not speak Russian.

But Holman had one thing in common with all truly successful people: He had a clear goal, even if he didn't know exactly how to get there. He was not naïve. He knew that unexpected difficulties would get in his way. But he had enough self-confidence to believe that he would be able to overcome any problems he encountered on his journey. He was convinced: "There are few obstacles which man's perseverance may not enable him to overcome, if he will but rightly exercise those faculties with which the beneficence of his Creator has endowed him."[74]

Once in Russia, he traveled by horse-drawn sleigh and hired a peasant, whose language he did not understand, as a coachman. The first stop on his journey was St. Petersburg, where he met many interesting people. Among his possessions, he carried numerous letters of recommendation that he had been given before the start of his journey, which opened quite a few doors and enabled him to make contacts. Once in the then capital of the Russian Empire, he researched possible itineraries. "I was always particularly cautious in divulging my real plans. On the contrary, I rather endeavoured to keep them concealed, by appearing to show a greater interest with respect to parts that I least contemplated visiting."[75] Holman had a relief map of Russia, which was of immense value to the blind man, because it enabled him to feel with his fingertips what he could not see. When he was unobserved, he would run his index finger over the map.

Although he kept quiet about his actual destination, he sometimes hinted in conversations that he also wanted to travel to Siberia. The reactions were unanimous: "When my intention first began to transpire at Moscow, every one made it his business to demonstrate the madness and absurdity of attempting so dangerous, uninteresting, and disagreeable a journey, in a country where, as respected myself in particular, nothing was either seen or heard! In short, the name of Siberia, probably from early associations, seemed connected in their minds only with sentiments of horror."[76]

But Holman found encouragement in conversations with another adventurer who had traveled through Siberia before him, one John Dundas Cochrane, who had just returned from Siberia with a young lady he had met on his trip.[77] The time he spent with Cochrane confirmed to Holman that such a trip—in part thanks to the hospitality of the region's villagers—would be fantastically cheap. Cochrane claimed that his travels throughout Russia had cost him only a little more than one British pound (the equivalent of about 120 euros today). This was certainly an understatement, but it set Holman's mind at ease. Holman bought a *povoshka,* a lightweight, open carriage with no padded seats and no suspension, from Cochrane. Nevertheless, the carriage did come with a team of three horses.[78] The coachman was a sinister-looking man with a huge beard and pungent body odor. Not long after setting off, they got hopelessly lost in the forest.[79]

Holman describes his feelings at the beginning of the journey through Siberia: "My situation was now one of extreme novelty, and my feelings corresponded with its peculiarity. I was engaged under circumstances of unusual occurrence, in a solitary journey of several thousand miles, through a country, perhaps, the wildest on the face of earth, and whose inhabitants were scarcely yet accounted within the pale of civilization; with no other attendant than a rude Tartar postillion, to whose language my ear was wholly unaccustomed."[80]

They tended to travel at night, which had advantages as rested horses were easier to come by in the evening. Another advantage of traveling in the dark was that the coachman was forced to travel a little more slowly on the rutted paths, gravel, and other 'road' surfaces, which at least somewhat mitigated the risk of bruises and broken bones. "The stress, indeed, violence, of traveling in this fashion has no modern equivalent," Roberts finds.[81] Then there was the bitter cold of Siberia.

In his book, Holman describes his journey across Russia as follows: "In short, no position within the carriage was tenable, and the shocks it gave my brain so excessive, that it felt very instant ready to burst out of its tenement."[82]

Holman had been warned about the inhospitable Barba steppe in Siberia, an area where "in addition to the risk of ague, fever, of being poisoned, or stung to death, there was no little chance of being robbed and murdered."[83] There were flies and mosquitoes everywhere, but Holman had neither a mask nor chain mail, which people normally used to protect themselves from bites and stings. Instead, he and his coachman wrapped their faces in gauze.

When he arrived in Irkutsk on the Mongolian border, he allowed himself some rest. During his stay, he met Alexander Stepanovich Lavinsky, the Governor General of Eastern Siberia, the highest-ranking official in an area twice the size of Europe. Lavinsky had already heard of Holman, and they spent a lot of time on long walks and engaged in conversation, both speaking in French. Holman gained more and more trust, a friendship developed and finally he decided to share his true goal, a trip around the globe, with at least one person. But the Governor General did not react quite as

Holman expected and told him that he was allowed to move freely in Siberia, but not to leave the country toward the East. Thus, his plans lay in tatters. He was ordered to start his return journey immediately, accompanied by a sergeant from the Tsar's elite troop: "Then they were off, at a speed that only a *feldjager* could choose. Despite the snow and subzero temperature, he kept the horses at a constant gallop for fifty miles, until one of them collapsed and died. The driver unhitched the corpse, already beginning to freeze solid, and resumed a pace only slightly diminished."[84]

Because of the high speed and the poor condition of the 'roads,' the sled overturned at least once a day and sent the supplies and passengers tumbling out. Every time this happened, the sergeant would explode in a fit of rage and thrash the poor driver. The cold was unbearable and despite many layers of clothing, Holman could not keep his arms and legs warm. "As touch was the primary sense by which he comprehended the world, numbness was a sort of second blindness. The threat of frostbite held special terrors."[85] Holman made it to Poland, but then he encountered new, unexpected difficulties. He applied for a visa to Austria but was denied on the grounds that he should have applied for it during his stay in St. Petersburg. It took a month and countless letters of protest from Holman before he was allowed to continue his journey to Vienna. From there he continued to his home in England, arriving on June 20, 1824, exactly two years and one day after he had embarked on his adventurous journey. Upon his return, Holman began writing his second book, which brought him much acclaim, including admission to the venerable Royal Society of London.

Despite his new-found fame, he got into trouble with the Visitors of the Naval Knights because his long absence had violated the rules of the order. He was admonished and ordered to refrain from further travel and to confine himself to saying his prayers in

Saint George's Chapel—as befitted a Naval Knight. Holman protested and claimed that he needed to travel for his health. His recuperation, he said, required a trip to Fernando Po, now Bioko Island in the Gulf of Guinea in northwest Africa. Objectively, this was an almost entirely absurd justification, especially as seamen stationed on the island were five times more likely to die of disease than others deployed closer to home. And indeed, the mission that Holman joined in would go down in the annals of the Royal Navy as the deadliest expedition ever: Of the original 135 crew members, only twelve survived, one of whom was Holman. Most died of malaria. "Although so many persons were dying around me, I still maintained my cheerful spirits, to which circumstance I attribute the restoration of my health, which was now daily improving."[86] Holman believed in positive thinking, even that his comrades' despondency and fear of death was "more fatal than the disease itself," and could be conquered with a healthy attitude and the sheer will to live.[87]

After Africa, the expedition headed for South America. Unlike other travelers, Holman avoided cities and was drawn to the unexplored wilderness. He joined a mule trek that meandered through a *sertao*, the term used in Brazil to describe remote inland regions. From Brazil, Holman returned to Africa, this time to South Africa, where he learned to ride and spent weeks on horseback. His third great journey, which he began on August 1, 1827, was to be his longest yet. After South Africa, he traveled to India, China, and Australia. It was not until August 1832 that Holman returned to London, where he was celebrated, and extensive articles were written about him in leading literary journals.

The Visitors, those guardians of the rules of the Naval Knights, finally lost patience with Holman after this five-year journey. Nevertheless, the globetrotter had no intention of staying in London and was already planning his next trips. But one request for leave after another was rejected. Holman used all his political and social contacts to obtain an exemption that would allow him to travel again. Meanwhile, his health took another turn for the worse.

The breakthrough came when one of the most prominent doctors in England confirmed that the only chance of restoring Holman's health would be a "continual change of scene and of climate, together with the unrestrained exercise of his mental and physical powers prolonged for a period of at least three years."[88]

The doctor who wrote this just happened to be an acquaintance of Holman and a fellow member of the Royal Society. Nevertheless, Holman's biographer Jason Roberts believes that this was by no means a called-in favor, but a serious diagnosis, especially since it was shared by another two of England's most respected physicians: "Personal sympathies aside, three of the most prominent physicians in the nation would not take such firm stands—under oath and in the face of escalating controversy—unless they honestly concurred. Mysterious as Holman's ailment was, the one seeming certainty was this: it was fueled by sedentary ways, and prolonged exposure to the familiar. The only known treatment was travel."[89] Today, one would perhaps say that Holman was addicted to traveling and that it made him downright sick when he had to stay in one place for any length of time. For Holman, his love of travel was a result of his blindness—losing his sight had created in him a restless urge to see the world.

Holman ultimately prevailed against all odds. Despite being poor and in extremely ill health, he again set off on journeys through Europe, Africa and the Middle East. This time, he experienced no alleviating effect, and his health deteriorated more and more. Returning to London, he set about writing an autobiography, tentatively titled *Holman's Narratives of His Travels*. One friend said

Holman felt "a very natural longing for fame beyond the grave."[90] His death spared him the indignity of seeing his autobiography go unpublished. No publisher showed any interest in publishing the once celebrated and best-selling author's final work. Today, the manuscript is considered lost. On July 28, 1857, less than a week after completing the manuscript, he died at the age of 70. "The most restless man in human history was finally at rest," as his biographer writes.[91]

In Holman's great work on the journey to Africa, South America and Oceania, he had written: "If my undertakings—for such they may without vanity be called—be productive of no other benefit than that of proving to the world how much may be done by a cheerful perseverance under a heavy affliction—how great obstacles may be subdued by resolution,—how the void of sight may be peopled by an active mind, and the desert fertilized by industry—how much hope exists even in the darkest pages of life,—and how many resources against discontent and loneliness this beautiful and varied earth presents—I shall be content to think that my labours have not been altogether destitute of utility."[92]

William Hickling Prescott: "Quiet energy, justifiable self-reliance, cheerful views of life are the best guarantees of success as I have hitherto succeeded. I will."

Credits: Falkensteinfoto / Alamy Stock Photo

# 3.  William Hickling Prescott
## America's First Scientific Historian

William Hickling Prescott is widely regarded as America's first scientific historian. His works, which include books on the conquests of Mexico and Peru and the reign of Ferdinand II and Isabella I of Spain, were praised by critics for their adept combination of historical sources and linguistic flourishes and were translated into many languages. Although Prescott maintained a distance from day-to-day politics throughout his life,[93] leading politicians sought his company—and he cultivated friendships with scholars such as Alexander von Humboldt. His library contained 5,000 books and, perhaps more importantly, a treasure trove of handwritten sources from throughout Spanish history. Nevertheless, for long periods of his life, he was unable to read at all or, at most, for a few short minutes per day—the greater portion of his life was spent as a listener. Prescott would sit in a chair, listening attentively to a paid reader seated behind him. And he wrote on the same writing instrument for the blind, the Noctograph, that was also used by the "blind traveler" James Holman.[94]

Prescott came from a prominent family that emigrated from England to America in 1640. His grandfather, William Prescott, was a colonel in the American War of Independence and led the American rebels in the famous Battle of Bunker Hill. To this day, he still has a bronze statue in his honor in Boston, Massachusetts, the city his son, William Prescott Jr. moved to in 1808.

The historian's father was a well-known and successful lawyer who had become affluent through a series of shrewd investments "in a number of Boston's leading manufacturing, banking, shipping, railroad, and insurance firms."[95] The family's wealth enabled

William Prescott Jr. to send his son, William Hickling Prescott, who was born on May 4, 1796, to a small and exclusive private school, where he and eleven other students received a classical education that included Greek and Latin. William Hickling Prescott was no more than an average student, but he worked diligently to overcome his weaknesses—especially in mathematics. Even as a schoolboy, he began setting regular goals and writing down resolutions in a journal. His friend William Howard Gardiner, his teacher's son, reports: "Thus was, as far as I remember, the feeble beginning of a process of frequent self-examination and moral self-control, which he afterwards cultivated and practised to a degree beyond all example that has come under my observation in cases of like constitutional tendency. It was, I conceive, the truly great point of his moral character, and the chief foundation of all he accomplished in later life as a literary man..."[96]

In anything and everything he turned his mind to, Prescott made resolutions, which he recited aloud and wrote down. And in order to force himself to keep his resolutions, he made small bets with his school friends. When he lost, he paid. But when he won, he forgave his friends' debts. For him, betting was a means of self-discipline, and he stuck with this method. Later in life, for example, he would wager with his secretary about how long it would take him to finish a chapter of whatever book he was working on, or he would agree to pay a fine if he did not get up immediately after being roused from his slumber. Such wagers were always committed to writing and signed by both parties.[97]

Admittedly, at least according to his friends, he sometimes undermined his own discipline. For instance, while attempting to limit his alcohol consumption, he resolved to drink a maximum of two glasses of wine a day. But the first thing he did upon entering a restaurant or bar was to inquire about the biggest glass on the premises. He would then demand that glass, even though it might be two or three times the size of a normal wine glass.[98]

In August 1811, at the age of 15, he enrolled at Harvard College. In his very first year, he was the victim of an accident that would determine the rest of his life. The accident happened after dinner in Commons Hall: "...when he was passing out of the door of the Hall, his attention was attracted by the disturbance going on behind him. He turned his head quickly to see what it was, and at the same instant received a blow from a large, hard piece of bread, thrown undoubtedly at random, and in mere thoughtlessness and gayety. It struck the *open* eye; – a rare occurrence in the case of that vigilant organ, which, on the approach of the slightest danger, is almost always protected by an instant and instinctive closing of the lid. But here there was no notice, – no warning. The missile, which must have been thrown with great force, struck the very disk of the eye itself."[99]

After the accident, Prescott collapsed. He was unconscious, and when he came to, he vomited repeatedly and was confined to his bed for several days. Worst of all, he could no longer see out of his left eye. His sight would never recover, and he remained almost entirely blind in that eye for the rest of his life. His reaction to the accident says a great deal about his character: He knew which young man had thrown the crust of bread into his eye and caused him such serious, lifelong damage. But he very rarely mentioned the boy's name—and when he did, it was not with an accusatory tone. In stark contrast, the perpetrator's conduct was far less honorable: he never once apologized to Prescott for the accident.

Some people blame negative events for their inability to do certain things, others look for culprits. But not successful people: Prescott's biographer writes that, "William would never use his damaged eye as an excuse, for in his mind God had seen fit to leave him with one good eye."[100] But the real difficulties began 18 months later, when Prescott also developed problems with his previously healthy right eye. It became so inflamed that, at times, he was unable to see anything at all. He also became extremely sensitive to light and, for weeks at a stretch, was forced to live in a pitch-black room.

One can only imagine how difficult this was for him, especially as he was terrified of being permanently blind. On top of everything, he also began to suffer from severe rheumatic attacks. His doctors saw a connection between these attacks and the inflammation of his right eye, but even in such a desperate situation, his behavior set him apart: "Throughout this long and painful ordeal William refused to allow these sufferings to dampen his spirits; he never complained or felt sorry for himself, and friends who visited made note of the fact that he was always in a cheerful mood."[101] Prescott's right eye did improve and, over the next few years, he even experienced periods in which he was almost symptom-free. Then the bouts of inflammation would return again and leave him almost totally blind. For the rest of his life, he alternated between almost total blindness and moderate vision.

Despite the coolness of his initial reaction, his blindness did trouble him. In March 1816, at the age of 19, for instance, he wrote to his parents: "The most unpleasant of my reflections suggested by this late inflammation are those arising from the probable necessity of abandoning a profession congenial with my taste, and recommended by such favorable opportunities, and adopting one for which I am ill qualified, and have but little inclination."[102]

After his graduation from Harvard, he initially considered following in his father's footsteps and becoming a lawyer. As he considered his future, he increasingly realized, however, that this was not his true calling. His thoughts and feelings are well documented because, by the age of 23, he had begun to keep a regular journal—a habit he was to maintain throughout his life. His journals comprise some 1,200 pages[103] and bear witness both to his single-mindedness and to his self-doubt and soul-searching. In the spring of 1822, he wrote in his journal: "I am now twenty-six years of age, nearly. By the time I am thirty, God willing, I propose with what stock I have already on hand to be a very well-read English scholar; to be acquainted with the classical and useful authors, prose and poetry, in Latin, French, and Italian, and especially in history."[104] He increasingly developed an interest in history, and in the same year he set down his objective in writing: "History has always been a favorite study with me and I have long looked forward to it as a subject in which I was one day to exercise my pen."[105]

Many successful people commit their goals to paper. For this approach to be effective, the goals need to be both specific and tangible—and preferably linked to a date by which they are to be achieved. Prescott had a habit of setting goals so that they would be achieved by his next birthday.[106] But he also kept a written record of his failures and setbacks, put these notes in an envelope, and read them over and over again to constantly improve and increase his determination and discipline.[107]

Given his father's wealth, he didn't have to worry about accepting a "bread-and-butter" job as he knew that his own financial security was taken care of. And he could also afford to hire secretaries to read to him for many hours a day. He did sometimes also read for himself, but he could often only manage a few minutes at a time before he needed to take a long break to rest his damaged eye.

Once he had decided to devote himself to history, he first considered the recent history of America. It wasn't long, however, before his interest turned to the history of Spain, which, after all, frequently overlapped with that of America. He spent a long time deciding on the exact subject of his first major work. His various ideas, along with his assessments of the pros and cons of each potential subject, are detailed in his journal, in which he finally recorded not only his decision, but also the reasoning behind it.[108]

Yes, he invested his time well and considered his subjects carefully. After all, he needed to hone in on a topic that, first of all, still offered something new to research, for which, second, he could discover new sources, and which, third, would also motivate him for years to come. When a writer decides on a subject, it is much like getting married, except that the writer will probably devote more time to the subject matter of his book than he will to his wife in the years that follow. Prescott was to spend about twelve years working on his first book—from initial research to publication.

As the subject of his book, he chose the "Catholic Monarchs," Isabelle I of Castile (1451–1504) and Ferdinand II of Aragon (1452–1516), whose reign coincided with an eventful period in world history. In 1478, the Spanish Inquisition was established to track down and punish "infidels" who had publicly converted to Catholicism but continued to practice their former faith in secret. Later in their reign, in 1492, Christopher Columbus discovered America, an event that temporarily established Spain as a Christian world power.

The work of any historian depends to a large extent on their sources. Prescott succeeded in uncovering a trove of previously unpublished materials. He had books and handwritten documents brought to him from Europe and spent a great deal of time evaluating them because of his eye disease. He had the documents and books read to him by his secretary and took notes as he listened. He then had his notes repeatedly read back to him—at least six times, but sometimes as many as twelve times.[109]

He was blessed with a very good memory, which allowed him to memorize everything he heard and, little by little, the structure and the story he wanted to tell would take shape in his mind. Every morning—he usually woke very early—he would start the day by going riding. While riding or on a post-lunch stroll, he would craft the next pages of a chapter in his mind, sentence by sentence and paragraph by paragraph. He explained: "I never take up my pen until I have travelled over the subject so often that I can write almost from memory."[110] Before committing ink to paper, he rehearsed what he was about to write five or six times—and sometimes as many as sixteen times.[111] Only once he was truly ready did he begin to write, using a new apparatus developed for the blind, the Noctograph.

Prescott's first biographer, George Ticknor, was a close friend from the age of twelve[112] until Prescott's death. On the subject of the historian's tremendous willpower, he writes: "That Mr. Prescott, under his disheartening infirmities, – I refer not only to his imperfect sight, but to the rheumatism from which he was seldom wholly free, – should, at the age of five-and-twenty or thirty, with no help but this simple apparatus, have aspired to the character of an historian dealing with events that happened in times and countries far distant from his own, and that are recorded chiefly in foreign languages and by authors whose conflicting testimony was often to be reconciled by laborious comparison, is a remarkable fact in literary history. It is a problem the solution of which was, I believe, never before undertaken; certainly never before accomplished. Nor do I conceive that he himself could have accomplished it, unless to his uncommon intellectual gifts had been added great animal spirits, a strong, persistent will, and a moral courage which was to be daunted by no obstacle that he might deem it possible to remove by almost any amount of effort."[113]

As already mentioned, Prescott not only suffered from impaired vision, but also from severe attacks of rheumatism. Even when he experienced such severe pain that he could no longer sit, he refused to interrupt his work. He simply lay down on his stomach on the floor with his Noctograph and continued writing.[114]

In writing, he set himself the goal of preserving his remaining vision for as long as possible and avoiding doing anything that might impair his sight yet further. With this in mind, his friend and biographer reports, Prescott "regulated his life with an exactness that I have never known equaled."[115]

Prescott planned his daily routine with the utmost precision, down to the hour and sometimes even to the minute. This might create the impression that he was an incredibly uptight person with little zest for life. But according to his friends and acquaintances, this could not be further from the truth. In fact, he made sure that his schedule always allowed him enough free time for his leisure pursuits and to socialize with his friends—even if he then tended to excuse himself at a precisely predetermined time. While attending such soirees, however, he was particularly easy-going and entertaining, and always friendly and gracious to those around him.

Thus, he was very different from Beethoven, whom you read about in Chapter 1, and Van Gogh, who is portrayed in Chapter 5. The great composer and the great painter were quick-tempered, got into frequent arguments, and had a hard time maintaining lasting and untroubled friendships. Prescott was the exact opposite. And his amiability was probably one of the keys to his success. He established a network of readers and fellow academics, not only in America, but also in England, Spain, France, Germany, and other countries. And this network of avid supporters was happy to supply him with the books and historical sources he needed and helped with recommendations and reviews of his books.

And yet, Prescott was by no means free of self-doubt. When, after a decade of painstaking research and writing, he finally finished his three-volume work on Isabelle and Ferdinand, he initially questioned the wisdom of publishing it at all. Few people knew that he had been working on the book for the last ten years, and they certainly had no idea that he was writing such a major work.[116] His father finally admonished him: "The man who writes a book which he is afraid to publish is a coward."[117] It took Prescott and his agent a year to find a publisher. Many authors think that once they have completed a manuscript, their work is done. Not Prescott. He devoted himself to every aspect of the book's publication—the paper, the binding, the illustrations—and set exacting standards for the overall quality of his three-volume work.

His doubts about how his work would be received proved to be entirely unfounded. Upon its release, it was highly acclaimed by reviewers and established him as an expert on the reign of Ferdinand and Isabelle. "He was also widely acknowledged for setting a higher standard of documentation for primary and secondary sources. William Hickling Prescott was the first American historian to be recognized as an equal of the European historians of his day."[118] The book was well received not only in academic circles, but also by a wider audience—it was regularly reissued and was translated into numerous languages.

Once the work was published, there followed another extended period—lasting about 18 months—during which he weighed up the subject of his next book. He finally settled on the Spanish conquest of Mexico under Hernán Cortés in the years from 1519 to 1521. This conquest led to the fall of the Aztec empire and established Spanish rule over Mesoamerica. For his book, Prescott had compiled a total of 8,000 pages of previously unpublished documents. They consisted of "instructions of the Court, military and private journals, correspondence of the great actors in the scenes, legal instruments, contemporary chronicles and the like, drawn from all the principal places in the extensive colonial empire of Spain, as well as from the public archives in the Peninsula."[119]

The book combines a history of the conquest of Mexico with a biography of the conquistador Hernán Cortés, which is why it ends not with the conquest of the Aztec capital, but with the death of Cortés. Prescott was convinced that the best way to make history more accessible to a wider audience was by writing biographies of the people involved: "Instead of a mere abstraction, at once we see a being like ourselves ... We place ourselves in his position, and see the passing current of events with the same eyes."[120]

While he was working on his history of the conquest of Mexico, Prescott grappled with a question that all historians face: Should he approach his task with the aim of reporting history "the way it really was" (to employ the famous formulation from the historian Leopold von Ranke, with whom he was also in contact)? Or should he, as many modern historians do, interpret the words and deeds of historical figures through the prism of present-day political and moral standards? Prescott was more closely aligned to Leopold von Ranke. "Prescott avoided passing judgement whenever possible," writes his biographer Peter O. Koch. "He understood that opinions are subject to changes caused by shifts in moral, political, and religious values, and therefore felt the facts of the story should speak for themselves."[121]

Prescott's position couldn't have been clearer: "It is far from my intention to vindicate the cruel deeds of the old Conquerors. Let them lie heavy on their heads. They were an iron race, who periled life and fortune in the cause; and as they made little account of danger and suffering for themselves, they had little sympathy to spare for the unfortunate enemies. But to judge them fairly, we must not do it by the lights of our own age. We must carry ourselves back to theirs."[122]

In the case of the conquest of Mexico, the problem was particularly acute. The continent's indigenous culture was largely wiped out and it is estimated that between 1519 and 1565, Mexico's indigenous population plummeted from 25 million to 2.5 million, primarily due to diseases introduced by the Spanish, but also as a result of forced labor on the Spanish latifundia. In the preface to his book on Mexico, Prescott warned that many readers were likely to take issue with his presentation of events: "The distance of the present age from the period of the narrative might be presumed to secure the historian from undue prejudice or partiality. Yet by the American and the English reader, acknowledging so different a moral standard from that of the sixteenth century, I may possibly be thought too indulgent to the errors of the Conquerors; while by a Spaniard, accustomed to the undiluted panegyric of Solis, I may be deemed to have dealt too hardly with them. To such I can only say that, while, on the one hand, I have not hesitated to expose in their strongest colors the excesses of the Conquerors, on the other, I have given them the benefit of such mitigating reflections as might be suggested by the circumstances and the period in which they lived."[123]

Having already started to collect material for his book on the conquest of Mexico, he found out that the well-known historian Washington Irving was also planning to write a book on the very same subject. So, on December 31, 1838, he wrote to Irving asking how they should best proceed. He explained to Irving that he had already collected a substantial amount of material, but also did not want to stand in Irving's way.[124] Irving was generous and replied that he had indeed considered writing a history of the conquest of

Mexico, but that Prescott had proved through his magnificent work on Ferdinand and Isabelle that he was the right man for the project—and put an end to his own work on the subject.[125]

In the preface to his Mexico book, published five years after he commenced his research, Prescott also openly addressed his eye condition and apologized to his readers: "Owing to the state of my eyes, I have been obliged to use a writing-case made for the blind, which does not permit the writer to see his own manuscript. Nor have I corrected, or even read, my own original draft."[126] His book did not suffer, however, and he is still praised to this day for his historiographical accuracy, fidelity to his sources and his vibrant, easily accessible style.

Peter Neumann, who wrote the afterword to the German edition of Prescott's *Conquest of Peru* (his follow-up to *History of the Conquest of Mexico*), perfectly captures the appeal of Prescott's works: "In striving, through the most exacting research, to provide an accurate portrayal of historical events, his works exhibit all of the progressive traits of the Enlightenment. At the same time, the influences of European Romanticism are evident in the style of his writing: he understands the art of vibrant and vivid representation, which he learned from Romanticism, but he always employs such techniques in service to the facts he wants to communicate and to brilliantly intensify the emphatic effect of his historical observations on the reader by enhancing the colorfulness and pace of the narrative. Thus Prescott, though he once described himself as a 'craftsman,' stands to this day as an outstanding researcher, famous for his fidelity to his sources, and as a great narrator, whose gift for portraying historically significant events has certainly stood the test of time."[127]

Prescott's style sets him apart from a number of contemporary historians who seem to believe that it is impossible to combine a descriptive, accessible style with the highest academic aspirations. Prescott often thought about style—and his notes document his clear-cut opinions on the matter: "Put life into the narrative, if you would have it take. Elaborate and artificial fastidiousness in the form of expression is highly detrimental to this. A book may be made up of perfect sentences and yet the general impression be very imperfect."[128]

According to his friend and biographer George Ticknor, Prescott's visual infirmity was even an advantage in some respects. The fact that Prescott was largely dependent on texts being read to him, and that he was compelled to rehearse every aspect of what he wanted to write down to the smallest detail in his memory before he started to work with his Noctograph, was extremely time-consuming, but it also proved to be beneficial to his work.[129] According to Ticknor, it was precisely as a result of this unique process that Prescott was able to develop such a natural and unmistakable style. What's more, Prescott frequently kept up to 60 pages in his memory for several days, until he could commit them to paper.[130]

The vision in his right eye continued to deteriorate, and by the time he wrote his third book, *Conquest of Peru*, he could only read for a total of 30 minutes a day—and he even had to divide this into smaller, five-minute chunks, followed by half-hour breaks. Thus, his work became ever-more arduous. Nevertheless, he felt that his eye disease was an advantage in some ways. At one point, Prescott even referred to the Greek philosopher Democritus, who is said to have put out his own eyes so that he might philosophize better—without the distractions of sensory input. Moreover, Prescott also credits blindness with being an extremely beneficial aid to disciplining the memory.[131]

Prescott's *History of the Conquest of Mexico* was an enormous success. His publisher expected to sell 5,000 copies of the expensive three-volume work in the first year—a large print run in that day and age. Nonetheless, the entire first print run of 5,000 copies sold out within just four months of publication.[132] This was helped by the fact that a total of 130 reviews of his work—most of them very positive—appeared in the first five months.[133] By 1855, the book had been published in 23 editions[134] and translated into ten languages.[135]

Having been congratulated on his work by none other than Alexander von Humboldt, Prescott noted: "Such testimonies – from a distant land are the real rewards of the scholar. What pleasure would they have given to my dear Father!"[136] His books made Prescott famous in America and Europe. He was admitted to the most prestigious scientific associations in Germany, France, and England,[137] including the Royal Academy of Berlin, which counted Alexander von Humboldt as its president and had a roster of famous members, including Barthold Georg Niebuhr and Leopold von Ranke.[138] Moreover, Harvard University, where Prescott had originally studied, awarded him an honorary doctorate.[139]

Prescott did not get involved in contemporary politics, repeatedly declaring that he only wrote about figures who had been dead for at least 200 years. Nevertheless, or perhaps because of this, he did occasionally move in the same circles as statesmen and leading politicians in America and England. Above all, however, he remained a man of books.

After a brief illness, Prescott died on January 18, 1859, at the age of 62. He had written two wishes before his death, both of which were granted. First, as he had always been afraid of being buried alive, he insisted that one of his principal veins be severed to ensure that no more blood could flow through his body. His second wish was also fulfilled: "He desired that his remains, before they should be deposited in the house appointed for all living, might rest, for a time, in the cherished room where were gathered the intellectual treasures amidst which he had found so much of the happiness of his life. ... Silently, noiselessly, he was carried there. Few witnessed the solemn scene, but on those who did, it made an impression not to be forgotten. There he lay ... in unmoved, inaccessible peace, and the lettered dead of all ages and climes and countries collected there seemed to look down upon him in their earthly and passionless immortality, and claim that his name should hereafter be imperishably associated with theirs."[140] If, after his death, his works were to be his legacy and his soul should mingle with those of other wise and good people of future generations, he wrote on his 48th birthday, he would not have lived in vain.[141]

Prescott possessed a trait that all very successful people exhibit: He was convinced that any disadvantage—such as his eye disease—could be turned into an equally significant advantage: "There is no higher evidence of drawing consolation from its own resources under so heavy a privation, so that it not only can exhibit resignation and cheerfulness, but energy to burst the fetters with which it is encumbered."[142] None of us has much influence over the problems we will face in life, but it is within our power to decide how we respond: "Whining about my troubles unmans me, and, is of itself the worst augury. Making light of these – quiet energy, justifiable self-reliance, cheerful views of life are the best guarantees of success as I have hitherto succeeded. I *will*."[143]

Margarete Steiff: "It was a long search for healing until I said to myself, God has ordained that I cannot walk. It must therefore be right so."

Credits: Margarete Steiff GmbH

# 4. Margarete Steiff
## The woman who made a fortune with Teddy Bears

In Germany, 95 percent of the population has heard of the stuffed toys company Steiff. Generations of children have grown up with Steiff products, the iconic cuddly animals with the distinctive "Button in Ear." According to the credit agency Creditreform, only just under 1.5 percent of German companies have been active for more than 100 years. In fact, Creditreform estimates that the average company is just 18 years old. Steiff, in contrast, is 140 years old, has 1,700 employees and an annual turnover of more than €100 million. Steiff toys from the company's early days through to the 1950s have become sought-after antiques and collectors' items, fetching record prices at international auctions.

As a child, Margarete Steiff's doctors made the following prognosis: "[She is] incapable of the full enjoyment of earthly life as well as of the later fulfillment of the claims which society is entitled to make on its individual members."[144] They couldn't have been more wrong.

Margarete Steiff was born in Giengen, Swabia, in 1847, the third of four children. In her diary she wrote: "At the age of 1 ½, I was stricken with an illness which left me unable to walk. My left foot was completely paralyzed, my right foot partially lame, and my right arm was very weak."[145] Three years later, a doctor diagnosed polio. After an incubation period of about two weeks, the disease, a viral infection, begins with headaches and pain in the limbs, difficulty swallowing, loss of appetite and bouts of diarrhea. The pathogen then invades the central nervous system, eventually leading to paralysis of the arms and legs. For Margarete's mother, Maria, this was another cruel stroke of fate, because years earlier her first husband had died, as had her two sons from her first marriage.[146]

Maria Steiff did not have much time to look after her paralyzed daughter because she had a family of six to support, a household to manage and also had to help her second husband Friedrich, whom she married two years after the death of her first husband, with his construction business. Despite her disability, Margarete was a fun-loving girl. She didn't want to sit around at home on her own: "I begged my neighbors: 'Carry me outside,' even though sometimes I almost froze to death."[147] She would not get a wheelchair until much later; in the early years she was packed onto a hand-pulled cart that was parked in front of her parents' house.

She couldn't run or walk, but used her vivid imagination to make sure she could still take part in life. She sat in her handcart, watched over the other children and, as she later reminisced, "organized games in which I was the center of attention."[148] Her biographer Gabriele Katz writes: "More than anything, she just got in the way of the other kids. So, Margarete decided to turn the situation around. The other children would have to follow her 'rules.' She would choose the games and organize them."[149] Everyone who knew her described her as a friendly and cheerful girl, who was happy taking center stage and had a great appetite for life.

Her parents left no stone unturned in an effort to cure their daughter. In her diary, Margarete Steiff writes that "no remedy was left untried, of course, and I can remember that my mother took me to countless doctors, many of whom were far away from home."[150] Her father applied to a foundation for financial support so that he could have his daughter admitted to the Ludwigsburg children's sanatorium run by the physician Hermann August Werner. And his application was successful. Margarete lived in the doctor's private residence as she wrote in her diary: "In Ludwigsburg I was fortunate enough to be taken in by Dr. Werner's family, who welcomed me to their home and also gave me more freedom than my parents ever had. Thus, I never experienced even a trace of homesickness."[151]

In the clinic, two of the tendons in her left foot were cut and her leg was put into a plaster cast with the hopes of straightening it. She was then taken to Wildbad to recuperate. She enjoyed the time she spent there, but her health did not improve. In 1856, at the age of nine, she spent a total of six months in the clinic and the spa, and another attempt was made the following year. But this second round of treatments was also unsuccessful. Nevertheless, as Gabriele Katz writes, her time in Ludwigsburg and the Black Forest was of great significance for her future life. "It helped her to broaden her horizons enormously. Margarete had been the center of attention, as she so loved to be, had seen, and learned new things, and didn't think of herself as being so disadvantaged compared to the other children. Her self-confidence grew."[152]

Some of the other children in the clinic, she wrote in her diary, could not walk at all, had much more troublesome ailments or suffered from debilitating pain—in comparison, she was the healthiest. She was tutored and even learned some English, which was very unusual at the time. The words of her doctor, who had told the children over and over again that what counted most was their attitude toward their illness, also had a huge impact on Margarete. She had seen more of the world outside her small town than other children—the sum total of new experiences and impressions must have made a strong impression on her. To make her life at home easier, she was allowed to keep the wheelchair she had used at the clinic. Until then, she had always sat in a handcart or been carried by adults.

Back in Giengen, she went to school. Her two older sisters took her to school every morning in her wheelchair, and a strong woman who lived next door to the school carried the paralyzed girl upstairs to her classroom and back down again after class. She enjoyed going to school and her ambition showed as she was always one of the best students. Since she had missed a lot of school due to her time in the hospital, she was determined to try all the harder. "She preferred to have soup brought to school from home so that she would not have to spend time on unnecessary journeys between morning and afternoon classes and could use the time she saved for some extra studying. It is said that Margarete would even skip lunch altogether in order to catch up with the other children as quickly as possible."[153]

Her heart's desire was to play the zither, which was particularly difficult given her disability. After her first pitiful attempts, however, she resolutely told her family, "I will learn." And she did. She practiced for several hours every day, and eventually the handicapped girl had reached the point where she could give zither lessons, which brought in even more money than her painstakingly produced handicrafts.[154]

From an early age, Margarete had to work and help her mother—sewing clothes, knitting, crocheting and so on. "But sewing was also very difficult for me," she reported. "My right arm hurt with the slightest effort, and I had no skill in my left. Instead, I stuck to crocheting and other light needlework."[155] Her parents could not imagine their daughter working in any other way than with her hands.

Margarete was very independent from an early age. Like many successful people, when she was young, she frequently butted heads with her parents. "I had never been as well-behaved and obedient as my sisters, I was often referred to as Ghastly Gret," she wrote in her diary. "Once, still in my school days, my mother was not at all pleased with my work, and yet I had crocheted diligently. I didn't touch any work for two days and told her that if my work wasn't good enough, I would simply stop."[156] Her mother prevailed, but such episodes are testament to her rebellious spirit.

For the strictly religious Maria Steiff, life consisted only of work, and she was not prepared to tolerate cheerful distractions. Margarete also rebelled against this. "So, I actually had to fight for everything, because my mother was a determined enemy of any pleasure or recreation. The word was simply not in her dictionary, only work and work again," she wrote in her diary.[157]

Clearly, Margarete expected more from life. And in the conflicts with her mother, she formed an independent personality and set goals for her own life instead of settling for what was considered 'normal.' Her disability even proved an advantage in certain respects. After all, the usual path for girls at that time was to take on domestic work in other people's homes, thus preparing them for their future roles as mothers and housewives. The first thing any young woman had to do was to find a suitable husband. Unfortunately, it was precisely this path to security that was closed to Margarete due to her disability.

The words of the Serenity Prayer, "God, grant me the serenity to accept the things I cannot change, courage to change the things I can, and wisdom to know the difference," commonly attributed to the theologian Reinhold Niebuhr, perfectly encapsulate Margarete Steiff's attitude to life and might also have become her motto. Margarete and her parents had initially tried everything to cure her illness, but after all of their efforts proved unsuccessful, she finally learned to accept her condition. In her diary she wrote, "From then on—I must have been about 17–18 years of age—I no longer allowed myself to be excited by advertisements for remedies or cures, for the useless seeking of cures does not allow a person to rest."[158] Elsewhere in her diary she writes, "It was a long search for healing until I said to myself, God has ordained that I cannot walk. It must therefore be right so."[159]

Despite the frequent arguments with her mother, her diaries share her gratitude to her parents for "not spoiling me, as mothers so often spoil and pamper their suffering children."[160] Together with her sisters she laboriously sewed and embroidered household linen, nightgowns, men's shirts, bed linen and pillows to earn money. Margarete was very thrifty and soon saved up enough to buy a sewing machine, the first one in her small hometown. Margarete Steiff was therefore ahead of her time and clearly open to the latest innovations. With her new sewing machine, she could not only sew about ten times faster than by hand,[161] but the clothes she made were also more robust and long-lasting thanks to the machined seams.

The first time she tried the new machine, Margarete found that her disability made it impossible to operate because her right arm lacked the strength to turn the flywheel. But she came up with an unconventional solution: "Then I'll sew the other way around," she explained. After just a few days, she was able to move the wheel with her left arm and guide the fabric through the machine with her paralyzed right hand. "Her skill and courage are greater than her disability," commented Margarete's father, praising his daughter.[162]

When her two sisters married early, as was the custom at the time, Margarete was left to run the business alone. She began to hire outside help and, in 1877, she took the next major step. A cousin by marriage—Adolf Glatz—encouraged her to turn her simple tailor's workshop for garments and trousseau linen, which she mainly sold to friends and acquaintances, into a felt clothing company that would also do business with a far larger customer base.[163] She had a small catalog printed and advertised in newspapers. "Margarete Steiff had risen to the class of entrepreneurs, albeit at first only small-scale entrepreneurs. She was now 30 years old," writes Katz.[164] In 1880, Margarete Steiff GmbH was officially founded.

Shortly before that, Margarete Steiff had discovered the pattern and manufacturing instructions for a "fabric elephant toy" in a fashion magazine. She made some of the toy animals, initially as gifts for the children in her family, using felt instead of the recommended cotton fabric. She had no idea how much the elephant would change her business.

At that time—unlike today—there were no cuddly toys for children, only toys made of wood, stone, metal, or porcelain. At first, the production of elephants was only a sideline; the manufacture of clothes had priority. Margarete Steiff was also a little skeptical as to whether the toy animal business would really be of any long-term significance. But her brother Fritz and, above all, strong demand from customers soon convinced her.

In 1880, she produced only eight animals, the following year 18, in 1883 over 100, in 1884 almost 300 and in 1885 almost 600. Then the numbers skyrocketed. In 1886, her company made more than 5,000 elephants and, for the first time, more than 100 monkeys. She constantly added new animals: a horse, a camel, a pig, a mouse, a dog, a cat, a rabbit, a giraffe and so on.[165] In 1892, the 32-page Steiff catalog listed 256 toy animals. For the first time, she added bears, but they were still on four legs—the bear was soon to play a major role.[166] Her stuffed animals were popular not only in Germany, but also abroad—a renowned toy store in St. Gallen, Switzerland, for example, invited Margarete Steiff to visit.

In 1893, the toy factory was officially entered in the commercial register. Margarete Steiff was now 46 years old; her company had grown but was still relatively small with just four female employees and ten home workers. It was at this point that she hired her first sales representative to visit stores across Germany to sign up new customers so that production could be expanded. Four years later, Margarete Steiff had ten in-house employees and 30 home workers, and sales had more than tripled.[167] Her brother Fritz Steiff and his sons continued to encourage and inspire Margarete.

The small family business quickly became an international success. Buyers from London and New York came to visit her factory and purchase her innovative toy animals for their customers in Great Britain and the USA. "The successful entrepreneur," writes her biographer Gabriele Katz, "existed in two worlds, operating on the world market and living with her family in Giengen."[168]

None of this would have been possible without the aforementioned bear, which would go on to become the Steiff company's flagship product. The idea came from Richard Steiff, one of Margarete's nephews. Richard had studied at the academy of applied arts in Stuttgart and spent all his free time in the zoo with a sketchpad under his arm. He observed the animals closely in order to capture their various poses as accurately as possible. He was particularly taken with one animal that had been missing from the collection so far: the bear.

Margarete Steiff was initially a little skeptical about whether a bear would appeal to children; moreover, the production costs for the bear's fur seemed too high.[169] The world's first stuffed toy bear with movable limbs, which bore the designation PB 55, was included in a batch of toy animals sent to New York, where another of her nephews, Paul, was working to sell Steiff products. But, he noted, Americans found the bear too big, too heavy, too hard, and also too expensive, which is why it was "rebuffed and did not sell."[170] In March 1903, the bear was introduced at the Leipzig Toy Fair, but, even there, buyers were not overly impressed. Buyers from the largest and most important toy stores not only spurned the bear with the movable limbs, but even feared that the bears would have a negative impact on the Steiff brand as a whole.[171] Was Margarete right to be skeptical? Had her nephew been overly optimistic?

But, as every entrepreneur knows: when one door closes, another one opens. Every report on the life of Margarete Steiff includes the following anecdote: The toy fair in Leipzig was almost over and the disappointed Richard Steiff was already packing up the collection, when an American toy buyer, one of the company's regular customers, showed up and asked, "Doesn't Steiff have anything new to offer for Christmas this year?" Richard Steiff did not even dare to open the box of bears again. After all, they had not been very popular at the trade fair so far. But the buyer persisted and when he saw the bears, he exclaimed: "Why aren't these soft, golden bears on display? Children will love being able to hold something so dear in their arms even as they go to sleep." The American immediately ordered 3,000 bears and for the next few weeks all of Giengen, from the pastor to the teacher, was busy stuffing bears.[172]

Perhaps the company's big breakthrough with the bear would still not have happened if Theodor Roosevelt had not been the American president at that time. Roosevelt was a passionate bear hunter. As the Steiff company history published in 1930 explains: "When the first samples of the new bear arrived in America, Americans took the whimsical fellow to their hearts. For them, he symbolized their president's happy hunts and christened him 'Teddy' Bear. Everyone had to have a 'Teddy Bear,' and in the first year, the company shipped 12,000 of this timelessly popular toy animal across the big pond. 'Teddy' became world famous overnight, a flagship product that drove the further growth of the house of Steiff."[173]

Production skyrocketed. Two years later, in 1906, the company produced 385,393 Teddy Bears, and in the record year of 1907, almost a million.[174] The total number of all Steiff animals produced per year had risen from 240,000 to 1.7 million between 1903 and 1907.[175] The economic crisis in the USA subsequently led to a slump in sales, but in Europe, the Teddy Bear came to increasingly dominate the stuffed toy market.

As always in business, success attracted imitators, some of whom produced cheaper and inferior knockoffs. In November 1904, Margarete's nephew, Franz, developed the signature "Button in Ear," which today, almost 120 years later, is still the instantly recognizable trademark of every Steiff animal. At that time, the "Button in Ear" was registered as a trademark for Steiff's high-quality toys. Margarete Steiff issued a bulletin: "Registered trademark; (elephant with S-shaped trunk), as of Nov. 1904, the company now attaches a nickel button to the left ear of every piece without exception. This type of attachment has been legally registered."[176] In 1908, the company published an obviously necessary clarification: "The 'jointed bears' that became world famous under the name 'Teddy Bears' are our sole invention. The model did not originate in America, nor did the idea." Margarete Steiff defended herself against fakes, saying, "Customers who are familiar with my goods will not possibly confuse them with inferior imitations. If any of the bears recommended above have been imitated, I kindly ask my honored customers to send me proof, as so many have often done. Only the Button in Ear brand is truly a durable, artistic, and beautiful toy."[177]

Margarete Steiff had come a long way. What would her life have been like without her disability? In the photos, you see a young woman with a beautiful face—presumably she would have married, and her life might not have differed from that of so many other women in her small town. However, her disability prevented her from following the well-worn path open to women at the time. On the threshold of adulthood, after all attempts to cure her paralysis had failed, she accepted that she would be permanently confined to a wheelchair. But she did not accept that this meant being condemned to a life without joy, without travel, without adventure, without success, and without money. Her life was shaped by her life-affirming attitude and her creativity. Her life's journey is all the more remarkable because, prior to 1914, Margarete Steiff was the only woman on the board of any major company, whether publicly traded or privately owned, in Germany—with the exception of the heiress Bertha Krupp von Bohlen und Halbach.[178]

Margarete Steiff died of severe pneumonia on May 9, 1909. In his eulogy, the priest said: "O, is it not a miracle when such a poor, weak, frail, and helpless child, of whom one probably worryingly inquired in childhood: How will she fare? How will she get by? in later life takes care of a thousand others, helps a thousand others, and becomes not only the head of her family, but also the founder and guiding light of a global company? Isn't it a miracle when one, who in childhood was at best granted glances of pity, at worst condemned to be shunned, so steps out into the light of the public stage and wins for herself, and with her, her hometown, a beloved and respected name in the farthest periphery and even across the ocean? Isn't that the kind of miracle you only see once every few centuries?"[179]

Vincent van Gogh (self-portrait, 1887): "Even if I didn't succeed, all the same I thought that what I have worked at will be carried on ... I feel so strongly that it is the same with people as it is with wheat, if you are not sown in the earth to germinate there, what does it matter?—in the end you are ground between the millstones to become bread."

# 5. Vincent van Gogh
## The Sower

You might be asking yourself whether Vincent van Gogh really fits into a book about successful people with disabilities. It is a justified question, especially since the founder of modern Expressionism was not in any way successful during his lifetime. In fact, everything he tried, whether professionally or privately, was a miserable failure. Although he had become a "fixture of the Parisian art scene"[180] as early as 1880 to 1890, he only truly achieved success as an artist after his death.

You might also wonder whether he really qualifies as a person with a disability. After all, classifying someone as "mentally ill" as opposed to "normal" or "healthy" is far less clear cut than is the case for physical disabilities. Van Gogh expert Manfred Clemenz objects to calling him "insane," but concedes that the artist did occasionally suffer from psychotic symptoms, depression, and epileptic seizures.[181] "His mood swung between euphoria and abject dejection, between frenzied activity and depressive exhaustion."[182] In the monumental biography by Steven Naifeh and Gregory White Smith, Van Gogh is described as "perhaps the most depressed and incandescently productive artist in history."[183]

By any measure, the Dutchman was never "normal." He was always an unusually difficult person, a struggling artist who could not find his place in the world and was also only able to support himself for a few years of his life. By the time he reached the age of 24, his parents had grown increasingly worried, and his mother wrote a letter in which she admitted that "we fear that he will become unfit for practical life."[184] Soon after this letter another family member reported that Vincent had suffered his first "mental break-down."[185]

People around him—and even Vincent himself—repeatedly had the feeling that he was descending into madness. At the time, his father even spoke of having Vincent committed to a psychiatric institution. But it wasn't until the last 18 months of his life that his mental illness became so serious that he voluntarily entered an asylum. And this was his most productive period, during which he created many of the works of art that would earn him such fame after his death. In many ways, it is Van Gogh's tortured mental state that makes his life and work so fascinating. Thus, any book on successful people with disabilities would be incomplete without him.

Throughout his life, fame and fortune eluded him. Although his uncle and brother were influential art dealers, while he was alive, Van Gogh only managed to sell one of his many paintings—and only for a distinctly modest sum. Today, he is ranked as the world's most significant modern artist, well ahead of Pablo Picasso, Claude Monet, Henri Matisse, Paul Cézanne, and Andy Warhol.[186]

At auction, Van Gogh's paintings are among the most expensive works ever sold. In 1990, his *Portrait of Dr. Gachet*, a melancholy study of his doctor, was auctioned at Christie's for $82.5 million (adjusted for inflation, that would be about $165 million in 2021). He painted it two weeks before his death. Over the years, some of his other works, such as *Field with Plowing Farmers*, *Self-Portrait without Beard* (both painted in 1889), *L'Allée des Alyscamps* (1875), *Vase with Cornflowers and Poppies* (1890) and *Wheatfield with Cypresses* (1889), have attracted prices ranging from just under $60 million to a little over $80 million. At €25 million, *The Park at the*

*Saint-Paul Hospital,* which he painted during his stay at Saint-Rémy psychiatric hospital, was the most expensive painting at the Tefaf fine art and antiques fair in 2009.

Vincent van Gogh was born in 1853 in Zundert near Breda in the Netherlands, the son of a priest. He was considered a difficult child. In the family's memoirs, which were otherwise relatively moderate in tone, he is described as "obstinate," "unruly," and "self-willed." He was "hard to deal with" and "a queer one" with "strange manners" and a "difficult temper."[187] Even as a child, he was noisy and quarrelsome, and he never gave a damn about what would commonly be called "form." According to his mother, "It is as if he purposely chooses the ways that lead to difficulties. It is a vexation of our souls."[188]

He was just as difficult at school as he was at home. His parents tried everything in their power to salvage his education: they engaged private tutors and enrolled him in evening classes, but to no avail.[189] They then sent him to boarding school, but at the age of 15 he left. At first, he did nothing, that is, he took long, solitary walks and collected beetles. He was told he had to choose a profession, but he didn't know what to do. His uncle, a wealthy art dealer, arranged a job for him in his art dealership in The Hague, where he soon clashed with his coworkers. He didn't think much of "social graces" and had no talent for sales. He quarreled with his bosses and customers and was transferred first to the dealership's London branch and then to Paris. But wherever he went, he had the same problems. He never shied away from saying what he thought of people—including customers. He became clearly exasperated at what he held to be the stupidity of some rich female customers, and when someone defended a purchase by saying *"C'est la mode,"* he would recoil in astonishment and anger.[190]

He worked in the art dealership for six years—the only time in his life when he actually had a regular job and earned his own money. Even then, Van Gogh was afflicted by extended bouts of depression. He didn't have girlfriends; instead, he began associating regularly with prostitutes—a habit he would maintain for the rest of his life. In his free time, he read countless books; another predilection he was to cultivate throughout his life.

Besides history, he was fascinated by religious literature and especially the Bible. When he took up a cause, it was always with a fervency that can only be described as fanaticism. When he discovered religion for himself, he wrote long, stirring letters to his family and friends, "letters fat with scripture, hymns, inspirational verses, and homiletic aphorisms."[191] Even his pious father became uneasy. Vincent admonished his brother Theo, with whom he was in regular (often daily) correspondence, in a commanding tone to "go to church every Sunday; even if the preaching is not good."[192] He commanded his brother not to read anything but the Bible and dismissed all other literature as "disgusting."[193]

At work, his behavior increasingly caused him problems and led to confrontations with his bosses. If his rich uncle had not done so much to protect him, he would certainly have lost his job much sooner. He was finally dismissed in January 1876, and the family chronicler noted: "Vincent received word that he is no longer employed in the house of Goupil...The gentlemen had noticed long ago that he was not fit for business, yet they had let him stay as long as possible for Uncle [Cent]'s sake."[194]

On his 23rd birthday, Van Gogh left Paris and took a job as a teacher at a small boys' school in Ramsgate, a seaside resort on the English coast. It wasn't much of a job; he didn't even receive a salary, just room and board. Vincent stayed only a short time and then traveled hundreds of miles crisscrossing the English countryside.

Although train rides were extremely cheap at the time, he preferred to walk, in any weather, at any time of day or night. "He read books about criminals on the run and consoled himself with daydreams about the ultimate escape of death."[195]

The young man was disoriented. For a short time, he taught at another boys' school, before deciding that he wanted to become a missionary or preacher, perhaps in South America. In a Methodist church in Richmond, Surrey, he gave his first sermon.[196] But he found no permanent position anywhere, and it was at this time that his parents wrote to his brother Theo, "We fear that he will become unfit for practical life. It is bitterly sad."[197] Vincent himself admitted to Theo feeling "heavy depression because everything I undertook failed."[198]

As a short-term solution, he took on a job with a bookseller. But here, too, he paid no attention to his employer's interests and could not be trusted with customers, bluntly telling them what he thought of each book's artistic value. Eventually, he was only allowed to sell "half-penny prints to children and blank paper to adults." As one long-time acquaintance recalled, "He was really next to useless, for he had not the slightest knowledge of the book trade, and he did he make any attempt to learn it."[199]

Vincent could not deal with the day-to-day routine of the kind of normal job that would pay for a regular living. His plans were constantly changing. His father admonished him, telling him that anyone who wanted too much from life was doomed to fail. But Vincent wanted more from life, even if he couldn't yet say exactly what that was. "The need is for nothing less than the infinite and the miraculous," he wrote long before he ever thought of becoming an artist, "and man does well not to be contented with anything less, and not to feel at home as long as he has not acquired it."[200] He was determined to join the ranks of authors, poets and artists who had "thought a little more deeply and searched and worked and loved a little more than the rest, who [had] plumbed the depths of the sea of life."[201]

We know that many famous and successful people, even from a young age, were driven by a desire to achieve something extraordinary in life—even if they did not always know from the beginning *what* that would be. All they knew for sure was that they did not want run-of-the-mill jobs like most of their peers. Sometimes, however, as in Vincent's case, this desire was also fueled by the fact that they knew they would never fit into preordained structures and had problems kowtowing to authority figures, let alone getting on with other people.

Now in his mid-twenties, Vincent was becoming more and more of a religious fanatic. The walls of his room were covered with biblical illustrations, image after image, mostly of Jesus. He spent his Sundays going from church to church, sometimes even attending as many as three or four sermons in a single day. He recited Bible passages and aphorisms to himself until he was numb. Finally, he decided that he wanted to be a pastor, just like his father. In order to study theology, however, he first had to enroll in a university. Although religious knowledge was not a condition of admission, he made long lists of parables and miracles, which he took from the Bible and arranged chronologically in English, French and Dutch.

His behavior became more and more erratic. He only ate bread; even when it was raining and cold, he went out without a coat. At night he denied himself sleep and consumed vast quantities of coffee and tobacco. When he did take short rests, he tortured himself by sleeping on his walking stick or beating himself across the back with it. Eventually, he suffered his first "mental breakdown." His parents and siblings watched in horror as the handwriting in his letters deteriorated along with his mind: "It became mere pen strokes without rhyme or reason," his sister recalled.[202]

It was during this period that Vincent, for the first time on record, contemplated suicide. He meandered alone for weeks, was seen with a sooty face, barefoot, clothed in rags, wandering out of doors in all weathers. Peasants who encountered him on his long, lonely walks simply called him "mad." Vincent would retort that "The Lord Jesus was also crazy," an answer that some took as further proof of his mental instability.[203] Like a tramp, he walked alone, lay down in old wagons or haystacks, and awoke covered with frost. Returning to the parental home, Vincent's father consulted a well-known "alienist" in The Hague, who was also an inspector of lunatic asylums. That was the first time the family considered committing Vincent to an asylum.

Vincent was a seeker. He knew what he didn't want—a conventional, middle-class job—but he didn't know what he wanted. "I know that I could be quite a different man! How can I be useful, of what service can I be? There is something inside of me, what can it be?" he wrote to his brother.[204] In another section of the same letter from July 1880, he writes: "But you will ask: What is your definite aim? That aim becomes more definite, will stand out slowly and surely, as the rough draft becomes a sketch, and the sketch becomes a picture—little by little, by working seriously on it, by pondering over the ideas, vague at first, over the thought that was fleeting and passing, till it gets fixed."[205] It is no coincidence that he invoked the analogy to painting. After all, it was during this period that he decided to become an artist.

Vincent's brother Theo had always encouraged him to concentrate more seriously on his drawing, probably for the same reason as their parents, "as one of Vincent's few remaining social graces, a connection to the bourgeois world that he seemed determined to reject."[206] In December 1881, Vincent wrote to his brother: "For, Theo, with painting my real career begins. Don't you think I am right to consider it so?"[207] And to himself: "Well at present I begin to feel 'that I have a draftsman's fist,' and I am very glad to possess such an instrument, though it may still be unwieldy."[208]

With the same obsession he had applied to his religious studies, Vincent now immersed himself in manuals on perspective drawing and home study courses on figure drawing, which he devoured page by page. He worked from morning to night, for as long as the light allowed, and in a single two-week period he reported finishing a hundred and twenty drawings. He also took some courses at the Royal Academy of Art in Brussels and even enrolled at the Royal Academy of Art in Antwerp, but, essentially, he taught himself to draw. Just as he had earlier believed he could become a priest without studying theology, he was now convinced he needed no formal training to become a major artist. He was probably even right to do so, for it is doubtful whether he would have been able to develop his own unique style if he had pursued and completed disciplined studies at either of these prestigious Royal Academies.

In the beginning, Vincent van Gogh mainly drew landscapes as well as workers and farmers. He initially lived off an allowance from his father and did not see why he should have to take a normal job to earn a living. Given the fact that he was always short of money, he was reluctantly driven to the "indignity" of looking for a job, only to be rebuffed everywhere he applied.[209] Later, looking back, he wrote contemptuously that he had "lost time in terms of earning my bread."[210]

In place of Vincent's father, who as a pastor did not earn all that much himself, Theo took on the role of paying Vincent an allowance for the rest of his life. But even Theo, as a salaried art dealer, was not rich and sometimes had to transfer as much as half of his salary to Vincent. On the one hand, Vincent had a guilty conscience and promised again and again in his letters that he would soon paint pictures that could be sold. On the other, he refused to earn money in any other way and had come to believe "that he *deserved* to be supported."[211] And when his brother insisted that he create more salable works to earn his own living, he countered, "It seems to me that it is much less a matter of *earning* than of *deserving*."[212]

In his letters, he demanded financial support from his brother as if it were an absolute entitlement, and repeatedly pressed Theo to increase his monthly allowance. Van Gogh's biographers write: "Armed with this delusional sense of entitlement, Vincent loudly asserted his artistic prerogative: eschewed formal training; disdained taking a job to help defray expenses; and demanded a large, well-stocked studio, prodigious supplies of materials, and a steady flow of private models—all while he was still little more than an unpromising novice."[213]

Like many artists whose works do not find favor with the public, Vincent developed a defiant attitude. On the one hand, he despised the market and money; on the other, he needed ever larger sums: "I do not pretend to be acquainted with the commercial value of things," he scathingly wrote, "I personally attach more importance to the artistic value, and prefer to interest myself in nature instead of calculating prices."[214]

In one of his regular letters to Theo he wrote: "For the rest, I will run after people less and less, whoever they may be, dealers or painters; the only people I will run after are models; for I think working without a model decidedly wrong, at least for me."[215] His pleas for money became increasingly desperate and were always one of the main subjects of his letters. When his brother wrote that he was not well off, Vincent replied, "If the situation becomes more difficult, let us double the energy. I will be doubly attent with my drawings, but you must be doubly attent on sending the money." The money was absolutely indispensable, he wrote, and warned Theo that "cutting it down would be something like choking or drowning me. I mean, I can do as little without it now as I can do without air."[216] He categorically rejected the idea of getting a job as a "nightmare."[217]

Vincent made Theo a proposal: Vincent would send him his work and Theo should choose what he liked—and any money Theo sent should thus be considered payment for the selected works, "money I have earned."[218] He refused to accept his brother's insistence that his works were not good enough to sell. Vincent said that as far as he was concerned, Theo could even tear his work to pieces. Outwardly, however, Vincent wanted to be able to justify himself in the eyes of the world by saying that his brother had bought his work and his money had been "earned."[219] And his need for money became even greater when Vincent took in one of the prostitutes he regularly consorted with. She had a child (though not by him) and he—or rather his brother—now had to provide for three people.

You could certainly consider Vincent selfish and inconsiderate towards his brother and father by refusing to take on a traditional job and living at their expense all his life. But there is no doubt that he would not have become one of the greatest artists of all time otherwise. It was only because he was free from having to earn a crust that he was able to concentrate entirely on his art without having to bend himself to the latest fashions or public tastes. Such an exclusive focus on one goal and one field of activity can only be described as monomaniacal and is a characteristic of almost all successful people.

Artistically, Van Gogh continued to develop and in 1885 he finished *The Potato Eaters*, which he considered his most successful painting of this period. Later in his career, he tended to paint his pictures very, very quickly. With *The Potato Eaters*, however, he spent a great deal of time on studies, sketches and refining the final version of the painting, which depicts peasants in a dark parlor, seated around a table eating their supper. Unlike his later works, in which he employed bold colors and striking contrasts, *The Potato Eaters* was similar to his early landscapes and portraits in its darkness of tone. For *The Potato Eaters*, Vincent began with lighter flesh tones at first, using yellow ochre, red ochre and white, before painting over them: "I immediately repainted them, inexorably, and the colour they are painted in now is like *the colour of a very dusty potato, unpeeled of course*."[220]

In 1886 he moved to Paris, but here too he failed. He had tried to draw illustrations he could sell, but none of the hundreds of magazines in Paris were interested in buying any of his works. Although his family gave him a direct line to the art market, all of his attempts to interest art dealers floundered. It was during this time, however, that he discovered color. Just as he had earlier praised dark drawings as the only true art, he now praised color: "What is required in art nowadays is something very much alive, very strong in color, very much intensified."[221]

In Paris he became acquainted with impressionism, which he, at first, rejected. But Vincent was always open to new things, and he tried to see the positive and useful in the works of other artists rather than what could be criticized. He soon declared that "though *not* being one of their club yet," he did much admire certain impressionists' works.[222] Despite his reservations about the style, he was nonetheless influenced by the impressionists, as can be seen, among other things, from the fact that he now started to use lighter colors. He was particularly taken with the doctrine of "complementary colors," which soon came to exert a strong influence on his work. In 1887, he even organized an exhibition with a number of well-known impressionists. He was obviously self-confident: the exhibition's largest room contained 100 of his own works, more than any other artist. Nevertheless, even on this occasion he was not able to sell a single one of his paintings.

In February 1888, Van Gogh moved to Arles in southern France. According to the art historian Uwe M. Schneede, Vincent settled in this town in Provence and, "in no time at all, set about creating the unique body of work that would shape the entire modern era."[223] In just two years, Van Gogh produced about 200 paintings. He virtually made speed into a philosophy. Brushstrokes could only express an artist's emotions and sense of nature if they were as fast as words in a conversation, he thought. However, this should not obscure the fact that the quickly painted pictures had often been maturing in his mind for weeks, months or years before he committed brush to canvas. Color played an increasingly important role for him, and he spent long days and sleepless nights planning the color "program" that would both differentiate and unite his images.[224]

But when he then began to paint, "Barrages of brushwork swept across the canvas again and again, like summer storms. Furious exhortations of paint, as intense as fireworks, were followed by wary, ruminating reassessments as he recoiled from the image, arms folded, plotting his next volley. Then, just as suddenly, his brush would dart to his palette, dabbing and stirring, dabbing and stirring, searching for a new color; then rush to the canvas, bursting with new arguments and fresh fervor."[225]

Van Gogh wanted to be inspired by the light of the southern sun and—again with his brother's money—bought a house in Arles, which he proceeded to paint yellow. It was during this time that he developed the concept of a community of artists. Artists who failed to succeed in the marketplace should, according to Vincent, combine forces with other, more successful artists and share the income they earned. Of course, he was unable to find a successful artist who wanted to join his community. Similar to other artists who fail to sell their works, Van Gogh took this as the highest confirmation of the artistic value of his work: "With a more austere talent, you cannot count on profit from your work," he wrote.[226] At the same time, he believed that anyone who was sympathetic to the new artists was likely to be too poor to afford any of their works.

For months, Van Gogh courted the artist Paul Gauguin, whom he deeply admired. And Gauguin did actually come to Arles and move into Vincent's yellow house to form the core of the planned artistic community. The two months during which they both lived and worked together are, as Schneede writes, among the "greatest moments in the history of art." Schneede goes on to write that, "First of all, the sheer volume of works created during this period between late October and the end of December 1888 is stunning. A sense of competition between the two artists seems to have energized them both. During these eight weeks, the two painters frequently tackled the same motifs, although their pictures often enough turned out to be as conceptually different as could be."[227]

And it was perhaps entirely predictable that the artists' community would quickly break up. Van Gogh simply didn't and couldn't get along with anyone. Sooner or later, he would lose his temper and get into heated arguments with everyone. Gauguin was no exception, and soon left the house. This was probably one of the triggers for the violent psychological crisis that haunted Van Gogh until his death, added to which came the news that his brother Theo was engaged to be married. All of this happened around Christmas when Vincent was notoriously sensitive anyway. Gauguin's departure on December 23, coupled with the fear of losing his brother to marriage, triggered an intense panic attack, which led to the famous incident in which he cut off part of his earlobe. Although he was bleeding profusely, he carefully wrapped the small piece of flesh in newspaper and went to look for Gauguin. He searched for him in the brothels they both frequented but could not find him anywhere. He asked for Gauguin's favorite prostitute, gave the package with the piece of the earlobe to the brothel's doorman, and asked him to convey it with the message, "Remember me."[228]

Van Gogh was admitted to hospital, bleeding and unconscious, later raving incoherently in a variety of languages. He was confined to a small, locked isolation room, a kind of padded cell with barred windows. The hospital's doctors declared him insane, but over the next few months, his psychotic episodes gave way to periods of almost complete lucidity. During his attacks, he was overwhelmed by nameless fears and unbearable hallucinations. They spoke to him and accused him of terrible crimes. They called him "a deplorable and melancholy failure," a "weak character" and a "miserable wretch."[229]

His family, notified of Vincent's descent into madness, was shocked, if not entirely surprised. His sister remarked "that he has always been insane," and his brother Theo explained, "I almost dare not hope for his complete recovery, because the attack was the culmination of a variety of things that had been pushing him in that direction over a long period of time. All one can hope for is that his suffering is brief."[230]

In May 1889, Van Gogh voluntarily admitted himself to the insane asylum at Saint-Rémy. He was distraught and wrote, "Now as a painter I shall never amount to anything important, I am absolutely sure of it."[231] But he found solace in the idea that, "As an artist, you are only a link in a chain, and whatever you find or whatever you do not find, you can find comfort in it."[232] It was a fact, he said, "that lots of painters go mad, it is a life that makes you, to say the least, very absent-minded."[233]

At first, he even preferred life in the asylum to life in Arles, where the citizens had united against the 'mad painter' and made life difficult for him. Although he was continually assailed by terrible cries and howls, "like beasts in a menagerie," there was a great sense of solidarity among the patients: "... in spite of that, people get to know each other very well and help each other when their attacks come on. When I am working in the garden, they all come to look, and I assure you they have the discretion and manners to leave me alone—more than the good people of the town of Arles, for instance."[234] Even if some of the patients howled or raved continuously, there was also much genuine friendship there: "... they say we must put up with others so that others will put up with us, and other very sound arguments, which they really put into practice...If someone has an attack, the others look after him and interfere so that he does not harm himself."[235]

Van Gogh would not give up. He continued to paint—and his final 18 months, many of which were spent in an insane asylum, were among the most productive of his life. In June 1889, he created what is probably his most famous painting, *The Starry Night*. "Well, I with my mental disease, I keep thinking of so many other artists suffering mentally, and I tell myself that this does not prevent one from exercising the painter's profession as if nothing were amiss,"[236] he wrote in a letter to Theo in mid-September 1889.

Again and again, his words speak of his hope that his paintings and his body of work would endure beyond his death. Painted portraits—in contrast to photographs—were, he asserted, "felt, done with love or respect for the human being that is being portrayed." In a letter in September 1889, he even asked, "What is left of the old Dutchmen except their portraits."[237] And he was right: one of his final portraits, of his physician Dr. Gachet, was created a few weeks before his death and is today one of the most famous works of art in the world.

Van Gogh died on July 29, 1890, at the age of 37, in a manner that remains unclear to this day. The only point researchers agree on is that he died as the result of a gunshot wound that he sustained in Auvers, a town about 30 kilometers outside Paris, on July 27, 1890. Most biographies speak of suicide, but in the Appendix to their biography, Steven Naifeh and Gregory White Smith cite numerous pieces of evidence that would seem to undermine the common version of events.[238] They suspect that he was killed by the leader of a rowdy group of boys who frequently tormented Vincent with crude jokes—possibly by accident. In his work, art historian Manfred Clemenz provides the best overview of all the theories of whether Vincent's death was suicide, an accident or murder.[239]

Although fame and recognition eluded him during his lifetime, Van Gogh did not fail, but succeeded. "My aim in my life," he once wrote, "is to make pictures and drawings, as many and as well as I can. Then, at the end of my life, I hope to pass away, looking back with love and tender regret, and thinking: 'Oh, the pictures I might have made!'"[240]

As part of the eternal chain of artists, he considered himself immortal. The recognition denied him during his lifetime cannot be taken as evidence of a lack of success, because that was not the standard by which Van Gogh judged his own life. In May 1888, he wrote: "And as for us who are not, I am inclined to believe, nearly so close to death, we nevertheless feel that this thing is greater than we are, and that its life is of longer duration than ours. We do not feel we are dying, but we do feel the truth that we are of small account, and that we are paying a hard price to be a link in the chain of artists, in health, in youth, in liberty...There is an art of the future, and it is going to be so lovely and so young that even if we give up our youth for it, we must gain in serenity by it."[241]

Ten months before his death, Vincent wrote a letter to his brother Theo expressing the hope that what he had begun would be taken up by others: "Do you know what I think of pretty often, what I already said to you some time ago—that even if I didn't succeed, all the same I thought that what I have worked at will be carried on. Not directly, but one isn't alone in believing in things that are true. And what does it matter personally then! I feel so strongly that it is the same with people as it is with wheat, if you are not sown in the earth to germinate there, what does it matter?—in the end you are ground between the millstones to become bread...Even faced with an illness that breaks me up and frightens me, that belief is unshaken."[242]

It was no coincidence that he used the metaphor of wheat and seed. Van Gogh saw himself as a sower, a motif that he returned to over and over again in his paintings. One of his most famous works symbolizes his belief that he was the sower, and his works were his seeds, destined to later become wheat fields, another of his frequent subjects.

A few months before his death, the journal *Mercure de France*, penned by Albert Aurier, published a first, highly regarded essay celebrating the exceptional genius of Van Gogh. And it took no more than a decade for the seeds of Van Gogh's work to begin to sprout. "In the second half of the first decade of the twentieth century, the stylistic influences of his fierce brushstrokes and bright colors have made their way into the work of an entire generation of artists," writes the art historian Uwe M. Schneede.[243] And as Pablo Picasso remarked, "Beginning with Van Gogh, however great we may be, we are all, in a measure, autodidacts."[244]

Helen Keller with her teacher Anne Sullivan Macy at the International Flower Show, New York City, 1913: "Of us it is as true as it is of the seeing that the most beautiful world is always entered through the imagination. If you wish to be something that you are not,—something fine, noble, good,—you shut your eyes, and for one dreamy moment you are that which you long to be."

Credits: Imago History Collection / Alamy Stock Photo

# 6. Helen Keller
## An American Icon

She was friends with the most famous people of her time, including the writer Mark Twain and the inventor Alexander Graham Bell, she was invited to the White House, was the first woman ever to be given an honorary doctorate by Harvard University in 1955, and in 1964 also received the highest civilian honor in the USA, the Presidential Medal of Freedom. She published several bestsellers, gave lectures in 35 countries on five continents and inspired millions—but she could neither see nor hear, and she never learned to speak properly.

Helen Keller was born on June 27, 1880, in Alabama. But in February 1882, at the age of one and a half, an illness robbed her of all hearing and sight. Frighteningly, she writes, she was suddenly plunged into darkness and turned into a "phantom."[245] She later described herself as not even knowing "that I am. I lived in a world that was a no-world...I did not know that I knew aught, or that I lived or acted or desired. I had neither will nor intellect. I was carried along to objects and acts by a certain blind natural impetus. I had a mind which caused me to feel anger, satisfaction, desire."[246]

Naturally, she felt the need to interact with those around her. She began to make simple signs: a shake of the head meant "No," a nod meant "Yes," a pull toward her meant "Come," and a push away meant "Go." If she wanted a piece of bread, she imitated the motions of cutting and spreading butter. If she wanted her mother to make ice cream, she motioned turning the ice cream machine and shuddered as if she were freezing.[247] She had made up about sixty signs, all of which imitated regular actions and were easily understood by other people. "In the years of her mental imprisonment she depended entirely on signs, and she did not work out for herself any sort of articulate language capable of expressing ideas."[248]

One day, she reports in her autobiography, she got her apron wet and spread it out to dry in front of the fireplace. Since the apron did not dry quickly enough for her liking, she stepped closer to the fire–causing her clothes to catch on fire, "so that in a moment my clothes were burning." She screamed terribly, the house servant threw a blanket over her and extinguished the fire.[249]

She often had furious outbursts of anger. She guarded her doll and the cradle where she lay with the most jealous care. But one day she discovered her little sister sleeping peacefully in the cradle. Helen became angry in response to her sister's "presumption," rushed toward the cradle and knocked it over—"the baby might have been killed had my mother not caught her as she fell."[250]

In search of a cure for her deafness and blindness, her parents consulted several doctors, but none could give them any hope. Their child would never be able to see or hear again. One day Helen's mother read an account of a woman named Laura Bridgman, who was also deaf and unable to speak, but had received instruction and made amazing progress thanks to Dr. Samuel Gridley Howe, founder of America's first school for the blind. It should be noted here that you have already met one of the school's most important early supporters in Chapter 3, the historian William Hickling Prescott, who also served on its advisory board.

A doctor told Helen's parents to contact the famous Dr. Alexander Graham Bell, who was already widely known as the inventor of the telephone and who might be able to help them. Bell suggested that they contact the Perkins Institute, which had been founded by Dr. Howe and was now run by Michael Anagnos. This marked the most important turn in Helen Keller's life. Anagnos recommended that Helen take lessons from a young teacher, Anne Sullivan. This woman, then 21 years old, was to play a pivotal role in Helen Keller's life over the next 50 years. Sullivan herself was severely visually impaired and had undergone a series of eye operations. She had extensively studied the methods Dr. Howe had used with Laura Bridgman at the time, but she herself had no experience as a teacher. Helen Keller described March 3, 1887, the day Anne arrived at her home to give her lessons, as the most important day of her entire life, indeed, as her second birth: "I am filled with wonder when I consider the immeasurable contrast between the two lives which it connects."[251]

But Sullivan didn't have an easy time of it at first—and that is a vast understatement. Helen had violent temper tantrums and was not used to any kind of discipline. During lunch, she would go around the table and take food from her parents' and siblings' plates. Her parents permitted this because they felt sorry for the deaf, mute, and blind child. When she did not get her way, she lashed out and screamed. Sullivan soon realized "that I could do nothing with Helen in the midst of the family, who have always allowed her to do exactly as she pleased. She has tyrannized over everybody, her mother, her father, the servants, the little darkies who play with her, and nobody had ever seriously disputed her will, except occasionally her brother James, until I came; and like all tyrants she holds tenaciously to her divine right to do as she pleases."[252] On one occasion, Helen even knocked out two of Sullivan's teeth.

Sullivan accused Helen's parents of not setting boundaries for her, telling them that it would be impossible to teach Helen until she learned discipline. "I have thought about it a great deal, and the more I think, the more certain I am that obedience is the gateway through which knowledge, yes, and love, too, enter the mind of the child," Sullivan said.[253] She had a number of heated discussions about the issue of discipline with Helen's parents, who were initially not sympathetic. Sullivan finally suggested that Helen be separated from her parents for a few weeks because, otherwise, she felt that it would be impossible to teach Helen discipline in the current environment.

Helen's parents finally agreed to let Sullivan and Helen move into a garden house—her parents could see her every day, but only through the window. Sullivan wanted to be alone with Helen. Although Helen initially raged in the garden house as well, the plan worked, and she became calmer. Sullivan was able to begin teaching her words. She used what is called fingerspelling, which was developed for the deaf and mute. In her book *The Story of My Life*, Helen herself describes fingerspelling as follows: "One who reads or talks to me spells with his hand, using the single-hand manual alphabet generally employed by the deaf. I place my hand on the hand of the speaker so lightly as not to impede its movements. The position of the hand is as easy to feel as it is to see. Constant practice makes the fingers very flexible, and some of my friends spell rapidly—almost as fast as an expert writes on a typewriter. The mere spelling is, of course, no more a conscious act than it is in writing."[254]

Sullivan taught her different words this way, but Helen didn't understand at first that each thing had a name. Her teacher spelled into her hand all day, even though she didn't understand what spelling actually meant at the time. But Sullivan didn't think she was doing anything different than adults who say phrases to a small baby whose meaning it doesn't understand at first. "I shall talk into her hand as we talk into the baby's ears," Sullivan said.[255]

Helen made a breakthrough about a month after her arrival. April 5, 1887, was a crucial day in Helen's life: she was pumping water, felt the wetness on her hands, and suddenly understood that the finger movements with which Sullivan spelled the word "water" into her hands meant a name. That "aha" moment, namely that everything has a name that can be spelled out with the finger movements into the hand, was the defining event in Helen's life and a breakthrough for Sullivan. "She spelled 'water' several times. Then she dropped on the ground and asked for its name and pointed to the pump and the trellis, and suddenly turning round she asked for my name. I spelled 'Teacher.'"[256]

Afterwards, Helen was very excited and asked the name of every object she touched. In a few hours she learned thirty words. After nouns, Helen began to learn adjectives and verbs. She had developed words for adjectives before, such as "small" and "big." But instead of communicating with a form of sign language she had invented herself, she now used the words her teacher taught her. At first, Helen spoke only single words and could not yet form sentences, but Sullivan persisted and taught her to communicate in complete sentences. Helen, Sullivan reported in one of her letters, "is as triumphant over the conquest of a sentence as a general who has captured the enemy's stronghold."[257]

Sullivan emphasized that her teaching method was special precisely because she did not use a set method. She did not believe in sitting down with her student at a certain time of day to teach words and phrases. Rather, she relied on what educational psychologists now call "informal learning." They went on outings and did other activities together and talked to each other—using fingerspelling—about whatever was of interest to Helen at the time. She learned through play. "The schoolroom," Sullivan opined, "is not the place to teach any young child language, least of all the deaf child. He must be kept as unconscious as the fearing child of the fact that he is learning words...Language should not be associated in his mind with the endless hours in school, with puzzling questions in grammar, or with anything that is an enemy to joy."[258]

Helen was fortunate to have a teacher with tremendous willpower, who set ambitious goals for herself and never gave up until she achieved them. Sullivan's greatest goal was to wrest Helen from darkness and teach her everything so that she could communicate and know at least as much as those who could see, hear, and speak. Later, Helen Keller wrote a book about her teacher (*Teacher*) and described her as follows: "She could not simplify herself or restrain her ambition (I prefer to call it love of perfection) or circumscribe her dream-nurtured plans for me. She was consumed by restlessness, and moderation was beyond her power to develop. She could not submit to any fate if it meant defeat for us."[259]

Helen Keller could have easily used the same words to describe herself. The fact that she was to achieve more in her life than any other deaf and blind person before her was due to the fact that she met and lived with Sullivan for 50 years in an inseparable bond, driven by great goals and a mutual enthusiasm for learning. "We both believed," Keller said, "that self-improvement is not too difficult if one sees its need with one's mind and realizes it as an inner experience of consciousness and will power."[260]

One can hardly imagine the perseverance, willpower and enthusiasm for progress and self-improvement required to accomplish what Sullivan did. All day long she spelled words into Helen's hand, often entire books. Sullivan did not go easy on herself in the process, for reading did not come easily to her, since she herself had very poor eyesight—which deteriorated further with each passing year.

Word of Helen Keller's extraordinary accomplishments spread quickly. She wrote reports which she sent to the director of the Institute for the Blind, who in turn embellished and exaggerated them in his own reports. The media, first in Boston, then in other cities, adopted the exaggerated reports and embellished them yet further—much to the chagrin of Sullivan, who complained in a letter on March 4, 1888: "Nearly every mail brings some absurd statement, printed or written. The truth is not wonderful enough to suit the newspapers; so, they enlarge upon it and invent ridiculous embellishments. One paper has Helen demonstrating problems in geometry by means of her playing blocks. I expect to hear next that she has written a treatise on the origin and future of the planets!"[261]

Some reports claimed, for example, that Helen had even learned to speak fluently in the meantime. This was a gross exaggeration. Helen had indeed tried for many years, with great effort and many, many hours of practice, to learn spoken language as well. But throughout her life she was never able to speak in a way that other people could understand. At the many lectures she later gave, Sullivan stood by her side and spoke for her while Helen spelled into her fingers. Nevertheless, she had made considerable progress and her family were able to understand Helen when she articulated words.

In May 1888, Helen, her mother, and Sullivan traveled to the northeastern United States. They visited Alexander Graham Bell, with whom Helen became friends, and were even invited to the White House by President Grover Cleveland.

Three years later, Helen became involved in a scandal. Helen, having now learned to read Braille and write, had sent a story she had supposedly written herself, entitled *King Frost*, to Michael Anagnos, the director of the Institute for the Blind. He published the story, but shortly afterward it turned out that Keller was not the author at all. It was a reproduction, even verbatim in parts, of a text previously published by another author. Helen was accused of plagiarism. She and Sullivan countered that Helen had been read the story at some point and, because of her superior memory, had later—unknowingly—written it down as her own without remembering the original source. The head of the Institute for the Blind convened a committee to decide the case. The eight members failed to agree a verdict and Anagnos initially sided with Helen. Nevertheless, the bond of trust between Helen and Anagnos was shaken, and a rift developed between the two.

Keller left the Perkins Institute, where she had been studying temporarily, and attended the Wright-Humason School for the Deaf in New York City. In October 1896, she was accepted as a student at the Cambridge School for Young Ladies, which prepared students for Radcliffe College. Her great dream was to study at a prestigious university. "The thought of going to college took root in my heart and became an earnest desire, which impelled me to enter in competition for a degree with seeing and hearing girls, in the face of the strong opposition of many true and wise friends."[262] Sentences like these reveal the strength of Keller's drive and competitive nature, and her urge to compete not with other blind, deaf, or deaf-blind people, for example, but against people without disabilities.

About a year later, she left school and continued to prepare for college admission with the help of private tutors. Sullivan accompanied Helen everywhere she went, even in school, and spelled into her hand. Helen had learned to read several variants of Braille, but not all of the books she needed at school were available in Braille. However, unheard-of perseverance and diligence bordering on obsession led her to success. By this point in her life, she had learned several languages. This was where she saw her greatest talent: "The first day I had Elementary Greek and Advanced Latin, on the second day Geometry, Algebra and Advanced Greek."[263] While German was her favorite language, she always struggled in mathematics, and her exams were made all the more difficult because she was presented with tasks in an unfamiliar variant of Braille, which she first had to translate into a version she knew. Despite all the difficulties, on June 29 and 30, 1899, she passed her final examinations and was accepted by Radcliffe College. Even so, many people doubted that she would really succeed in her studies and were worried that her time at college would end in great disappointment. Even the dean advised her against studying—even though she had passed the entrance exam.

But it was other people's doubts that really spurred her on. When asked later why it had to be Radcliffe College, Keller replied without hesitation, "Because they didn't want me."[264] She began studying there in late 1900. Her first day was overwhelming: "I had looked forward to it for years. A potent force within me, stronger even than the pleadings of my friends, stronger even than the pleadings of my heart, had impelled me to try my strength by the standard of those who see and hear. I knew that there were obstacles in the way; but I was eager to overcome them."[265]

Psychologists call this "self-efficacy." The term, developed by psychologist Albert Bandura in 1970, is not synonymous with "optimism," but denotes something similar: a person's confidence in being able to cope with even the most challenging situations and to overcome "unexpected" obstacles along the way. The willpower that united Helen Keller and her teacher Sullivan is evident from Keller's book *Teacher*: "I was to her a little explorer of life, and she did not pet nor praise me unless my efforts equaled the best of which normal children are capable."[266] This idea of comparing oneself not to other people with disabilities, but to people without disabilities, was a common theme of Helen's books—whether it was her autobiography or the biography of her teacher Anne Sullivan published many years later.

The university disappointed her to some extent. This was partly because Helen was very emotional and had no use for scientific analyses of literature, for example. "Many scholars forget, it seems to me, that our enjoyment of the great works of literature depends more upon the depth of our sympathy than upon our understanding," she wrote in her autobiography.[267] Differing interpretations and scientific debates confused her. She criticized the "endless comments and confusing criticisms, from which only one thing emerges, that there are more views than people." This, however, is precisely the core of science—controversy. She was relieved when a professor proclaimed what she believed to be the truth: "But when a great scholar like Professor Kittredge interprets what the master said, it is 'as if a new sight were given the blind.' He brings back Shakespeare, the poet."[268]

At the suggestion of her English professor, Helen began writing about her life. He passed her work on to *Ladies' Home Journal*, which offered her $3,000 for a serialized story about her life. The book rights were to remain with her. Keller signed the contract and—while studying—began writing her life story, which would later be published as an autobiography, *The Story of My Life*.

This was not an easy task, especially since it was not possible for her to immediately reread (and rewrite) what she had written. John Macy, who later became a well-known literary critic and whom Helen's teacher Sullivan married, was a great help. He learned fingerspelling, helped her, and when her book, *The Story of My Life*, was published in 1902, he supplemented it with his own comments as well as letters and reports Sullivan had written about Helen. Macy, whose understanding of Helen was only rivalled by Sullivan and Helen's family, described Helen's personality thus: "Her life has been a series of attempts to do whatever other people do, and to do it as well. Her success has been complete, for in trying to be like other people she has come most fully to be herself. Her unwillingness to be beaten has developed her courage. Where another can go, she can go. Her respect for physical bravery is like Stevenson's—the boy's contempt for the fellow who cries, with a touch of youthful bravado in it. She takes tramps in the woods, plunging through the underbrush, where she is scratched and bruised; yet you could not get her to admit that she is hurt, and you certainly could not persuade her to stay at home next time."[269]

Helen graduated cum laude from Radcliffe College with a Bachelor of Arts degree on June 28, 1904. Over the next few years, she published several more books, including *The World I Live In* (July 1908), in which she emphasizes the power of imagination. Helen was a woman of great imagination, and that imagination enabled her to set great goals and to visualize those goals in her mind's eye.

According to the Irish essayist Jonathan Swift, "Imagination is the gift of seeing invisible things." Indeed, imagination allows us to see even those things that we do not yet have. It enables us to see ourselves today as we want to be in the future. Imagination is the launchpad for every discovery and invention, it is the foundation of every business success and every career, but it is also the basis of all great changes in our lives. Einstein once said, "Imagination is more important than knowledge, because knowledge is limited."

-Helen expressed the same sentiment in her book *The World I Live In*: "Of us it is as true as it is of the seeing that the most beautiful world is always entered through the imagination. If you wish to be something that you are not,—something fine, noble, good,—you shut your eyes, and for one dreamy moment you are that which you long to be."[270] This process is also called "visualization," which is one of the most important techniques used in autosuggestion. Undoubtedly, it is also a technique Helen used. The fact that she was deaf and blind probably even made this easier for her because she was not distracted by external stimuli as she dreamed of things with her inner eye.

In many ways, Sullivan served as Helen's motivational coach. In *Teacher*, Helen writes that Sullivan encouraged her with phrases such as: "No matter what happens, keep on beginning and failing. Each time you fail, start all over again, and you will grow stronger until you find that you have accomplished a purpose—not the one you began with, perhaps, but one that you will be glad to remember."[271]

Helen Keller also became an American icon because she was an exponent of positive thinking—similar in this respect to authors Dale Carnegie, Joseph Murphy, Napoleon Hill, Norman Vincent Peale, and others. "...as I regard my country, I find that to be an American is to be an optimist,"[272] she said in *Optimism. An Essay*, in which she strongly opposed any form of pessimism and exalted optimism as a typically American virtue from which, however, other nations could also benefit: "In America the optimist finds abundant reason for confidence in the present and hope in the future, and this hope, this confidence, may well extend over all the great nations of the earth."[273]

While her pleas for optimism were embraced across America, she remained an outsider with her political views. In 1909, John Macy—Anne Sullivan's husband—and Helen Keller joined the Massachusetts Socialist Party. Helen was very much guided by emotion throughout her life; a fact that is clear from all her writings. An exuberant idealism based on strong emotions, combined with a lack of understanding of economic affairs, leads many intellectuals to socialist convictions, which of course did not prevent Helen—after initial reluctance—from accepting the financial support of one of the richest capitalists of her time, the steel magnate Andrew Carnegie. He had offered her a generous pension, and she had proudly refused at first. Three years later, she wrote him a meek letter confessing her difficulties and her helplessness to meet them. "It was the hardest thing she ever did," writes her biographer, Helen E. Waite. "Back came a check, and the most heart-soothing letter the generous Scot ever wrote: 'There are a few great souls who can rise to the height of allowing others to do for them what they would like to do for others. So you have risen.'"[274]

In her autobiography, Helen did not mention Carnegie by name, but was effusive in her thanks: "To the other friend I am also deeply indebted. He is well known for the powerful hand with which he guides vast enterprises, and his wonderful abilities have gained for him the respect of all. Kind to every one, he goes about doing good, silent and unseen." Of course, she was not allowed to mention his name.[275] Carnegie died in 1919, and in her 1955 book *Teacher*, Keller then referred to the entrepreneur by name, calling Carnegie a "wonderful friend." He had helped her by granting a pension that allowed her to "climb up the steep hills of self-support," which she called "ultimate happiness."[276]

In 1913 Helen began to tour widely giving lectures, first in the USA, then in other countries. As long as Anne Sullivan was alive, she accompanied Helen everywhere she went. Helen spelled words into Sullivan's hands and Sullivan then verbalized them for the audience. Since she could not earn enough money from these lectures, Helen also began performing in vaudeville theaters with Anne Sullivan in February 1920, which brought in significantly more money.

In the years that followed, she became involved with the American Foundation of the Blind, becoming a board member in December 1932. Helen wanted to spread her messages for the blind and deaf worldwide. In 1931, she traveled to France and Yugoslavia, in 1936 to England, Scotland, and again to France, and in 1937 to Japan, Korea and Manchuria.

During World War II, she visited blind, deaf, and invalid soldiers in hospitals and spoke words of encouragement to them. After the war, she made her first trip on behalf of the American Foundation for the Overseas Blind, lecturing in London, Paris, Italy, Greece, Scotland, South Africa, Latin America, India, and many other places. In all, she visited 35 countries across five continents.

One of her most important messages was that pity was the wrong attitude to adopt toward people with disabilities. She even called pity the "main obstacle for the blind": "Such an attitude almost neutralized an act of genuine good will. There may be poetry in tears shed over the unfortunate and in the overwhelming sense of fate over human beings, but that is not the way God wishes us to lift their spirits above the infirmities of the flesh." In Helen's words, a person with a disability does not know "his hidden sources of strength" until "he is treated like a normal human being and encouraged to try to shape his own life."[277] Again and again, she denounced "the destructive element of pity" and concluded that the habit of viewing people with disabilities as "objects of charity...was incredibly hard to break."[278]

What Helen said about her teacher also describes her own attitude: "She could not bear anyone who thought it was wise and clever to be gloomy. Her scorn fell upon those who peeped between the curtains of life's shrine, found it empty and went away grumbling, never suspecting the dimness of their own spiritual vision."[279]

In 1961, Helen suffered a stroke and withdrew from the public stage. President Lyndon Johnson awarded her the Presidential Medal of Freedom. Helen died in her sleep on June 1, 1968. She found her final resting place next to her teacher Anne Sullivan Macy, who had died in October 1936, in the Episcopal Washington National Cathedral in the American capital.

It was the deepest inner conviction of Helen Keller and Anne Sullivan that "every human being has hidden away in him capabilities waiting to be discovered... Achievement is a pleasure—the most satisfying of all pleasures, but it is won only at the price of a valiant fight. It is the palm that crowns the creator. Achievement is a part of the boundlessness of life tamed."[280]

Not giving up, even in the face of the most challenging difficulties, was one of Helen's defining personality traits from childhood on. Sullivan provided a perfect example in her notes, which perhaps shows better than anything else why Helen was so incredibly successful. One day, as Sullivan was showing Helen how to build a tower with building blocks, she recalls: "As the design was somewhat complicated, the slightest jar made the structure fall. After a time I became discouraged, and told her I was afraid she could not make it stand, but that I would build it for her; but she did not approve of this plan. She was determined to build the tower herself; and for nearly three hours she worked away, patiently gathering up the blocks whenever they fell, and beginning over again, until at last her perseverance was crowned with success. The tower stood complete in every part."[281]

Frida Kahlo: "Since my subjects have always been my sensations, my states of mind and the profound reactions that life has been producing in me, I have frequently objectified all this in figures of myself, which were the most sincere and real thing that I could do in order to express what I felt inside and outside of myself."

Credits: Jerónimo Alba / Alamy Stock Photo

# 7.   Frida Kahlo
## Latin-America's Most Famous Painter

Frida Kahlo is the most famous painter from Latin America. During her lifetime, however, she was overshadowed by her husband, Diego Rivera, who was widely regarded as the most popular painter in Mexico at the time. Nonetheless, she is now far more widely known than Rivera and, in recent decades, a "veritable cult has formed around her life and works. In fact, it has even developed its own name—*Fridamania*—which, since the 1990s, has created an entire merchandising machine that has come to stamp the artist's face, including her trademark fused eyebrows, onto almost every object you could possibly imagine."[282]

At auction, her paintings sell for millions. Her 1939 painting *Dos desnudos en el bosque*, which shows two nude women sitting in a meadow on the edge of a forest, changed hands for $8 million at Christie's in 2016. At the time, that was the highest price ever paid for a painting by a Latin American artist. Ten years earlier, Kahlo's *Roots* had sold for $5.6 million at auction (adjusted for inflation, that would be around $7.5 million in 2021).

Kahlo was born on July 6, 1907, although she always insisted that she had been born in 1910, to coincide with the first year of the Mexican Revolution. Even her fake date of birth was a calculated fabrication for this "master of self-promotion."[283] Her father was German and had emigrated to Mexico at the age of 18. When Frida was six, she contracted polio and was bedridden for nine months. As a result, the growth of her right leg was retarded, and it remained noticeably thinner than her left. To hide her suffering, she wore three or four layers of socks and elevated her right shoe with a stacked heel.

At the age of 15, Frida was admitted to the Escuela Nacional Preparatoria, then the best school in Mexico, in order to prepare for university. Frida's attendance at the school was certainly unusual. In fact, she was only one of 35 girls among a total of 2,000 students.[284] Her mother opposed the idea of sending Frida to the school, but her father firmly believed in his daughter's abilities. Nevertheless, he was only willing to allow her to attend the school on one condition: Frida was forbidden from talking to the male students. Of course, she did not comply with her father's wishes. She joined a rebellious gang that was well known for its frequent pranks—and the beautiful Frida fell in love with the gang's leader, Alejandro Gómez Arias.

On September 17, 1925, at the age of 18, she was riding a bus with her boyfriend. That day was to change her life forever. The bus they were on was involved in a serious accident. She later described sitting in the back of the bus, near the handrail, with Alejandro sitting next to her. Moments after they had taken their seats, the bus collided with a slow-moving trolley car from Xochimilco. "When the trolley car went around the corner the bus was pushed against the wall...It was a strange collision. It was not violent but rather silent, slow, and it harmed everybody. And me most of all."[285]

The steel handrail had broken, skewering her body through her left hip and coming out through her vagina. Her boyfriend tried to lift her but was horrified to see the iron bar piercing her body. The man next to him said, "We have to take it out." He braced his knee against Frida's body and said, "Let's take it out." Thinking back on the aftermath of the accident, Alejandro later recalled, "When he pulled it out, Frida screamed so loud that when the ambulance from the Red Cross arrived, her screaming was louder than the siren."[286]

In the hospital, the doctors did not think she would survive. Her spinal column was broken in three places in the lumbar region, her collarbone was broken, her third and fourth ribs were broken, her right leg had eleven fractures, her right foot had been crushed and her pelvis was broken in three places. She spent a month laying on her back in a cast, despairing: "I was completely pierced through from the hip forward, for such a small thing I'll be a wreck for the rest of my life or else I'll die..."[287] Having spent a month in hospital, she was discharged, but still had to stay at home for several more months.

She had originally planned to study medicine, but that now seemed impossible, especially as the hospital and medical fees associated with her accident meant that her parents no longer had enough money to fund her studies. Over the next few decades, Frida Kahlo endured at least 32 operations, most of them on her spine and right foot, until she finally succumbed to her suffering 29 years after the accident. "She lived dying," said the writer Andrés Henestrosa, one of her closest friends for many years.[288] She was frequently desperate and, two years after her accident, she wrote to Alejandro that she sometimes wished she were dead, because, as she confided, "I'll never be able to do anything with this wretched sickness."[289]

It was at this time that Kahlo discovered her true talent, painting. She painted her first serious work of art as a gift to her boyfriend in late summer 1926, during a relapse that again confined her to bed for several months. It was a self-portrait, the first of many. There was no subject Frida Kahlo returned to as often as she painted herself. More than a third of her nearly 200 paintings were self-portraits.[290]

In 1947, when she applied to the Instituto Nacional de Bellas Artes, which was organizing an exhibition of 45 self-portraits by Mexican painters from the 18th to the 20th centuries, her application tersely stated: "I began painting...out of sheer boredom. I was in bed for a year on account of an accident that fractured my spine, foot and various other bones. I was 16 years old at the time [she was actually 18, R.Z.] and was desperate to study medicine. When a bus from Coyoacán hit a trolley car from Tlalpan, all of my plans were ruined...But I was young, so the accident was no great tragedy at the time: I felt strong enough to do something other than study medicine. And without wasting too much time thinking about it, I began to paint."[291]

One element of Kahlo's self-promotion strategy was to portray herself as neither particularly vain nor ambitious, and so she added to the brief application, "I have painted but little, without the slightest ambition or desire for fame, but mainly for my own pleasure and later in the hope of earning a living through my work."[292]

Painting offered Kahlo a way to express her physical and psychological pain. In many of her paintings, she turns her body inside out—depicting her internal organs on the outside of her body, as a form of artistic X-ray vision, or even floating beyond her physical form. "The girl whose ambition was to study medicine turned to painting as a form of psychological surgery," writes her biographer Hayden Herrera.[293] Later in her biography of Frida Kahlo, Herrera explains: "And, friends have noted, Frida's most passionate love affair was with herself." In Kahlo's self-portraits, Herrera observes, there is "a strong element of self-fascinated autoeroticism in her display of wounds in paintings like *Remembrance of an Open Wound* and in later wounded self-portraits."[294]

Kahlo wanted to know if she really had any talent for painting and was confident enough to set off to see by far the most famous painter in Mexico at the time, Diego Rivera, whom she greatly admired. Rivera was working on murals for the Ministry of Education and Kahlo asked him to come down from his scaffolding and look at her paintings. She knew, of course, his reputation as a ladies' man, so she got straight to the point, "Look, I have not come to flirt or anything even if you are a woman-chaser. I have come to show you my painting."[295] She showed him the three canvases she had brought with her and asked him for his honest opinion, because she said she could not afford to continue with her art merely to appease her own sense of vanity. If he thought she had no talent, she would accept his opinion and find another way to help her parents and support her family. He was immediately impressed and told her she had talent, which of course delighted Kahlo. And yet she remained somewhat skeptical, because she was worried that the famous painter was only expressing an interest in her art because she was a beautiful young woman. On the one hand she was right, on the other hand she wasn't: Rivera couldn't resist beautiful women and, just a few days after they first met, he kissed her for the first time. But he also believed in Kahlo's great artistic talent, regardless of his personal interest in her—and remained a firm believer for the rest of his life.

Not long after their first meeting, the two became a couple, and soon there was talk of marriage. One of Kahlo's friends even advised her, "Marry him, because you will be the wife of Diego Rivera, who is a genius!"[296] Her mother was skeptical for several reasons: first, there was the age difference (she was 22, he was 42); second, the famous painter, despite his ugly face and considerable excess weight (130 kg), was a well-known playboy; finally, there was his political convictions—Rivera was an ardent communist, a conviction he shared with Frida, who had also joined the Communist Party. In the 1920s and 1930s, it was fashionable in intellectual circles to be a communist. Their hatred of capitalism had blinded them to the crimes of communism and closed their eyes to the atrocities of Stalin, whose murderous regime claimed millions of victims.

On August 21, 1929, Frida Kahlo and Diego Rivera became man and wife. Only six weeks later, Rivera was expelled from the Communist Party, in large part because they resented his close contacts with the government, for whom he regularly painted. Frida also resigned from the party in solidarity, although they both remained staunch communists.

The following year, the couple traveled to the United States, where Rivera accepted several commissions, including one from the Rockefeller family to paint murals at Rockefeller Center in New York City. The fact that the Rockefellers commissioned an artist known for incorporating communist symbols, such as the hammer and sickle, into many of his works, is testament to their political naiveté, a trait they share with many wealthy heirs. In fact, Rivera's mural at Rockefeller Center even included a likeness of Lenin.

The *New York World-Telegram* ran an article under the headline "Rivera Paints Scenes of Communist Activity—and John D. Jr. Foots Bill."[297] Nelson Rockefeller, John D. Jr.'s son, wrote to Rivera: "I am afraid we must ask you to substitute the face of some unknown man where Lenin's face now appears." Rivera then claimed that the figure of Lenin had been present in his original design (which was not true), but nonetheless suggested a compromise: Lenin should remain where he was, but on the opposite side of the fresco, Rivera offered to insert "in perfect balance with the Lenin portion, a figure of some great American historical leader, such as Lincoln."[298] The Rockefellers rejected Rivera's proposal. Shortly thereafter, representatives of the architectural firm responsible for the center came and demanded that Rivera, who was working on his painting, descend from his scaffolding. They handed Rivera a check for $14,000 dollars to settle his fee and instructed him to stop work.[299]

Kahlo was not particularly enthusiastic about the U.S. at first, and her political views are evident in her letters: "It is terrifying to see the rich having parties day and night while thousands and thousands of people are dying of hunger," she wrote to her doctor.[300] Rivera, despite his politics, was revered in the United States. In fact, New York's famous Museum of Modern Art selected Rivera to be the subject of only its second ever one-man show (the first exhibition featured the work of Henri Matisse). The exhibition was a great success.

Kahlo, initially completely overshadowed by her husband, now began to paint more seriously. In July 1932, while she was hospitalized in Detroit after suffering one of her several miscarriages, she painted *Henry Ford Hospital*. In the painting, Kahlo lies naked in her blood-stained hospital bed, surrounded by symbols of her failed pregnancy. Her self-portraits were brutal and terrifying as she sought to express her suffering. According to Rivera, "Frida began work on a series of masterpieces which had no precedent in the history of art—paintings which exalted the feminine qualities of endurance and truth, reality, cruelty, and suffering. Never before had a woman put such agonized poetry on canvas as Frida did at this time in Detroit."[301]

For her own part, Kahlo continued to downplay the significance of her art. In January 1933, she wrote to Abby Aldrich Rockefeller that she painted "a little bit" but not because she considered herself "an artist or something like that." She only painted because she had nothing else to do and because working allowed her to forget her many troubles.[302]

In December 1933, the couple returned to Mexico and shortly thereafter Rivera began an affair with his sister-in-law Christina. Frida was devastated. Throughout their marriage, her husband was never faithful. He had a procession of affairs and Kahlo consoled herself with the fact that, as she wrote to her husband in July 1935, the other women only "represent flirtations, and that at bottom *you and I* love each other dearly..."[303] Kahlo was hospitalized at least three times that year. She had another miscarriage and needed surgery on her foot. Five of her toes were amputated. The same year, she painted *A Few Small Nips*, in which she projected her psychological and physical suffering onto the fate of another woman. The painting depicts a naked woman on a bed, covered in blood, towered over by a man with a knife in his hand.

It wasn't only Diego Rivera who had his affairs, she did too. However, she kept her affairs secret, while Rivera conducted his openly. Her most unusual affair was with the communist revolutionary Leon Trotsky, who, in fleeing Stalin, was forced to live in exile in Mexico from January 1937. Trotsky had been one of Lenin's closest comrades-in-arms but had lost out to Stalin in the struggle for power after Lenin's death. In 1938, he established the Fourth International and founded the ideology that would later be referred to as Trotskyism. Rivera had helped Trotsky and his wife come to Mexico. The two couples met on a regular basis—and a sexual relationship developed between Trotsky and Frida behind Rivera's back. Perhaps it was in revenge for her husband's numerous infidelities that Frida had an affair with the man Rivera so admired.

Trotsky was afraid of being killed in exile by Stalin's agents. And he was right to be so afraid. On August 21, 1940, he was murdered by one of Stalin's agents with an ice pick. Later in her life, having returned to the Stalinist Communist Party, Kahlo participated in the party's defamation of her former lover, claiming that she had always been against inviting Trotsky to Mexico: "He went out very little because he was a coward. He irritated me from the time that he arrived with his pretentiousness, his pedantry because he thought he was a big deal."[304] Back in 1938, however, she had written to a friend, "Now I can only can tell you his [Trotsky's] coming to Mexico has been the swellest thing ever happened in my life."[305] Similarly opportunistic, Rivera later tried to ingratiate himself with the Stalinists with the claim—invented, of course—that he had arranged Trotsky's asylum in Mexico only so that the Russian could be killed there.

In 1937, Kahlo began to focus more seriously on her art and, in 1937 and 1938, she produced more paintings than in the previous years of her life combined. In 1938, for the very first time, she participated in a group exhibition at a gallery in Mexico City, and an art collector bought four of her paintings for $200 each (the equivalent of $1,800 per painting in today's currency). The experience had a major impact on her, because now she saw painting not just as a hobby, but as a way to become financially independent. "This way," she told herself, "I am going to be able to be free, I'll be able to travel and do what I want without asking Diego for money."[306]

Most of her paintings were self-portraits, a fact she explained in an application for a Guggenheim Foundation fellowship in October 1939: "Since my subjects have always been my sensations, my states of mind and the profound reactions that life has been producing in me, I have frequently objectified all this in figures of myself, which were the most sincere and real thing that I could do in order to express what I felt inside and outside of myself."[307]

In 1939, at the invitation of André Breton—the influential pioneer of Surrealism—she traveled to France for an exhibition of her paintings. Kahlo was repeatedly plagued by pain, especially in her spine and feet. In addition, she suffered from other illnesses and was repeatedly hospitalized, including during her stay in Paris.

She did not like Paris or what she saw as the empty posturing of its intellectual scene. In a letter she wrote: "You have no idea the kind of bitches they are. They make me vomit. They are so damn 'intellectual' and rotten that I can't stand them any more...They sit on the 'cafes' warming their precious behinds, and talk without stopping about 'culture,' 'art,' 'revolution' and so on and so forth, thinking themselves the gods of the world, dreaming the most fantastic nonsense, and poisoning the air with theories and theories that never come true. Next morning—they don't have anything to eat in their houses because *none of them work*."[308]

Her private life was dominated by a series of ups and downs in her relationship with her husband—they divorced in 1939 but remarried just one year later. They remained in constant touch, even in the period after the divorce, although they both started seeing other people. Her most intense love affair was with the photographer and Olympic fencer Nickolas Muray.

Rivera once remarked that she created her best works during their period of separation. And indeed, she was particularly industrious at that time because she was determined to stop accepting money from Rivera. She wanted to earn her own living entirely from her art. She had tried to rent her house to tourists, but when nothing came of it, she wrote: "So now I am hoping only in my own work."[309]

It was immediately after her divorce from Rivera that she completed one of her most famous works, *The Two Fridas*. It was her first large-scale work and is widely regarded as one of her most remarkable paintings, depicting a double self-portrait with two different versions of Kahlo sitting together. One is wearing a white Victorian dress in the European style, while the other wears a traditional Tehuana costume. Then, in 1940, she created her *Self-Portrait with Cropped Hair*, in which she looks like a man. Karen Genschow writes that Kahlo's heightened productivity during her time apart from Rivera "suggests that pain, whether psychological or physical, was a central impetus of her painting. Thus, she was able to process it, transform it into something tangible, and make it 'speak.'"[310]

Kahlo's art was increasingly attracting attention, including from an international audience. After the Paris exhibition, Picasso wrote to Rivera: "Neither Derain, nor I, nor you are capable of painting a head like those of Frida Kahlo."[311] In 1940/41, she exhibited with a group of Surrealist artists in Mexico City, New York and Boston. She did not describe herself as a Surrealist and did not want to be pigeonholed. "I never knew I was a Surrealist till André Breton came to Mexico and told me I was. The only thing I know is that I paint because I need to, and I paint always whatever passes through my head, without any other consideration."[312] Despite her misgivings, she benefited from interest in this new artistic movement and, as long as it remained fashionable, she had no problem with being called a Surrealist in public.

She was repeatedly troubled by illness—a consequence of the injuries she had sustained in the accident at the age of 18. She was ill and depressed throughout the autumn and winter of 1939/40. Above all, she was plagued by terrible pains in her spine. Out of desperation, she drank as much as one bottle of brandy a day. In November 1940, during a stay in New York, she wrote, "Before I came to the States, a month and a half ago, I was very ill in Mexico. Three months I was lying in bed with a plaster corset and an awful apparatus on my chin which made me suffer like hell. All the doctors in Mexico thought I had to be operated on my spine. They all agreed that I had tuberculosis on the bones due to the old fracture I suffered years ago in an automobile accident. I spend all the money I could afford to see every specialist on bones there, and all told me the same story. I got so scared that I was sure I was going to die."[313]

Fortunately, it turned out that she did not have bone tuberculosis, although her health was becoming more and more troublesome. In 1941, she wrote to her doctor: "If I felt better healthwise one could say that I am happy—but this thing of feeling such a wreck from head to toe upsets my brain and makes me have bitter moments."[314]

In the 1940s, Kahlo's international standing grew. She participated in international conferences and, in 1942, she began teaching at Mexico City's renowned La Esmeralda Art Academy. By the mid-1940s, she was so well known that she was included in every major group exhibition in her native country. In 1946, she was awarded second prize in the international exhibition at the Palacio de Bellas Artes for her painting *Moses*, which had been commissioned by Don José Domingo Lavin, who asked her to read *Moses and Monotheism* by Sigmund Freud and paint her interpretation of it. She later said that after rereading Freud's book, she found her painting incomplete and no longer felt that it did justice to Freud's analysis—but it was too late to change it once it had been painted. Unlike some other artists, she was very reluctant to "interpret" her art anyway. She believed that her works should speak for themselves and reveal their meaning to each viewer.

In the meantime, her health continued to deteriorate. In 1950, she spent nine months in hospital and underwent a total of seven operations on her spine. In 1953, her lower right leg was amputated. Toward the end of her life, she described the succession of orthopedic corsets she wore after 1944 and the treatments that went with them as a "punishment." In all, she had to wear 28 corsets, one made of steel, three of leather, and the rest made of plaster. One of these corsets in particular did not allow her to sit or even recline. It made her so angry that she took it off and used a sash to bind her torso to the back of a chair in order to support her spine. At one point, she spent three months in a nearly vertical position with sacks of sand tied to her feet to straighten her spine.[315]

In her self-portraits she depicted herself as bleeding, broken open, without a foot and even headless. She transformed her pain into art. To numb her immense pain, she was given high doses of morphine and eventually became dependent on Demerol, a painkiller that would become widely known decades later as one of the pop star Michael Jackson's regular drugs of choice. The active ingredient in Demerol is pethidine, which mimics the body's own pain and stress relievers, endorphins. Depending on the dosage, Demerol can inhibit the transmission of pain or even block it completely.

Despite the pain, she continued to paint and, in April 1953, had her first solo exhibition in her native Mexico. Until shortly before the exhibition opened, nobody knew for sure whether the seriously ill painter would be able to attend in person. She was carried into the exhibition and took center stage in a four-poster bed. The scene is depicted in the Oscar-winning film *Frida*, which, by the way, sticks far closer to the facts than many other movie adaptations of the lives of major historical figures.[316] From the bed, Kahlo soaked up the adulation and affection of 200 friends and admirers; it was something of a farewell for her. According to Genschow, the exhibition's opening celebration documents an important part of the Frida Kahlo myth: "She is presented as a woman who, despite a litany of physical adversities, created extremely personal (and celebrated) art and, even marked by death, still wrings the last out of life and, bedecked in vibrantly colorful costume, embodies a true zest for life."[317]

Although she was still recovering from pneumonia, she joined a communist demonstration on July 2, 1954. Her husband pushed her wheelchair along the bumpy streets as the leading lights of the Mexican art scene marched in her wake. For Kahlo, communism was something of a comforting religion. Karen Genschow writes that "the party" increasingly became her religion and even came to manifest itself in some of her later works. Her 1954 painting *Marxism Will Give Health to the Sick*, for instance, features Karl Marx as a saint.[318]

At her bedside, Kahlo kept pictures of Marx, Engels, Lenin, Stalin, and Mao. She saw men like Stalin and Mao as saviors of mankind, despite the fact that they were responsible for the deaths of over 80 million people. Unfortunately, she was not alone in this great error; she shared it with a great many intellectuals and artists. At one point she wrote: "I understand clearly the materialistic dialectic of Marx, Engels, Lenin, Stalin and Mao Tse. I love them as the pillars of the new Communist world."[319] The last painting she left on her easel was an unfinished portrait of Stalin.[320] In her art, however, she never adhered to the principles of "socialist realism," as she herself admitted.

On July 13, 1954, Frida Kahlo Rivera died in her sleep. The official cause of death was listed as pulmonary embolism, although there are indications that she had taken an overdose of painkillers. The last words she wrote in her diary were "I hope the exit is joyful—and I hope I never come back—Frida."[321] In her husband's own words, it was "the most tragic day of my life." At first, he refused to believe that she was dead. A doctor had to prove it to him by making a small incision in her carotid artery—it was the only way he could convince Rivera that no more blood was flowing through her body and that she was really dead. Frida Kahlo had specified that she wanted to be cremated and, when her ashes emerged from the crematorium's oven, Rivera took some in his hand and ate them.[322]

Frida Kahlo lived beyond death. Although she had suffered physically and emotionally all her life due to the accident she had in her youth, she lived life in all its facets to the full, combining an extraordinary relationship with a famous artist, numerous affairs with both men and women, and creating a body of work with which she made herself immortal.

John Forbes Nash, Jr. in New York, November 2010: "I think mental illness or madness can be an escape also ... If things are not so good, you may be one to imagine something better. For me, I was able to imagine myself as in a role of greater importance than I would seem to be ordinarily."

Credits: Patrick McMullan / Getty Images

# 8.   John Forbes Nash, Jr.
## A Schizophrenic Nobel Prize Winner and Math Genius

John Forbes Nash, Jr. was awarded the Alfred Nobel Memorial Prize in Economic Sciences in 1994, along with two other scientists, for their joint achievements in the field of game theory. Nash was one of the very few mathematicians ever to receive this award. In 2015, he also received the Abel Prize, worth 6 million Norwegian kroner (about €600,000), one of the highest honors for mathematicians. Some readers may have seen the 2002 multi-Oscar-winning film *A Beautiful Mind*, about the schizophrenic mathematician. However, the film has little to do with Nash's actual life or with the biography by Sylvia Nasar on which it is based.

Nash's life was unusual in many respects. At first glance, it can be divided into three phases: First, prior to the age of 30, he accomplished numerous brilliant mathematical feats; then he fell ill with schizophrenia; finally, after decades, he eventually recovered (which is unusual enough). But at second glance, the transitions between these phases are not so clear.

Nash was born in Bluefield, West Virginia, on June 13, 1928, the son of an engineer. As a child, he loved books and conducting experiments with electrical and chemistry kits but had little interest in playing with other children. When he was 13, he got his hands on the book *Men of Mathematics* by mathematician and science fiction author E.T. Bell. It contained 40 biographies of the lives of famous mathematicians, and Nash was fascinated. Perhaps reading it awakened his ambition to later achieve similar great feats himself as the heroes in this book.

As early as high school, it was clear that he was more intelligent than his classmates. When he entered the George Westinghouse competition, he won one of a total of ten full scholarships awarded nationwide.[323] At 17, Nash was accepted by the Carnegie Institute of Technology in Pittsburgh. His original ambition was to become a chemist, not a mathematician. All through school, he had a reputation for being difficult and often had arguments with his teachers, which continued at university, where he once got into a dispute with the professor over the lack of rigor of the mathematics in the course.[324] His math professors recognized his talent—one even called him "a young Gauss"[325]—and recommended that he major in mathematics.

After the first half of his sophomore year, he focused almost exclusively on mathematics. At the age of 19, he had already adopted "the style of a mature mathematician."[326] He was different from the others. Mathematician Raoul Bott recalled: "He was a much more dreamy person. He'd think a long time. Sometimes you could see him thinking. Others would be sitting there with their nose in a book."[327]

In spring 1948, at age 20, he was accepted by the prestigious universities of Harvard, Princeton, Chicago, and Michigan, the top four doctoral programs in mathematics in the United States. Nash chose Princeton, where the best mathematicians in the world gathered. Albert Einstein was also conducting research at the university's Institute for Advanced Study at the time.

The environment was just right for a young, brilliant, but eccentric man like Nash. He rubbed shoulders with the most talented math students in America and benefitted from the combination of informality and fierce competition that is so characteristic of the

United States. As one former student recalled, "Competitiveness, it was sort of like breathing. We thrived on it. We were nasty. This guy, he's dumb, we'd say. Therefore he no longer existed."[328]

Everyone seemed somewhat arrogant, but Nash was even more so. He always wanted to draw attention to himself and make it clear to everyone that he was more intelligent than everyone else. Nash attended few seminars and read little because he felt that too much second-hand learning would inhibit his creativity and originality. He thought a lot, and especially thought while interacting with others. Many mathematicians prefer to work alone, but for Nash, sharing ideas was most important. "Nash's main mode of picking up information he deemed necessary consisted of quizzing various faculty members and fellow students. He carried around a clipboard and constantly made notes to himself. They were little hints to himself, ideas, facts, things he wanted to do..."[329]

Nash was brimming with self-confidence. Only a short time after arriving at Princeton, he told Einstein's assistant that he had a topic he absolutely must talk to the great professor about. No other student would have come up with such an idea. Nash got the appointment; he wanted to talk to Einstein about improving quantum theory. For most of the meeting, Nash stood at the blackboard, scribbling equations. The conversation lasted almost a full hour, but at the end Einstein just said with a friendly smile, "You had better study some more physics, young man."[330]

Nash struck fellow students as odd. One summed it up by saying, "If he was in a room with twenty people, and they were talking, if you asked an observer who struck you as odd, it would have been Nash."[331] He was respected, but hardly anyone liked him. Nash irritated students by saying things like, "What was happening on the earth when the Martians took over and there was a period of violence and why such and such?"[332]

Among the Institute's top mathematicians, however, he had advocates who considered him "very brilliant and original but rather eccentric."[333] Nash polarized, even among professors. Some accepted his peculiarities, others refused to.

One of his favorite pastimes was playing games. Fellow students recalled that Nash seemed to spend all of his time at Princeton sitting at game tables in the common room, playing board games such as chess, go, or "Kriegspiel" (a cousin of chess that uses three chessboards or a map), which was particularly popular at the time.

It was typical of Nash, however, that he wanted to do more than play games according to other people's rules so, at the age of just 19, he invented his own ingenious game, which his fellow students and professors loved to play. He later recalled, "At Princeton University, where I invented it, everyone called it 'Nash.' I worked on it with some other guys, and a friend of mine made the board. But later we found that someone in Denmark had invented a similar game. He called it 'Hex,' and that's the name it's known by now."[334]

It was for his work in the field of game theory that Nash would not only earn his first merits, but also became famous and win the Nobel Prize many decades later. "When Nash arrived at Princeton in 1948, it had already become game theory's world capital."[335] The founder of game theory was John von Neumann, then a professor at the Institute for Advanced Study. Neumann was considered a mathematical genius, and at Princeton there was a standing joke that he was really an extraterrestrial who had learned how to perfectly imitate a human being.[336] In 1944, together with the philosopher and economist Oskar Morgenstern, a professor in the economics department at Princeton, von Neumann had published *The Theory of Games and Economic Behavior*, which is considered the foundational work of game theory. The two authors criticized economics as hopelessly unscientific and wanted to put it on a new footing. With the exception of Einstein's theory of relativity, their work received more attention than any other highly mathematical book had ever received, including a breathless front-page story in *The New York Times.*[337]

Game theory involves decision-making situations in which the outcome for a decision-maker depends not only on his own decisions, but also on the behavior of other decision-makers. Game theory has little to do with parlor games; it is a theory of social action. "A decision situation in which several rational decision makers influence the outcome and pursue their own interests is called a strategic game, strategic interaction, or strategic conflict."[338]

Nash was becoming more and more interested in game theory, and he saw the potential to expand on von Neumann's work and highlighted the weaknesses of the latter's approach. A few days after Nash took his general examination, he knocked on the door of von Neumann's secretary's office and told his secretary he wanted to discuss an idea with him. "It was," as Nash's biographer writes, "a rather audacious thing for graduate student to do. Von Neumann was a public figure, had very little contact with Princeton graduate students outside of occasional lectures, and generally discouraged them from seeking him out with their research problems. But it was typical of Nash, who had gone to see Einstein the year before with the germ of an idea."[339] Neumann's reaction to the meeting, however, was less than enthusiastic, and Nash felt rebuffed. Perhaps this was what motivated him to write his doctoral thesis on von Neumann's field, game theory.

At the age of 21, Nash wrote his brilliant doctoral thesis on game theory, which was only 27 pages long but packs a punch. Von Neumann had been primarily concerned with zero-sum games, in which one player's gain is another's loss. In the capitalist economy, however, such zero-sum situations are the exception (although many people believe otherwise). Nash extends game theory to co-operative games in which mutual gain is possible. "By formulating the problem of economic competition in the way that he did, Nash showed that a decentralized decision-making process could, in fact, be coherent—giving economics an updated, far more sophisticated version of Adam Smith's great metaphor of the Invisible Hand."[340]

It seems astonishing that someone who attended only one course on economics in his entire life should develop a theory for which he was to receive the Nobel Prize in Economics decades later. But Nash's strength lay precisely in his unorthodox and completely surprising approaches to problems—and his ignorance of economics was probably even an advantage, because it meant he was not blinded by routine and did not fall into the temptation of thinking along well-worn lines.

After earning his doctorate, Nash spent the four years beginning in 1950 working for a number of organizations, including the RAND Corporation, a think tank founded in 1948 to advise the U.S. Army. This think tank was a perfect fit for Nash. The atmosphere was similar to the Internet start-ups in Silicon Valley decades later: the mathematicians came to work in short-sleeved shirts, and no one was addressed as doctor or professor. Everyone had the greatest possible freedom, which suited Nash. Even then, he struck many as somewhat peculiar, roaming the corridors without pause, chewing on an empty paper cup clamped tightly between his teeth. "He would glide through the corridors for hours at a time, frowning, lost in thought, shirt untucked."[341] Colleagues reported seeing Nash tiptoeing exaggeratedly along the street, stalking flocks of pigeons, and then suddenly rushing forward, "trying to kick 'em."[342]

At that time, game theory was not just a topic for the scientific ivory tower: the military had initially hoped that it would make significant contributions to solving strategic questions. Soon, however, disillusionment set in. And Nash's dissertation on game theory was also "greeted with a mix of indifference and derision" by the pure mathematicians,[343] so he sought other topics on which to focus his research. "Strange as it may now seem, the dissertation that would one day win Nash a Nobel wasn't highly regarded enough to assure him an offer from a top academic department."[344]

Nash now turned his attention to other areas of mathematics, in particular to so-called algebraic manifolds. He gained a reputation as a first-class expert in pure mathematics with a paper in this field, which he published in 1952. Nevertheless, he did not get an offer for a position in the mathematics department at Princeton. He had the impression that he was rejected not because of his achievements but because of his personality. Instead, the now 23-year-old received an offer to lecture at MIT, the Massachusetts Institute of Technology in Boston, also world-renowned, where he worked for the next few years. Nash's behavior became ever more outlandish. His typical sayings included, "You're a child. You don't know crap. How trivial! How stupid! You'll never do anything!"[345]

He looked for difficult problems in mathematics that others had not been able to solve, no matter what the field. "He was not a game theorist, analyst, algebraist, geometer, topologist, or a mathematical physicist. But he zeroed in on areas in these fields where essentially nobody had achieved anything. The thing was to find an interesting question that he could say something about."[346] Before turning to a new topic, he often spoke with other experts to find out how relevant and difficult they thought a given topic was. He only wanted to deal with problems whose solution would guarantee the highest possible recognition within the mathematical community.

In his office at MIT, he worked mostly at night, from 10 p.m. to 3 a.m. One mathematician described the way Nash approached difficult problems: "The difficulty [that Levinson had pointed out], to anyone in his right mind, would have stopped them cold and caused them to abandon the problem. But Nash was different. If he had a hunch, conventional criticism didn't stop him. He had no background knowledge. It was totally uncanny. Nobody could understand how somebody like that could do it. He was the only person I ever saw with that kind of power, just brute mental power."[347]

In 1958 Nash published a solution to a particularly difficult mathematical problem. It was one of the famous 23 problems that David Hilbert had announced in 1900 at the Mathematical Congress in Paris as the great unsolved questions in mathematics. As it happened, an Italian mathematician had solved the problem at the same time, but independently of Nash. This came as a shock to Nash, who was convinced that, had he been the only one to solve the problem, he would have been awarded the Fields Medal, the highest honor in mathematics, the equivalent of the Nobel Prize. Nash, however, did not let up and took on the biggest unsolved problem in mathematics, which was also on Hilbert's list of 23 unsolved questions, the Riemann hypothesis.

But at the same time, his behavior had evolved from crankiness to insanity. He showed his colleagues a copy of *The New York Times* and explained to them that aliens or some foreign government had contacted him through the newspaper. They had sent him secret messages through an article that only he could decode. He gave one of his students his expired driver's license and wrote the student's nickname "St. Louis" above his own name. The ID, he told the student, was an "intergalactic driver's license." He himself was a member of a committee, he said, and was putting the student in charge of Asia.[348] The student thought Nash was joking, but he wasn't. This and similar behaviors were signs that Nash was suffering from schizophrenia.

He wrote a letter to a colleague in four different colors, complaining that his career was being ruined by aliens. Sometimes he wrote letters all day—to ambassadors, heads of state, the Pope, the FBI and the United Nations. He gave a confused speech at the university and was laughed at. He believed he was the "left foot of God" and that God had come to earth.[349]

In an interview much later in his life, Nash explained why he had become schizophrenic at that time. The explanation is characteristic of his thinking, for, as in game theory, he tried to discover a rational and subjective benefit to the sick person, even in insane behavior. Most people, Nash argued, believed that the mentally ill were suffering and that it was the job of doctors to alleviate their suffering through medication or other treatments. But in fact, the situation, as he saw it, was more complicated: "I think mental illness or madness can be an escape also. People don't develop a mental illness because they are in the happiest of situations usually. One doctor observed that it was rare when people were rich to become schizophrenic. If they were poor or didn't have too much money, then it was more likely. And this is natural, if things are very good, you can find satisfaction with the world as it is, as it seems to be. If things are not so good, you may be one to imagine something better.

For me, I was able to imagine myself as in a role of greater importance than I would seem to be ordinarily. At the time, I had some recognition. I was making some progress professionally, but I wasn't really at the top. I didn't have top level recognition, and so when I started thinking irrationally, I imagined myself as really on a Number 1 level. I was the most important person of the world, and people like the Pope would be just like enemies, who would try to put me down in some way or another, or the president."[350]

Nash's behavior became increasingly unusual and disturbing. He later recalled, "I believed that other people were planning things in secret. I thought they were having secret meetings where they were conspiring, but I didn't know where they were taking place or when. I believed that coded messages were being sent, through newspapers, and that all I had to do was find them. So, I looked through the newspapers to find the codes. I was disturbed, but I seemed normal at first. I was making it all up with myself. At that time, I was offered a position at the University of Chicago, and I turned it down on the grounds that I had been chosen to become Emperor of Antarctica...I discovered that many men wore a red tie. You see, I don't wear a red tie (Nash points to his tie). I thought at the time that they were part of a communist secret movement."[351]

His wife Alicia, whom he had met as a student at MIT and married in 1957, became increasingly desperate and finally saw no other option than having him admitted to a psychiatric hospital. His first hospital was McLean Hospital in Belmont, Massachusetts, where many celebrities had also been treated, including Ray Charles. Nash was hospitalized for 50 days, after which he and his doctors believed he was healthy again. His behavior was completely 'normal' again. But he soon suffered a relapse.

He was now obsessed with the idea of establishing a world government. In the 1950s, the idea of a world government was quite widespread. Its supporters wanted to give up their respective national citizenships because they felt they were citizens of the world and advocated global citizenship. Nash traveled to Paris and intended to surrender his American citizenship at the U.S. Embassy. When this was refused, he tried the same thing in Geneva. He wanted to be recognized as a refugee from "all NATO, Warsaw, Middle East and SEATO pact countries."[352]

But everywhere he went his requests were rejected and finally, in a fit of desperation, he destroyed his passport. In his own eyes, he was now stateless. But in the eyes of the authorities, he was simply a man without the necessary identity papers. He was eventually arrested in Geneva and sent to prison. But he refused to have a new passport issued or to return to the United States. A police escort accompanied Nash to the train station bound for France. He managed by some unknown means to travel from Paris to East Germany without a passport. His biography stated that he probably sought asylum there, but Nash later denied this.[353] In any case, the East German authorities also asked him to leave the country.

Eventually, he returned to Princeton. He was now 32 years old. "The man who walked up and down the main street of Princeton in the stifling summer of 1960 was clearly disturbed. He would go into restaurants with bare feet. With dark hair to his shoulders and a bushy black beard, he had a fixed expression, a dead gaze. Women, especially, found him frightening,"[354] writes Nasar.

The situation escalated to the point where his wife again agreed that he needed to be committed to a mental institution. But she didn't have the money for an expensive private facility, so he was now incarcerated in Trenton Hospital, an overcrowded clinic with 2,500 patients, where he had to live in a room with 30 or 40 others. He was treated with electroshocks and insulin. This "therapy," invented in 1933 and for a time considered standard treatment for schizophrenics, is no longer used. Nash had to endure this "therapy" five days a week for six weeks—he later described insulin therapy as "torture."

Once again, Nash's condition improved, and he was discharged from Trenton four weeks after his 33rd birthday. His mental state remained volatile. He had periods when he and others believed he was well, only to relapse again.

He remained connected to mathematics despite his illness and his former colleagues helped him, collecting money for him. For a time, he even worked again at MIT, gave a seminar there and published an essay in the renowned journal *Annals of Mathematics* in 1966. Another essay followed. "The quality of these two essays—the first of which geometer Mikhail Gromov calls 'amazing'—constitutes the single strongest reason for questioning Nash's diagnosis of paranoid schizophrenia. Producing papers that broke new ground was a remarkable feat for someone who had, by 1965, been psychotic for most of six years and suffered substantial memory impairment," writes his biographer.[355]

But he soon sank deeper and deeper into his illness. A national economist was planning an anthology on mathematical economics and wanted to include an older contribution by Nash and wrote to Nash to ask permission. The only response that came back was an envelope with the economist's address painted on it with various crayons. Enclosed was a list of words meaning "You" in various languages: Du, Vous, You...

From the 1970s to the 1990s, Nash lived at Princeton, where he could be seen regularly on campus. When no one was in the lecture hall, he went in and wrote jumbled messages on the blackboard, such as: "Mao Tse-Tung's Bar Mitzvah was 13 years, 13 months and 13 days after Brezhnev's circumcision."[356] Students who saw him on campus called him "The Phantom." Rumor had it that he was a mathematical genius who "flipped" during a lecture. According to other students, he either lost his mind when he was trying to solve an incredibly difficult problem or after it was revealed to him that someone had beaten him to a major discovery. Alternatively, he descended into madness when he learned that his wife had fallen in love with a mathematical rival.[357] Among students, he served as a cautionary tale. Nerds were admonished that they would "wind up like the Phantom." But when a freshman complained that he felt uncomfortable around Nash, he was soon put in his place: "He's a better mathematician than you'll ever be!"[358]

Normally, schizophrenia is considered incurable, but there are studies that show that between eight to 20 percent of sufferers can permanently recover. At first, it's not easy to distinguish whether improvements are temporary and will be followed by new episodes, or whether they are the first steps on the road to permanent recovery. Some people who spoke with Nash observed significant changes as early as the mid-1980s. A professor who met him in 1985 recalled, "He seemed so much better. He described his work in the theory of prime numbers. I'm not competent to judge it, but it seemed like real mathematics, like real research. That was very gratifying."[359] In the early 1990s, reports began to accumulate that Nash had overcome his illness. In 1992, the mathematician and economist Lloyd S. Shapley visited Princeton and met Nash: "He was free of this distraction. He'd learned how to use the computer. He was working on the Big Bang. I was very pleased."[360]

Nash's recovery was not the result of any treatment or medication. He himself explained the process thus: "Gradually I began to intellectually reject some of the delusionally influenced lines of thinking which had been characteristic of my orientation. This began, most recognizably, with the rejection of politically-oriented thinking as essentially a hopeless waste of intellectual effort."[361] Nash himself was convinced that he ultimately forced his recovery through willpower: "Actually," he wrote, "it can be analogous to the role of willpower in effectively dieting: if one makes an effort to 'rationalize' one's thinking then one can simply recognize and reject the irrational hypotheses of delusional thinking."[362]

Whether willpower alone can cure decades of schizophrenic illness seems very unlikely, but Nash certainly felt that way—and you have to consider that even before his illness he was different from other people and had enormously strong willpower. When I first read about Nash, I was reminded of an experience from my own life: In my early 20s, I suffered from hypochondria for several years. Although I was in perfect health, I visited up to nine specialists in one three-month period. All of them assured me that I was in unusually good health. Unlike many other hypochondriacs, I knew I was one. And at some point, I decided to throw the health encyclopedias I had been reading into the trash and to stop paying attention to any articles, TV shows, etc. that dealt with diseases. After that, my hypochondria disappeared and I was no more worried about my health than other people. I recognized parallels between Nash and myself when I read the following words from Nash: "A key step was a resolution not to concern myself in politics relative to my secret world because it was ineffectual. This in turn led me to renounce anything relative to religious issues, or teaching or intending to teach."[363]

In a 2010 interview, the scientist explained that his recovery was at least partly due to the fact that he saw his name appearing more and more frequently in economics publications. "I think that changed my thinking and helped bring me back to my senses...After all, life is not so bad if you get a certain amount of recognition. I wanted to be something better, even a misunderstood prophet."[364]

In another interview, when asked how he had recovered, he explained, "My work was accepted, and I also felt more accepted again. The recognition helped me. The sensible life finally became more attractive."[365] This explanation corresponds to his rational theory, according to which his schizophrenia was caused by the lack of initial recognition he felt he was entitled to from the scientific community. As soon as he felt that his achievements got the recognition they deserved, he was able to recover—according to Nash's own explanation.

As game theory received increasing attention, that fueled Nash's perception of his own growing stature. One consequence of this was that Nash's name was now frequently mentioned whenever the Nobel Prize in economics was being considered. As early as the 1980s, the committee responsible for awarding the Nobel Prize in Economic Sciences had considered Nash. They initially had doubts, however, because of his mental state. However, Assar Lindbeck, who played a key role in awarding the prize, had heard in the late 1980s that Nash was on the road to recovery. He asked for research to be done on Nash's health. The research revealed that Nash was healthy again, but doubts remained: was he really cured? How would Nash react to being awarded the Nobel Prize, would he embarrass the committee in his acceptance speech? People also cited other arguments against Nash, such as that his achievements dated back almost half a century and that it was mathematics rather than economics. But Nash's supporters prevailed, and in October 1994 Nash, together with Reinhard Selten and John Harsanyi, was awarded the Alfred Nobel Memorial Prize in Economic Sciences in the field of game theory.

At a press conference in Princeton after the decision was announced, Nash said he hoped that winning the Nobel Prize would boost his credit rating because he desperately needed a credit card. He added that he was aware that a laureate was expected to express genuine joy at being one of the winners of the prize. However, he wished he had won the whole prize alone, because he really needed the money badly.[366]

Nash was not only interested in money privately but also academically. Over the next few years, he became deeply involved in monetary theory and criticized Keynesian economics for allowing manipulative short-term inflation and sovereign debt tactics that ultimately undermine currencies. As an alternative, he advocated "index money," which would link the value of money to a price index. In 2011, he explained in an interview with René Scheu: "I contrasted the ideal money with money that is devalued by inflation. My idea is to make money more stable through a price index. I have in mind the establishment of a kind of 'Industrial Consumption Price Index' based on global prices of industrial goods, including gold, platinum and copper. With such an index, prices would be less volatile. One could replace fiat money—money created out of thin air by banks—with this index money."[367] Nash noted on several occasions that some of his thoughts had parallels with those of Friedrich August von Hayek, who had received the Nobel Prize in Economic Sciences exactly 20 years earlier.

On May 19, 2015, a few days before his death, Nash, together with Louis Nirenberg, was awarded one of the most prestigious mathematics prizes, the Abel Prize, by King Harald V of Norway at a ceremony in Oslo. Nash and Louis Nirenberg received the award for their "striking and seminal contributions to the theory of nonlinear partial differential equations and its applications to geometric analysis." Just days later, on May 23, he died while riding in a cab with his wife—the cab driver had lost control of the vehicle. Neither of the passengers were wearing seat belts and were thrown out of the vehicle. A few weeks later he would have been 87 years old.

Nash's game theory, which was initially ridiculed, has since strongly influenced numerous sciences—including economics, evolutionary biology, political science, psychology, sociology, anthropology, neuroscience and even physics.[368] "There is no doubt, that game theory's wide application throughout the intellectual world was made possible by Nash's math."[369]

Ray Charles in July 1982: "A lot of my dreams were coming true, but there were still others. They might have been crazy, but they were dreams, and dreams, if they're any good, are always a little crazy."

Credits: United Archives GmbH / Alamy Stock Photo

## 9. Ray Charles
### The High Priest of Soul

He is known as "the high priest of soul." In *Rolling Stone's* ranking of the "100 Greatest Singers of All Time," Ray Charles is the number one male singer, ahead of superstars such as Elvis Presley, John Lennon, Bob Dylan, and Paul McCartney. Only one singer, Aretha Franklin, makes it onto the list ahead of him, relegating him to second place among the 100 greatest in music history. And he wasn't just a singer, he was also a songwriter and producer and won 17 prestigious Grammy Awards—from 37 nominations. With a net worth of $100 million, he was also one of the richest singers of his day and age.[370] He conquered the charts and achieved world-wide acclaim with hits such as "Hit The Road Jack," "What'd I Say" and "I Can't Stop Loving You." One of his most famous songs, "Georgia on My Mind," was even proclaimed the official state song of Georgia on April 24, 1970.

Ray was born in Albany, Georgia, in September 1930. He grew up in Greensville, Florida, without his father. His mother, Aretha Williams, was among the poorest of the poor in their small hometown.[371] "Even compared to other blacks in Greensville we were on the bottom of the ladder looking up at everyone else. Nothing below us 'cept the ground,"[372] Ray remembered. He later added: "Didn't bother us any that we were poor. Didn't bother us 'cause we didn't know any better. Folks who don't have much—and ain't ever had much—can get along just fine. Just fine, that is, till they start seeing that there's more to be had."[373]

Ray and his mother were both left distraught when his little brother, George, drowned in a wash tub. Ray watched on as his brother struggled for his life but could do nothing to save George.

And only a few months later, this tragedy was followed by a second shock: Ray developed a serious eye condition, probably glaucoma. Everything he saw became blurred—and he saw less and less. "When I woke up, my little eyes were shut tight as a door, crusted over and so sticky that my eyelids were matted together. Sometimes Mama took a damp cloth and gently mopped around my eyes. After five or ten minutes, I'd slowly start blinking and adjusting to the morning light."[374]

Ray's mother took him to the doctor, but there was nothing that could be done: her son would go blind. Ray writes in his autobiography that going blind sounds like a fate worse than death, something that should get a little boy down, make him afraid, half-crazy, and sad. But that was not how he felt. Perhaps it had to do with the fact that it took two years for him to lose his sight completely. "It slipped away gradually. And I suppose that's the reason I was never too frightened."[375] In his first year at school, his right eye started aching and throbbing from morning to night. His doctors told him that the eye would have to be removed. In comparison to losing an eye, going blind didn't seem half as bad, he said. But there was no alternative. The pain was unbearable, so his mother took him to hospital, where the eye was removed.[376]

Ray's mother was not an educated woman, but she instinctively acted in his best interests and raised her son to be independent. "One of these days, I ain't gonna be here,"[377] she kept hammering into him. Some of their neighbors gave Ray's mother a hard time, criticizing her whenever they saw him working in the garden or helping her in the house. "He's blind," his mother told them, "But he ain't stupid. He's lost his sight, but he ain't lost his mind."[378]

She also allowed him to walk around on his own, despite the fact that he was blind. He even rode his bike around the small town. No, that's not quite true—he didn't ride, he raced. "If you go to Greensville today and ask about me, I bet the thing they remember most is the way I raced around town on my bike, as though I had 20/20."[379] His hearing was good, and his instincts were so sharp that he was able to ride as if he could see. A little later, he took up the motorbike and—riding behind a friend—learned to orient himself by the sound of their exhaust alone.[380] One day, some people saw him riding the motorbike around the city and didn't believe that he was blind, so they reported him. Since Ray was going to a state school for the blind and receiving a form of state aid, they insisted he be examined by a state board. "I was examined and, of course, they learned I really couldn't see. So I hopped right back on the motorcycle."[381]

In his autobiography, Ray writes: "Now most mamas would die rather than let a blind child scoot around on a bike. And at first I know Mama was scared for me. She had to be. But she let me do it. She let me find out for myself. She let me stray, little by little, further and further away from her...In her own way, she was preparing me for tougher times—times which weren't very far off."[382] Aretha Williams was a strict woman, "I mean discipline was her middle name,"[383] Ray said. She never let him get away with anything just because he was blind. "I was treated like I was normal. I acted like I was normal. And I wound up doing exactly the same things normal people do."[384]

Ray loved his mother more than anything. She sent him to the school for the blind in a neighboring town despite the fact that he objected because he couldn't imagine being without her. At Christmas, when all the other children went home to their families, he had to stay on campus, all alone, because his mother simply did not have the money for a train ticket.[385]

Physically, Ray's mother was not very strong. From an early age, she was convinced that she would not live very long and set about preparing her son for the time when she would no longer be there to take care of him. She did indeed die young, at the age of 31, and Ray recalls that this was by far the worst experience of his life—worse than his brother's death or going blind. He was utterly distraught, but a wise woman in his small hometown, Ma Beck, who had spent time looking after his mother, took the crying boy in her arms and told him: "Your mama spent her whole life preparing you for this here day. You gotta carry on. That's all there is to it. That's what she'd want. And that's what you gotta do. You gotta carry on, RC."[386]

At school, Ray was difficult, rebellious even. One day, after provoking a teacher, he was told that the school had given him plenty of second chances—enough was enough and they were now going to expel him. But Ray said he had already decided to leave school anyway. The last entry on his official student card reads: "Sent home Oct. 5, 1945. Unsatisfactory pupil."[387] Ray was 15 years old at the time and left home to start a new life in Jacksonville, Florida. This was a daunting challenge for him, because in his hometown he knew his way around very well, was familiar with every street, every corner and could move quickly and safely. He vehemently refused a seeing eye dog or a cane. "It wasn't that I wanted to fool myself. Hell, I knew I was blind as a bat. But I didn't want to go limping around like I was half-dead. I didn't want to have to depend upon anyone or anything other than myself."[388]

He had taught himself numerous tricks to find his way around his hometown, tricks he now used in every new city. Whenever he was in a new part of town and needed to find his way somewhere, he would ask someone to take him there. He would pay close attention to the path they took, remember the buildings they passed, where they took a step down from the sidewalk, listening to the changing sounds and memorizing as much of the trip as he could. "I'd never count steps; that'd be too complicated. I'd keep the method simple."[389] Then, on the return trip, he would check the path again. That's how he found his way around Greensville and countless other towns.[390] "I don't want to sound like I'm bragging," Ray said, "but when I walked around those towns, my pace wasn't halting or even cautious. Man, I moved. I set my own rhythm, and I do believe it was usually a little faster than most other people's, blind or not."[391]

When Ray describes it, he makes it sound easy, but of course it wasn't. Especially at first—especially in a new city. Other people might have been overjoyed to finally learn their way around their own hometown. And it certainly takes courage to give up the security of the familiar once gained. But that's precisely what Ray did. He only spent one year in Jacksonville before moving—at the age of 16—to Orlando,[392] then, one year later, to Tampa,[393] Seattle,[394] and finally to Los Angeles.[395]

Even at this early stage of his life, Ray's frequent moves reveal a personality trait that he shares with all successful people: they are open to new experiences. Like Ray, they dare to leave their comfort zone—their desire for new experiences is greater than any fear of the unknown. And Ray's thirst for freedom put all other concerns in the shade. As his biographer Michael Lydon writes: "Again and again he would move away from people and places previously known, cut himself out of webs of the past when they threaten his freedom in the future. Independence became in time an ingrained habit of the man, an element of his makeup that some found grouchy, others cold-blooded."[396]

Ray was destitute for many years. But, he writes, he was never going to "get a tin cup, a cane and find myself a street corner."[397] At the same time, it was difficult, if not impossible, for him to take on a 'regular' job because of his blindness. But more importantly, Ray had a dream. He wanted to be a musician and music was the only way he ever thought of making a living.[398] He says that perhaps he could have become a mechanic, an electrician, a carpenter, or even a lawyer ("since I love to argue"), but he never thought about any of those things in the early days: "It was music which drove me, it was my greatest pleasure and my greatest release, it was how I expressed myself."[399]

And in music, he sensed, his blindness was an advantage, not a disadvantage. As his biographer notes, "Blindness posed no handicap in learning song forms and chord sequences—all musicians visualize the structure of music in the darkness of the mind's eye—and his aptitude for math gave him an advantage."[400] Ray was highly intelligent. Even from an early age, he had an aptitude for mathematics and later, for example, he became an outstanding chess player.

But before he could make a career in music, he first had to overcome some major challenges. In Jacksonville, he had found accommodation with friends of the family, but now, he reports, he wanted to "see what living *completely* alone was like."[401] Once in Orlando, he lived in abject poverty. He had less money than at any other stage of his life. "These were my hardest days, and sometimes in Orlando I actually wondered whether I was going to starve to death. For a while I thought I was dealing with malnutrition...A couple of days might pass without me having a meal...It was me—all by myself—getting a feel for what being busted was all about."[402] Everywhere he looked there were failing bands and musicians were a dime a dozen. No one was looking for yet another musician. "I didn't know many people, and like I said, the competition among musicians was ferocious."[403]

Nevertheless, Ray was not about to give up and, drawing on his natural stamina, somehow struggled through. He earned a few dollars here and there playing the piano in bars and clubs. Even then, he never gave up on his dreams of a brighter future. One day, Lucky Millinder, a big name in the music business at the time, came to Orlando with his 16-piece band. Ray had been listening to Lucky's records for years and had heard a rumor that the band was looking for a new piano player. Friends encouraged Ray to audition and even helped get him past Millinder's Road Manager. Ray had his chance—he played and sang his songs. Millinder didn't say anything at first, but after Ray had finished, he issued his verdict: "Ain't good enough, kid."[404]

What a shock! Ray went off by himself and wept. He even started to think that Millinder might be right, that maybe he wasn't good enough, maybe his dreams would never come true. After a few weeks, Ray's initial doubts were supplanted by a simmering determination to practice more than ever before and show the world what he was capable of: "Someday that s.o.b. Lucky Millinder would eat his words."[405] Ray later recalled what he had learned from this early defeat: You are not good (enough) just because the people around you say you are![406]

Ray was not a quitter and, after a string of disappointments, got his first taste of success. In February 1949, his very first single, "Confession Blues," was released and shot to No. 2 on the Rhythm & Blues chart. His early recordings were all blues tunes, the most popular style of music among African Americans in the 1940s. At that time, Ray had not yet developed his own signature style and made a living imitating other singers. His greatest idol was Nat

King Cole and Ray adopted many of Cole's earliest songs into his own repertoire. "I stole many of his licks. And I got his vocal style down to a T."[407]

In his earliest on-stage appearances, Ray took to the stage without sunglasses. Given the fact that one of his eyes had been removed, however, his friends advised him that it wasn't a good look. Ray quickly hit on a glamorous solution: the sunglasses that would soon become his unmistakable visual trademark. Posters and publicity materials even played up his blindness, branding him "The Blind Sensation, Ray Charles."[408]

Bit by bit, he developed his own musical style by combining elements from different musical traditions. Ray had been singing spirituals and listening to the blues since he was three. "These were my two main musical currents. So what could be more natural than to combine them?"[409] It would later be called soul music, but for Ray it was always a mixture of gospel and blues.[410]

Charles learned what resonated with the audience and what didn't, and this became a valuable point of reference. One thing that really bothered him at the time was what he describes as the strange attitude of some jazz players, who would say, "This is my music. If you like it, cool. If not, fuck it!" He thought that was wrong: "People give you their bread and are entitled to some kind of musical return on their dollar. I don't mean you got to give them *exactly* what they want. But you do have to keep them in mind."[411]

Charles had thus systematically formulated an attitude that many artists never come to understand. At the one extreme, many—unsuccessful—artists defiantly insist that they live and work only to their own standards, believing that they are never appreciated by a larger audience because most people are simply too stupid to understand their 'art.' At the other extreme, many artists compromise their artistic vision and become slaves to what they think audiences want in pursuit of commercial success. Charles found his position between these two extremes. He rightly said that it was arrogant to completely ignore what people wanted, but it was equally mistaken to blindly follow popular tastes, although, as he said, "you do have to keep them in mind." He gauged his success by how many people came to his concerts and bought his records.[412] And the themes of his songs were problems or feelings everyone could relate to: "love heartaches, money heartaches, pleasures of the flesh and pleasures of the soul."[413]

1953 to 1955 were the years when Charles, in his own words, "became myself. I opened up the floodgates, let myself do things I hadn't done before, created sounds which, people told me afterward, had never been created before."[414] He took gospel arrangements, for example, and turned them into soulful pop songs. His record company from 1952 to 1959, Atlantic Records, gave him all the freedom he wanted. The company's owners understood that Charles was at his best when they didn't try to cajole him but let him make his own decisions for himself. At first, both Charles and Atlantic needed to learn to be patient: they released four singles in one year, but none of them "caught fire."[415] Charles finally hit the big time with his sixth single, "I've Got a Woman," recorded in November 1954. It was his first No. 1 hit on the R&B chart. Even though the single, in many ways, marked a breakthrough, Charles never liked talking about his career in those kinds of terms. In fact, as he himself describes it, his career never zoomed along. No one could say, "This was the day it happened. No, my progress was slow. Steady, but very, very slow."[416]

The patience of Atlantic's owners, Ahmet Ertegun and Jerry Wexler, started to pay off: "They knew they had passed a milestone with Ray. It had taken two and a half years, but with a band that Ray had made an extension of himself, they had begun to get the special quality of Ray's music in record."[417] What impressed Ahmet most was Ray Charles' incredible self-confidence. One night in his hotel room in Atlanta, Charles said "Let's go to get some coffee" and ran down three flights of stairs ahead of Ahmet, who warned him, "You're going to kill yourself." But Charles replied that he had memorized the number of stairs. Ahmet was still taken aback: "Not so much by the physical skill, but because he was absolutely sure of what he was doing."[418]

Ray Charles undoubtedly had musical talent and a fantastic voice. Above all, however, his success was the result of his unswerving will to succeed. As Ray himself observed, there was no shortage of really great musicians who never made a name for themselves, "Cats who just hung around home and lacked the drive to go after fortune and fame."[419] But he was different.

There was, however, a darker, more negative side to his life: Charles had been using drugs since an early age. And not just marijuana, but also heroin. At the height of his habit, he was shooting up every day. In 1964, following a federal drug bust, he was sentenced to five years' probation for possession. He had been using drugs for 16 or 17 years and decided that now was the time to either kick his habit or end up in jail. He always believed that it was nobody else's business whether he took drugs or not: "Why do we need laws which tell me what I can or can't put into my own body?"[420] More importantly, he took responsibility for his drug use. In his autobiography, he also writes: "No one did it to me. I did it to myself. It wasn't society that did it to me, it wasn't a pusher, it wasn't being blind or being black or being poor. It was all my doing. And besides—as crazy as it sounds—I have no regrets. It was another lesson in life."[421]

When he was arrested in 1964 after going back to his plane to fetch some heroin he had left there, he blamed himself: "I was pissed off something fierce that I'd been caught. I sure as hell didn't want to go to jail. But I saw the bust as my own doing. After all, I was the cat who went back to the plane. I was the addict."[422] Throughout his autobiography, he stresses that he was in no way the victim of dealers or pushers: "No white cat or black cat got me hooked or encouraged me to turn on. Hell, the stuff cost money. And no one was giving it away. I had to look for it myself. I had to seek it out. And I wanted the shit bad enough so I found a way to get it."[423]

His lawyers said it would improve his chances in court if he named one or two pushers who had sold him the heroin. Charles flatly refused, stating: "I've always had to seek out the pushers; they never came looking for me. No one ever made me spend my money on dope. I dug it, and I did it."[424] And Charles did not only apply this attitude to his drug use. When, in 1977, his 22-year marriage to Della Beatrice Howard ended in divorce, he accepted the blame for "80 or 85 percent of the damage to our marriage."[425]

Like all incredibly successful people, Charles did not look for the roots of his successes or the reasons for his failures in external circumstances, nor did he blame others. Most people are happy to take the credit for each minor or major success in their life but are quick to blame others whenever they experience setbacks. Charles was so successful because he was different in this respect. As early as the age of 15, he recalls in his autobiography, he began to understand how the world worked: "If I got into trouble, that was *my* doing. Or if I did something halfway worthwhile, *I* could take the credit. Responsibility came awfully early to me."[426]

Whenever Charles met new people, he started off by trusting them and giving them the benefit of the doubt. He was sometimes asked whether being blind was not a disadvantage in this respect.

People wanted to know if club owners or others ever tried to steal from him because he couldn't see. "I don't think so. I basically trust people, and for the most part the trust has been justified."[427] That is not to say he was naïve. For example, he always asked to be paid in one-dollar bills and waited patiently until the money was counted out because he could not tell the difference between dollar bills of different denominations.[428] But even when he was cheated, he took responsibility for it: "I was even taken to the cleaners once for a lot of money. But that didn't make me furious or bitter. Just taught me to keep my nose closer to the books."[429]

Four years after the success of "I've Got a Woman," he landed another huge hit with "What'd I Say." For his record company Atlantic, it meant the first-ever million-dollar month in gross sales and Charles also earned handsomely from this record.[430] But Charles and his advisors did not want to rest on their laurels. The success of "What'd I Say" made them realize he had even greater potential—but that Atlantic was too small to take him to the next level. The perfect opportunity presented itself when Charles heard that ABC-Paramount, only four years old and the youngest major label in the business, was looking for promising stars. ABC-Paramount knew, however, that they could not lure the loyal Charles away from Atlantic just like that, so they decided to make him an unbeatable offer: "The company would finance Ray's recording costs and put out the records, recouping their basic costs before sending Ray a dime. Records that did poorly might earn Ray little or nothing. But once a record got into the black, 75 cents of every dollar would go to Ray."[431] To prove just how much they believed in Charles, they even offered him a guaranteed $50,000 a year, a spectacular sum at the time, for the three-year term of the contract.

It was a sensational offer that would have tempted any musician, but especially one as entrepreneurial as Charles. If he were successful, he would become rich, and any downsides would be covered by the guaranteed $50,000 a year. His skills as a negotiator were evident from his reaction. Any other artist would have been delighted at such an offer and accepted without a second thought. But Charles played high-stakes poker and went one better: "Look, since I'm producing my own music, I want to own my own masters."[432] The ABC negotiator's jaw dropped. This was an entirely unheard-of gambit! In normal circumstances, no record company ever gave up ownership of the master recordings. One of ABC's stunned representatives tried to explain to Charles that they had never done anything like this before and it was entirely out of the question. The other ABC representatives agreed. Ray, however, stuck to his guns. In all honesty, he would have signed the contract without the concession, but bluffed and said he would have to think it over.[433] Despite his hesitancy, ABC were determined to get the contract over the line. They wanted to send a signal to other R&B and jazz musicians, so they agreed to give him the master tapes after five years.[434]

Charles also wanted to be as fair as possible to Atlantic, so he went to them with the ABC offer. He told the owners Ahmet and Jerry that if they would match ABC's conditions, he would stay with Atlantic. But they were in no position to agree—and so Charles switched to ABC. Ahmet and Jerry were frustrated, because after all, they had believed in Ray and got him into the big time; they were the ones who had waited two and a half years for the first fruits of success; they had given him full artistic freedom. But Ray Charles was different. He was, of course, grateful for what Atlantic had done for him, but, as his biographer notes: "Forward motion had become an ingrained habit of his life. It took him to places and away from places, into people's lives, out of people's lives...The crew at Atlantic had done what they could for him during the time he was with them; now that time was over...'Seventy-five cents out of a dollar and owning my own masters, that's why I left Atlantic,' Ray recalled later. Friendship and sentiment had nothing to do with it. He was moving on; it was as simple as that."[435]

At the end of 1960, Charles received a check from ABC for $800,000,[436] the equivalent of $7 million in today's money. His second million-seller, "Georgia on My Mind," released in August 1960, contributed to a triumphant year for Ray and marked the first time he reached the top of the pop charts. Ray Charles had finally made it and was now being mentioned in the same terms as Elvis. Billboard wrote: "Ray Charles and Elvis Hit with Sweet Stuff; two pioneers of the rock 'n roll school are bigger than ever on Billboards' Hot 100, and they're doing it with ballads."[437] In August 1961, another major hit followed with "Hit the Road, Jack" and, in April 1962, he sold more than two million copies of his version of the country classic "I Can't Stop Loving You."

His backing vocals were provided by a girl group, The Raelettes, all the way into the 1970s. In the current #MeToo era, Charles would certainly have been named and shamed because he regularly had sexual relationships with his female singers. When a new girl joined the Raelettes, he would call her at night in the hotel and pretend to have dialed the wrong number: "Since I got you on the phone, why don't you come up? We can talk about a few things." Most of the women knew what to expect—and few ever refused.[438]

Ray claims in his autobiography: "When sex happens between me and one of the Raelets, it happens naturally."[439] Charles is adamant that it never had anything to do with the women's pay or their place in the band. And he never allowed any cross-over between his lovemaking and his music. His biographer writes: "As a venerable joke declares, to be a Raelet, a lady must let Ray. With many, many exceptions, the joke is true. From St. Louis onward Ray would sleep with one of his lady singers while seducing a second and going cold and silent on a third, all of it happening at once, in plain view and behind doors."[440]

Sex was one of the main themes of his life, together with music and business. "Then, like now," he confesses in his autobiography, "I was pouring all the energy I had into women and music."[441] Everyone, he said, has certain indulgences, certain habits. And, while some people chase money, power, or position, "My obsession centers on women—did then and does now. I can't leave them alone."[442] One of his girlfriends had this to say: "As long as he can get it up, Ray will go with any woman who gives him great sex and great talk."[443]

He may have been married twice, first to Eileen Williams for two years and then to Della for 22, but he didn't see either of his wives all that often because he was on tour most of the time. He had three children with Della, and another nine children with different girlfriends. Charles knew his wife Della was hurt by his sexual dalliances, but he didn't feel bad about it: "One rooster, many hens," he would say. He also liked to tell Della the Bible story of Solomon and his many wives.[444]

He made no secret of the fact that he was usually seeing several women at the same time—his biographer refers to his harem and describes his love life as follows:

"In the early 70s, Ray assembled a harem of such variety and delight that, when officially in LA, he seldom got back to Southridge by the six A.M. curfew that Della set to maintain a last vestige of respect. Susaye [whom he met at the age of 18, R.Z.] was his first lady on the road, Ruth in LA, but they shared him with Norma, a radio executive who moved from New York to LA to be close by, with

Arlette in Paris and another French flame who lived in a distant suburb, with Dorothy and Stella among the Raelettes, and with assorted newcomers, old timers, and occasionals along the way. Ray punched the names and numbers of his women into a thick leather address book...As many a working day ended, Ray took out the book and made his calls to plan the nights ahead, shading his voice to each woman in the tones of their unique intimacy."[445]

Ray Charles often had sex with multiple women at the same time. In his autobiography, he recounts several such episodes: "If two women are making love, I see everything they're doing to each other. I touch. I feel. I listen. And oh man, I've seen some exciting things! ...Many of those beautiful scenes are still alive inside my brain, and I wouldn't trade those evenings for a truckload of solid gold."[446]

These party nights, as he called them, became his passion, "long sweaty hours of surprise and pleasure in which he lost himself as both participant and blind voyeur. He planned his party nights weeks in advance, slowly feeling out possible participants, sometimes including one of the men."[447] To Charles, this lifestyle was an expression of unrestrained freedom: he refused to tie himself to a place, to a woman, to a record label, not even to a certain style of music.

He also understood that one important aspect of freedom is financial freedom. He never wanted to be like so many other artists who get into money trouble or debt.[448] Unlike other musicians, he never fell into the trap of living beyond his means. When other people called him stingy, Charles admitted they were right. He only employed people who really had a job to do. And he could live on $250 to $300 a week: "A warm bed, food to put in my mouth, a car, phonograph, TV, and, Lord help me, a decent piece of pussy to set off my day."[449] He added that he had owned decent cars, but never more than one at a time. He also had his airplanes, but they were for his day-to-day work because he was usually on tour.[450] And he was careful to put money aside to pay his tax bills.[451]

Of course, none of this means that he had no interest whatsoever in money. On the contrary, to Charles, having money meant freedom. And that was more important to him than being able to buy luxurious things. "Wealth," his biographer writes, "inspired Ray to take up the adult game of making money. He had come to love the cut und thrust of fighting it out as an independent entrepreneur, and he proved himself a quick study of business forms and language."[452] Whenever he heard a legal term (such as 'debenture') his curiosity was roused and he would ask what it meant, filing it away in his own mind for later use.[453]

Charles did not become rich just through his music, but by being a clever businessman. One of his employees reports: "For every hour he spends as an entertainer, he spends ten as a businessman."[454] All too many musicians fail to take care of the business side of things, but Charles, once again, was different. He founded his own record label, Tangerine, which proved to be a very astute move because, "Tangerine Music moved Ray a big step up the music business food chain: all royalties from record sales and airplay would be paid direct to Tangerine, and anyone who wanted to use Tangerine songs would have to deal with him personally."[455] ABC wondered why Charles wanted to own his own label. He responded: "That's like me asking you why you want to own your own car. Why do people want their own anything? It was natural. I am a musician, and I was saying to myself: 'I see what the record companies are doing. I don't know if I'll be successful at it, but I'd like to try.'"[456]

People like Charles, for whom freedom is so important, also need a great deal of discipline. Charles had this discipline in spades, not only in terms of how he handled his money, but above all in his day-to-day work. As we have seen, he had learned the importance of discipline from his mother at a very young age. Some of his band members said that working for him was like being in the army—and Charles didn't disagree.[457]

Artists are not usually known for their discipline, but Charles was different. During interviews for his band, he made a point of telling musicians what to expect: they had to be backstage half an hour before the first note was due to be played. If they were late, they would be fined. In the early days, that was just five or ten dollars, but when he realized that didn't do much good, he increased the fine to $50. Anyone who was late three or four times was fired.[458] And anyone who turned up without their bow tie or with the wrong socks on also had to stump up $50.[459] When the tour itinerary said the bus would leave at six o'clock, it was gone at one minute past. The concerts also started on time—to the second. His band manager Joe Adams, who ran the band like an army officer, stood in the wings with a stopwatch to make sure that their concerts always started on time.[460]

Despite all these measures, his big band often drove him to despair. Around 1963, he writes, he got "fed up" and decided to break up the band. However, one of the band's only two punctual musicians persuaded him not to: "Brother Ray, you've worked your whole life to have a big band. Don't you think it's dumb to let five or six cats mess up the works?"[461] Ray fired the band members who had been running wild and hired new people in their place. Ray basically formed a new band.

Like all successful people, Charles also had to overcome very challenging phases—periods riddled with self-doubt and defeat. At the end of the 1970s, for example, the difficulties mounted: His second wife Della filed for divorce—and it was to be expensive for Charles. In the early 1980s, he began to suffer from strange sensations in his left ear.[462] For a while, he even thought he might lose his hearing. He believed that it was possible to overcome blindness and still live a fulfilling life. But silence as well as blackness? "I'm too old to be Helen Keller,"[463] he remarked. If he lost his hearing, he worried, he would not be able to hear music and would eventually lose the ability to speak or sing properly.[464] And: "I'd probably have to lock up with one woman, and then I'd be telling myself that the only reason she hung around was 'cause she felt sorry for me."[465]

In the 1980s, interest in his music dwindled, he had few hits and pop music passed into the hands of newer, younger stars. In the eyes of the masses, he was yesterday's man. Worse than this, though, was that he lost his positive attitude. He started to complain about his blindness. If he could see, he moaned, he could have been a lawyer, an engineer or an even bigger star.[466] Despite reaching the lowest point in his career, he staged an amazing comeback. His return to the upper echelons of the music business was helped, of all things, by the 'cola wars' waged between Coca-Cola and Pepsi Cola. In the early 1990s, Pepsi featured Ray in a multi-million-dollar advertising campaign[467] and one of his songs "A Song for You" won the Grammy Award for Best Male R&B Vocal Performance.[468]

During his lifetime, Ray Charles became a legend. He sang at the inaugurations of Ronald Reagan and Bill Clinton. He embodied and still embodies the American dream. Here was a Black man who climbed all the way to the top of his chosen profession, in the face of strong racial discrimination in the U.S. at the time, a poor man who earned a fortune and a blind man who never saw himself as a victim. Here was a man who led the kind of interesting, happy, and successful life most people without disabilities will never know. If his mother had given him a religion, it was: "Believe in yourself."[469]

Ray Charles died of liver cancer on June 10, 2004, at the age of 73. He was buried on June 18 and B.B. King, Glen Campbell, Stevie Wonder and Wynton Marsalis all played at his funeral. As he once wrote in his autobiography: "A lot of my dreams were coming true, but there were still others. They might have been crazy, but they were dreams, and dreams, if they're any good, are always a little crazy."[470]

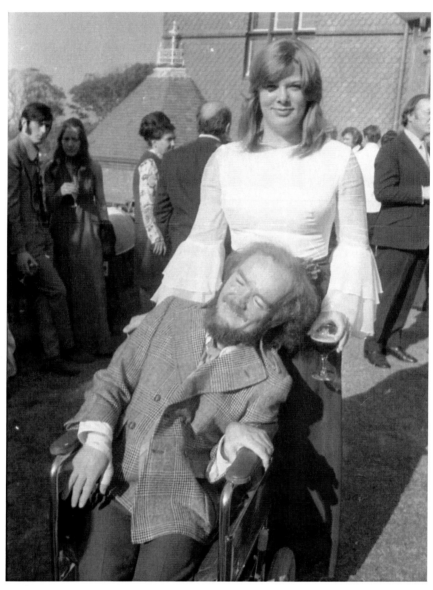

Christy Brown with his wife at their wedding in 1972: "I was born to be rich and rebelasian and to wallow in mistresses and Napoleon brandy ... I was not born to spend my days on cabbage and potatoes and to perish of TB or pneumonia in a damp smelly peeling little dungeon in the concrete wilds of south-west Kimmage with not even a dog never mind a mistress to my name."

Credits: Hulton Archive / Getty Images

# 10. Christy Brown
## My Left Foot

In 1989 the film *My Left Foot* was released and soon after was showered with prizes. It was nominated for 31 awards and won 16,[471] including the Oscar for Best Actor in a Leading Role (Daniel Day-Lewis) and Best Supporting Actress (Brenda Fricker). The film—based on the book of the same name—tells the life story of Irish writer and artist Christy Brown. He was born in Dublin, Ireland on June 5, 1932, his mother Bridget Brown's tenth child. She would go on to give birth to twelve more children. The Browns lived in humble circumstances in Kimmage, a suburb of the Irish capital, his father was a construction worker.

Just a few months after his birth, Christy's mother noticed that something was wrong with him, as his head fell back every time, she tried to feed him. Over time, she realized he had other physical impairments: his hands were clenched almost continuously and writhed behind his back. "My mouth," Brown writes in his autobiography, "couldn't grasp the teat of the bottle because even at that early age my jaws would either lock together tightly, so that it was impossible for her to open them, or they would suddenly become limp and fall loose, dragging my whole mouth to one side."[472]

His mother took him to several doctors, but they believed the child was feeble-minded—and would remain so. She refused to accept their diagnoses and later recalled in an interview: "The day that the doctors told me that Christy was mentally defective and should be sent to a home was the darkest in my life. I pushed the pram, with two babies in it, all the way from the centre of the city to Crumlin, and I was glad it was raining because I cried all the way home. Mind you, I knew Christy was as bright and as intelligent as any of the others…I made a vow that day coming from the hospital that Christy would lead as normal a life as possible. I promised myself I wouldn't spoil him, but that I would see to it that he was the centre of family life—no pushing him away in the back room."[473]

Brown suffered from athetosis, one of the most common forms of extrapyramidal disorder. Presumably, his brain had received too little oxygen at birth, but only the part of the brain responsible for coordinating muscle movement was affected, while the region of the brain that controlled his intellect was entirely unharmed.[474] Brown himself described his condition as follows: "I could not speak or even mumble, nor could I sit up without support on my own, let alone take steps. But I wasn't inert or motionless. I seemed indeed to be convulsed with movement, wild, stiff, snakelike movement that never left me, except in sleep. My fingers twisted and twitched continually, my arms twined backwards and would often shoot out suddenly this way and that, and my head lolled and sagged sideways. I was a queer, crooked little fellow."[475]

Most of the time he lay on his back in the kitchen or on warm days in the garden. He could not make himself understood, he was disconnected from his family and his environment. As the film of My Left Foot impressively portrays, one day in 1937, when Christy was five years old, something incredible happened: The family was sitting in the kitchen and his sisters were writing with yellow chalk on an old, crumbled slate. Christy suddenly reached out for the piece of chalk with his left foot, snatched it from his sister's hand, and scribbled something on the slate. Why he used his left foot in particular he was never able to explain—until then he had never made any attempt to use his feet in any way, nor his hands. The whole family was stunned into silence and couldn't take their eyes off him.

His mother went over to him, wrote the letter 'A' on the floor with chalk and told him to copy it. But, at first, he couldn't. He made several attempts, trying very hard, but in vain. His mother kept gently asking him to try again. What happened next, he and his family never forgot for the rest of their lives: "Out went my foot. I shook, I sweated and strained every muscle. My hands were so tightly clenched that my fingernails bit into the flesh. I set my teeth so hard that I nearly pierced my lower lip. Everything in the room swam till the faces around me were mere patches of white. But—I drew it—*the letter 'A'.*"[476] His father bent down and hoisted Christy onto his shoulders. "It had started," Brown said, "the thing that was to give my mind its chance of expressing itself."[477]

Brown's mother spent many hours teaching him the alphabet. She would write a letter on the floor with chalk for him to trace—always with the chalk gripped between his toes. Although he still could not speak intelligibly, he had found a way to communicate. He had acquired, as he writes, "a sort of grunting language which the family understood more or less,"[478] but other people could often not make out what he was trying to say. His left foot was "the only key to the door of the prison I was in."[479]

His siblings and friends took him outside—usually pulling him along in an old wagon. Christy was determined not to miss out on all that life had to offer. One day, when his brothers were bathing in a local canal, he felt the urge to join them and jump into the water. One of his brothers warned him, "But you'd drown!" But Christy, "being a fellow always willing to try anything once," was not deterred. And indeed, he somehow managed to stay afloat and even swim.[480]

Only as the years went by did he understand that he was very different from the others—and he began to suffer terribly as a result. When he was ten years old, he began to realize how helpless he was. "Now I saw everything, not through the eyes of a little boy eager for fun and brimming with curiosity, but through those of a cripple, a cripple who had only just discovered his own affliction."[481] When he looked at himself in the mirror, he hated the sight of his "wobbly head and lop-sided mouth," he hated his hands, he hated everything about himself.[482]

One day he climbed out of bed crying and ripped the mirror off the wall with his foot, causing it to shatter to pieces on the floor. When he was outside with his brothers, he felt the eyes of the people on the street as they looked at him and their stares pierced him to the core of his being. He withdrew more and more into himself and was deeply unhappy, "a tense, silent, great-eyed creature who had nerves as sharp as broken glass and as taut as telegraph wires."[483]

One Christmas, one of his brothers was given a box of paints and Christy got a box of toy soldiers, which didn't interest him in the slightest. He was fascinated by his brother's paints and pushed the box of toy soldiers to his brother with his foot and asked him to "swop" the box of paints for the toy soldiers. From that moment on, he painted every day, and it did him a lot of good. "I was changing. I didn't know it then, but I had found a way to be happy again and to forget some of the things that had made me unhappy...I had a feeling of pure joy while I painted, a feeling I had never experienced before and which seemed almost to lift me above myself."[484]

When he painted, he experienced what is known as a 'flow' state in which a person forgets everything around them, is completely absorbed in themselves and becomes totally immersed in the activity they are performing. As he described it, "I lived within the orbit of my paints and brushes."[485] In a newspaper he read about a painting competition for children aged 12 to 16, he had just turned 12. He won the contest, and after journalists learned that he had painted the picture with his foot, they visited him at home to write about him. It was to be the first of many newspaper articles about Christy Brown.

In the long run, however, painting did not satisfy him. He was regularly overcome by despair and a feeling of loneliness. At the age of 17, he discovered writing for himself as a form of expression alongside painting. As he wrote, he entered the same flow state he had earlier done when painting. Whenever he was depressed, he took up a pencil—with his left foot—and wrote exciting detective stories. Nevertheless, the older he got, the more he suffered. He longed for the things that filled the daily lives of other young men: football, beer parties and, above all, girls. "It seemed that instead of coming to a better understanding of my own handicap as I got older I only became troubled and bitter."[486] He felt like he was in a prison—and above all helpless and dependent. He was 18 now, but still had to be fed, dressed, washed and taken to the bathroom. "When *I* spoke all that came out was queer, jumbled noises. My brothers could use their hands without any trouble, but when I attempted to use mine they flew this way and that. They were useless to me. They were just lumps of twisted flesh."[487]

Brown was going through a deep crisis. He felt crushed and meaningless. He looked on as his brothers started dating, and he too had a longing for girls. Sometimes he would look out the window, and when a girl smiled at him, it meant the world to him. He joined a group of people with disabilities and flew to the Catholic Marian pilgrimage site of Lourdes in southwestern France. In his autobiography, he mentions the smallest friendly gestures from girls and women, such as a smile or a kind word from a stewardess. He was unable to satisfy his emotional and sexual needs, and he suffered from feelings of futility and emptiness. "I wanted something to live for, and there was nothing. I wanted my life to have a purpose, a value, but there was none. It was hollow, meaningless."[488]

During this time, he was visited by a doctor who had seen him once before as an infant. Dr. Robert Collis was to play a pivotal role in Christy Brown's life, giving him hope that there might yet be a way to alleviate the disability and, if not cure it, at least make it much more bearable. Brown was already following a treatment plan that involved special physical exercises at home with a doctor. This physiotherapy had, for the first time, given him hope that he might not be doomed to live his whole life without any chance of improvement.

He traveled to London and was examined by doctors, who were confident that something could be done about the disease. Brown was encouraged but there was a catch, a very big catch. "You must first make a big sacrifice," one doctor explained to him, "Nothing good is ever obtained without one, and yours is—you must resolve never to use your left foot again."[489]

While one of the doctors had recognized how much his life was enriched by the use of his left foot, she also believed that a cure would be impossible unless he stopped relying on it. "Since he controlled this foot with such extraordinary dexterity, the rest of his body had been left to run wild."[490] The condition of his atrophied muscles, he was told, had been aggravated by years of neglect. As long as he could make himself understood by using his left foot, he would never think of trying to use his hands. However, if he was no longer allowed to use his foot, he would then have to concentrate on making some use of the rest of his body.

On the one hand, Brown had gained hope, but on the other hand he was shocked. He recognized that the doctor was being entirely logical when she explained why he should no longer use his left foot. But his foot was until now his only means of communication with the outside world, his only way of making himself articulate and intelligible. After seeing the doctor, he wrote a friend: "I am writing this letter with a mixed feeling of regret and determination: regret as this is the last letter I shall write for the next five years: determined to write the next letter with my hands...who knows what the dim and distant future may hold? If determination and grit has a say it holds happiness, prosperity, independence and good living, as far as our correspondence is concerned it is au revoir, but as to our friendship—that is endless!"[491]

He knew that he could no longer afford to rely on his left foot and would have considered using it again as a sign of surrender. At the same time, he felt even more helpless now than ever before. "I felt the way anyone would feel with their hands and feet tied and a gag in their mouth."[492] At the cerebral palsy clinic where he received treatment, he saw children whose conditions were far worse than his own. Some lay huddled on the floor, inert and motionless. Others were convulsed with wild, endless movement, "...movement that shook their small bodies as if an electric current were constantly passing through them, making them shake, wriggle and jerk in endless writhings."[493]

The hope he drew from his therapy was accompanied by an increasingly painful awareness that he would never really lead a "normal life. The old 'difference' would always remain."[494] But Christy Brown did not give up. He found other ways to express himself, even without his left foot. His brother Eamonn could understand him, so he decided to dictate a book to him. His first book. The story of his life.

He was 18 years old when he first attempted to write—or rather dictate—his autobiography. The working title was: *The Reminiscences of a Mental Defective*. It was meant to be ironic; it was meant to be a punch on the nose for the doctors who had doubted his sanity when he was five years old. The style, however, was a disaster, gorgeous but impossible, as he later came to realize. In the first chapter he described his life at home: "I was brought up amid an environment of working-class doctrination and morality. As the world knows, the pursuit of literary…knowledge is not widely practiced by this class of the human race…Intellectualism is not a characteristic of this breed."[495]

He wrote long, unstructured sentences that would have bamboozled readers had the book ever been published, liked to use seven- and eight-syllable words, and deliberately tried to imitate Charles Dickens, whose books were the only ones he had read up to that point. He became increasingly disillusioned with the whole writing process. He became angry, angry with himself, angry with his brother and angry with his family. Sometimes he was so annoyed that he wanted to burn the whole manuscript. "I had by this time spent nearly two years at it and I couldn't bear to admit, even to myself, that all the work had been in vain, that I had failed."[496]

In desperation, he wrote to Dr. Collis, who was himself a writer, the author of several books and plays. Collis didn't mince his words: The manuscript was absolutely awful, nor could it be improved. The doctor did, however, give him a crumb of hope: "You have written one sentence here that stands out like a rose among a lot of weeds, one shining little gem thrown in amongst stones. It shows me that you could write if you knew how."[497] Collis gave him books that—unlike Dickens—were written in a modern style and told him that if he wanted to be a writer, he must learn to write. Brown abandoned his manuscript and started afresh. In response to a chapter of the second draft of Brown's autobiography, Eamonn said, "It's all right, but you'd want the dictionary beside you when reading it!"[498] Brown was angry at his brother's words, but he also knew he was right. He gave the second version of his book to Dr. Collis, who said it was better than the first, but not good enough. "Scrap it and start over again," he said. "This time you can make it, I know." Brown feigned a smile, "but actually I swore to myself as I contemplated the awful piles of useless manuscript. Would it never come out right?"[499]

How many other people would have had the strength and willpower to persevere for two years writing a book, despite feeling that the whole undertaking was beyond their capabilities? How many people would have had enough self-critical distance to recognize their weaknesses and then seek help from a professional? And how many people, in his position, would have had the guts to start all over again, even after a second failed attempt, and truly learn to write? Successful people have a tolerance for frustration that sets them apart from others. They don't give up after the first or second attempt, they learn from their mistakes and start again, as many times as it takes.

All of this would be difficult enough for someone who could easily type on a typewriter (or today on a computer). But Brown had to dictate every single word, sometimes even letter for letter. He still found it very difficult to make himself understood verbally, which made dictation even more stressful for him and his brother. Language lessons had led to some improvement, but throughout his life it remained impossible for Christy Brown to speak anywhere near as well as other people could.

On the third attempt at writing his life story, however, he decided not to dictate everything to his brother. Although the doctors had forbidden him to do so, he started writing again with his left foot.[500] This version of his book was much improved. Dr. Collis was so impressed with the first chapter that he asked Brown for permission to read it aloud at a cerebral palsy fund-raising event. The audience listened with rapt attention and Brown, on the stage with Dr. Collis, was overwhelmed by the applause that followed.[501]

When *My Left Foot* was published in Ireland, Great Britain, and the USA in 1954, it became clear that all his efforts and perseverance had paid off: it was a major success and attracted interest from international publishers. It was later published in French, German, Italian, Dutch, Japanese, and Braille.[502] Journalists asked for interviews, but Brown was not always comfortable with them. All too often, he felt, the interviews centered on his disability, and paid too little attention to his book. He became incensed when journalists spoke to his brothers and sisters about him rather than speaking directly to him. He even referred to this type of attitude as "Does he take sugar?"[503] But Brown proved quick-witted in interviews. When one journalist asked him what he might have done had he not been born with a disability, he replied: "I know. I would have been a good bricklayer like my father."[504]

After the book was published, his life changed dramatically. He became a well-known figure in Ireland and also became something of a celebrity in the USA. He finally had some money—and his first love. However, the woman, who was ten years older, lived in the USA and was already married.[505] Nevertheless, Brown and Beth Moore, who was even willing to get divorced for him, maintained a secret relationship for years.

At the age of 24, he made an important decision: he decided to stop physiotherapy, as he now wanted to concentrate entirely on his career as a writer. With the income from his book, he hoped that he could make a living as a writer. But of course, it wasn't enough. The Disabled Artists Association asked him to work for them for £100 a month. In return, he would have to paint in public—with his left foot. However, in the years to follow, he became increasingly dissatisfied with this activity: It was too poorly paid, and he did not really enjoy it; he saw his real vocation in writing.

"Even with proper training and education," he had realized, "I would never be more than an average artist; on the other hand I had set my heart on becoming a rather good writer and poet...because writing is not only a passion—it is a necessity, as vital to my nature as the presence of beauty itself and the pursuit of beauty."[506] His biographer, Georgina Hambleton, writes: "He felt writing was what he was really made for and that it was only writing that afforded him his truest means of self-expression and self-knowledge."[507]

But even with his writing, things didn't really work out at first. He wrote a few short stories and plays over the next few years, but several of his works for the stage were rejected. The situation became ever more difficult as he increasingly turned to alcohol. He spent hours alone at night writing—and usually drank excessively while doing so. There can be no doubt: Christy Brown was an alcoholic. In 1961, he wrote in a letter: "A lot of good people are irreconcilably convinced that poor old C. Brown has become so addicted to the bottle that he'll never write anything of value again."[508]

Every artist, he explained, dreams of creating something that will be respected long after their death and will still be read, seen, and appreciated by posterity 50 or even 100 years later.[509] In his own estimation, his debut work *My Left Foot* was not that kind of work. "He called it his immature juvenilia, decrying it as the bleating of a naive cripple."[510] The book, he now said self-critically, was not real literature but a corny story of the miracle of a boy who survives against all odds.[511] Moreover, he feared that Dr. Collis, who had helped him with the book, might be seen as the actual author. In 1969, he wrote to his brother: "I had such a horrible fear, all these years, that I was a literary freak, a one-book-man, a real literary flash-in-the-pan...For years, I lived with this dilemma, for years I lived in the shadow of my first book, in the shadow of Bob Collis, the man who helped me shape the damn book and who many people thought was the author of that damn book."[512]

He had spent so long working on his great work. He had poured everything into it in the hope that it would bring him the breakthrough he so desired and prove to himself and the world that he really was a writer. In 1970, 16 years after *My Left Foot*, his second book, *Down All the Days*, was published and immediately became a great success—both in terms of enthusiastic reviews and impressive sales. *Down All the Days* became an international bestseller and was translated into 14 languages.

It is a semi-autobiographical novel, but since it is a novel, it is not always clear which passages are based on his own life experiences and which are entirely fictional. After the success of *My Left Foot,* many readers were perhaps expecting a sequel, i.e. a book in which the author provides the next installment of his life story after the publication of his first work. But anyone who was expecting that was probably disappointed. It is a book about sex, death, alcohol, but it is also a social piece about the slums of working-class Dublin where his family lived.

In its review, *The Irish Times* wrote: "*Down All the Days* will surely stand beside Joyce and in front of all the others...has Dublin writ large and writ for all time." In England, the *Sunday Express* described it as "A great novel. Unforgettable." *Life* called the book "a joy to read," *Cosmopolitan* praised it as "an instant classic," and *The New York Times* exulted, "Nothing quite like this book has been known in literature."[513]

Brown flew to the U.S. for a major tour to promote the book. He appeared to an audience of millions on NBC's *Today Show*, one of the most popular breakfast shows in America. He demonstrated a talent for PR on several talk shows, and although he could barely make himself understood, he won the hearts of viewers and made them laugh. As his income increased, so did his self-confidence. In January 1970, he wrote in a letter: "Being poor, or even semi-poor, is such a drag, it's positively degrading, and destructive to one of my extreme fastidiousness and sensitivity. I was born to be rich and rebelasian and to wallow in mistresses and Napoleon brandy...I was not born to spend my days on cabbage and potatoes and to perish of TB or pneumonia in a damp smelly peeling little dungeon in the concrete wilds of south-west Kimmage with not even a dog never mind a mistress to my name."[514]

In 1971, he met Mary Carr, a former prostitute, at a party and married her just one year later. Brown's biographer, Georgina Hambleton, portrays Mary in an extremely negative light. According to Hambleton, Mary increasingly cut Brown off from his former friends and family and he didn't see them more than once or twice in the last years of his life.[515] Mary, Hambleton alleges, did not provide the same level of care as his sister had done in the past. In addition, Mary was reportedly also an alcoholic. At the same time, Brown was drinking more than ever before. "Christy was not drinking and working any more; he was simply drinking."[516]

Brown did manage to publish another book, *Wild Grow the Lilies*, in 1976, but this proved to be a complete flop.[517] Two weeks before his death, he reported in a letter: "I've been in and out of psychiatric wards on at least half a dozen occasions...The period of my incarceration in the hospitals varies: the 'drying out' process supposedly lasts for about ten days, with doses of anti-booze pills and in between regular meals; I think my longest stay was about a month, during which I became insufferably bored and just about able to function as a human being except on the most banal levels...I'm just not the man I used to be, I've only dim recollections of that individual, like an old friend I used to know and with whom I've lost contact."[518]

Christy Brown died on September 7, 1981, in Somerset, England, where he had set up a new home with his wife. The 49-year-old choked on his food—and Ann, his sister, was furious at Mary for not paying attention as she fed him, even though she knew that he sometimes needed help eating, especially when food got stuck in his throat.[519]

The end of Brown's life was particularly sad. He was by no means the first successful person to seek refuge in alcohol or drugs, and his abuse destroyed his life. In summing up Brown's life, his biographer lists many positives, but the question still remains what else he could have achieved if he had stopped drinking in time: "Christy Brown fulfilled in his life his greatest wishes: to fall in love, marry and become a successful writer. According to his *New York Times* obituary, he had earned $370,000 just from his writing career. He had bought the Brown family home in Kimmage, had provided for his mother after his father's death, and indeed before that had given his whole family large sums of money. He had written a novel that had transgressed boundaries and cultural taboos and had pointed out the hypocrisies of the Irish culture in its attitude towards religion, sex, and tradition. Christy achieved all that simply by doing what he loved to do. In his writing, he became an inspiration not just for disabled people but for anyone who feels unable to achieve whatever they set out to do."[520] More than anything, his story lives on in the film about his life, which became an international box office success seven years after his death.

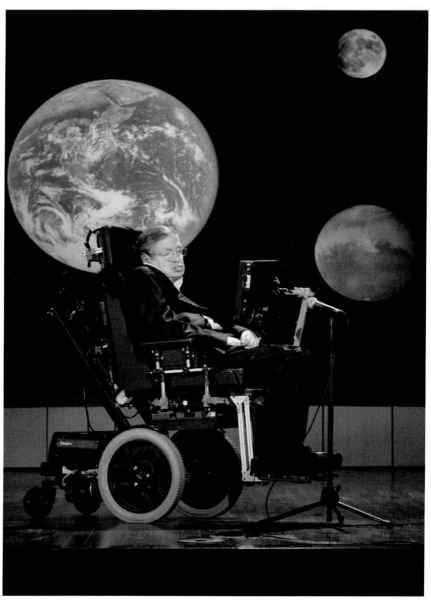

Stephen Hawking: "It has been a glorious time to be alive and doing research in theoretical physics. I'm happy if I have added something to our understanding of the universe."

Credits: NASA Photo / Alamy Stock Photo

# 11. Stephen Hawking
## Black-Hole Physicist

S tephen Hawking held the prestigious Lucasian Chair of Mathematics at the University of Cambridge for 30 years and was a cultural icon. No scientist before him had ever written books that attracted such popular acclaim and stayed on the bestseller lists for so long. He is the subject of numerous films, and, at his own request, he even played himself in an episode of *Star Trek*, in which he played a game of poker with Isaac Newton and Albert Einstein.

His regular appearances on television shows around the world helped cement his status as the most famous scientist on the planet. His name appears in eight documentary films or series, including *Stephen Hawking: Master of the Universe*, which aired in 2008. As one biographer writes, Hawking "may not have been the greatest cosmologist since Einstein or even in the top rank of modern physicists," but "he created a publishing phenomenon, met with popes and presidents, and filled concert halls in the manner of a rock star. He travelled the world, experienced zero gravity and hot air balloon flights, guest-starred in the world's most popular television series and was portrayed on the silver screen by movie stars."[521]

Stephen Hawking was born on January 8, 1942. As he repeatedly enjoyed pointing out, his birthday was the 300th anniversary of Galileo's death. He was always quick to add that approximately 200,000 other children were born on that same day, but the synchronicity of his date of birth nevertheless became part of the self-created legend of Stephen Hawking, who was not only a great physicist, but above all a genius of self-promotion.[522]

As a teenager, he spent many happy hours building model trains, boats, and airplanes. While he was not particularly skilled with his hands, his goal was always to build models that he could control. He did this, he says, because he had an "urge to know how systems worked and how to control them. Since I began my PhD, this need has been met by my research into cosmology. If you understand how the universe operates, you control it, in a way."[523]

At school, he was not among the best in his class, but his classmates, he remembers, gave him the nickname Einstein, "so presumably they saw signs of something better."[524] When he was twelve, one of his friends bet another friend a bag of sweets that he would never amount to anything. Nevertheless, the fact that the other friend accepted the wager proves that at least one person believed in him.

In 1959, Hawking won a place to study mathematics and physics in Oxford, his hometown. Fellow students recalled that Hawking only needed a few minutes to solve physics problems that took them a week. But Hawking was not particularly hardworking. In Oxford at that time, he reports, it was not considered good manners to work hard. You were either supposed to be brilliant without effort or accept your limitations and get a third-rate degree. Anyone who worked hard to get a better class of degree was regarded as a "grey man," the worst epithet in the Oxford vocabulary.[525] He later calculated that in his three years at Oxford he had worked a combined one thousand hours, averaging just one hour of work per day. "We affected an air of complete boredom and the feeling that nothing was worth making an effort for."[526]

The only thing that changed his attitude was his illness. In his final year at Oxford and shortly before he was due to transfer to the University of Cambridge, he noticed that he was becoming increasingly clumsy. On two occasions he lost his balance and fell over for no apparent reason. Worried, he went to the doctor, whose only advice was, "Lay off the beer." While skating on a lake over Christmas, he fell down and could not get up again. His mother noticed these problems and took him to the family doctor, who referred Hawking to a specialist. Shortly after his 21st birthday, he was admitted to hospital for a series of tests.[527]

For weeks, Hawking, the son of a tropical medicine researcher and an economist was subjected to a wide variety of tests. The doctors didn't tell him what he was suffering from, but he realized that he was suffering from an incurable disease that was likely to end his life within a few years.

Eventually, the doctors told him that he was suffering from amyotrophic lateral sclerosis (ALS), a disease that causes the nerve cells of the brain and spinal cord to first atrophy and then scar or harden. He learned that people with this disease gradually lose the ability to control their movements, speak, eat and, ultimately, breathe. His doctors then issued a dire prognosis and told him he probably only had two years to live – in fact he lived another 50 years.[528]

Of course, the news of his illness came as a massive shock. Hawking initially descended into a severe depression, which became even deeper as he spent hours listening to Wagner operas at full volume. "Holed up in his room at Cambridge, Hawking listened to music, read science fiction, struggled with terrifying nightmares and showed little interest in his PhD."[529] But looking back, the news about his illness also had a very positive effect on him. "My dreams at the time," Hawking recalled, "were rather disturbed. Before my condition was diagnosed, I had been very bored with life. There had not seemed to be anything worth doing. But shortly after

I came out of the hospital, I dreamed that I was going to be executed. I suddenly realized that there were a lot of worthwhile things I could do if I was reprieved."[530]

To his great surprise, he found that he enjoyed his life more now than ever before. This was partly because he had just fallen in love. And he knew that, if he was to marry, he had to find a job and finish his PhD. "I therefore started working for the first time in my life. To my surprise, I found I liked it."[531] Now that his disease had been diagnosed, he buried himself in his research: "When you are faced with the possibility of an early death, it makes you realize that life is worth living and that there are lots of things you want to do."[532] It was his research, together with his wife Jane, whom he had married in 1965, that helped him discover meaning in life.

In this, Hawking displays one of the key characteristics he shares with many great figures, namely to turn something bad into something good, and to draw energy from even the most debilitating crises. Rather than feeling sorry for himself and complaining about his disability, he soon came to see it as a great advantage: "I haven't had to lecture or teach undergraduates, and I haven't had to sit in on tedious and time-consuming committees. So I have been able to devote myself completely to research."[533] In his opinion, disabled people should "concentrate on things that their handicap doesn't prevent them from doing and not regret those they can't do."[534] According to his biographers Michael White and John Gribbin, Hawking would never have reached such dizzying heights so quickly if he had been expected to spend vast amounts of time on committees, conferences or overseeing undergraduate applications.[535]

Hawking quickly made a name for himself in the scientific community. In 1974, he predicted that black holes would emit thermal radiation, which subsequently became known as Hawking radiation. In the same year, he was also elected a fellow of the prestigious Royal Society—at that time he was not even a professor, just a lowly research assistant. Three years later, he was promoted to the position of professor. "My work on black holes had given me hope that we would discover a theory of everything."[536] A series of important discoveries followed, for which Hawking received numerous scientific honors and accolades.

Undoubtedly a great scientist, Hawking was well aware of his status within the scientific community: "To my colleagues, I'm just another physicist, but to the wider public I became possibly the best-known scientist in the world."[537] It is not possible to explain Hawking's fame in terms of his scientific discoveries alone, especially as their true ramifications – as with Einstein – were impossible for most people to understand. Hawking enjoyed a far higher profile than many Nobel Prize winners, despite the fact that he never won the Nobel Prize, most likely because according to the award's guidelines, any eligible discovery needs to be confirmed experimentally, which was not possible with Hawking's theoretical physics. His theories and predictions were based on mathematics, but they could not be confirmed by experiment.

And when it came to his standing within the scientific community, Hawking was right. To his peers, he was by no means the exceptional scientist the public perceived him to be. For instance, a survey of physicists around the millennium by *Physics World* magazine did not even place him among the top ten most important living physicists.[538]

So, how did Hawking, fully aware that his colleagues saw him as just one physicist among many, become the most famous scientist of his era? Well, Hawking provides the answer in his autobiography: "This is partly because scientists, apart from Einstein, are not widely known rock stars, and partly because I fit the stereotype of a disabled genius. I can't disguise myself with a wig and dark glasses—the wheelchair gives me away."[539]

But no scientist, no matter how groundbreaking their research, could become a global cultural icon and celebrity without actively pursuing fame at least to some extent, even if like Hawking, they are in a wheelchair or have a rare disease. To achieve the kind of fame requires actively cultivating a public image. Einstein had paved the way: the father of the Theory of Relativity was, as I explain in my book *The Art of Becoming Famous*, a genius in the art of self-marketing.

At the very beginning of his career, Hawking was smart in choosing his field of research. He based his decision on the fact that, at that time, elementary particle physics was a highly regarded and rapidly changing field that attracted most of the best scientific minds in the world. By contrast, cosmology and general relativity were stuck where they had been in the 1930s.[540] Hawking realized that it was easier for him to attract attention with new research and began to establish himself as an authority on a subject that captured everyone's imagination – black holes. A black hole is a region of spacetime where gravity is so strong that nothing – no matter, no light and no information – can escape. A black hole can be formed by the death of a massive star when, at the end of its life, the core becomes unstable and gravitationally collapses inward upon itself to a point of zero volume and infinite density called the singularity.

White and Gribbin write: "He was becoming the black hole cosmonaut trapped in a crippled body, piercing the mysteries of the Universe with the mind of a latter-day Einstein, going where even angels feared to tread. With the arrival of black holes in the public consciousness, the mystique that had begun to gather around him in Cambridge at the end of the sixties started to extend beyond the cloistered limits of the physics community. Newspaper articles and TV documentaries about black holes started to appear, and Stephen Hawking began to be seen as the man to talk to."[541] As with Einstein, the media and the general public were inspired by the mysterious nature of his theories, which were essentially incomprehensible to the layman. The fact that these cosmological messages were being delivered by a man with a mysterious illness—a man who communicated with ordinary mortals in an unearthly, computerized voice—served to heighten the overall effect.

As a result of his illness, Hawking's speech became progressively more indistinct and slurred. Even his children had difficulty understanding him. After a bout of pneumonia, he needed a life-saving tracheostomy. From then on, he completely lost the ability to speak. His only means of communication at first was to spell out words, one letter at a time, by raising his eyebrows when someone pointed to the correct letter on a spelling card.[542] He later used a computer program and a speech synthesizer. A special device allowed him to select blocks of words and letters, which were then converted into spoken words by a speech synthesizer. As time went by, he got better and better at using the system, and although it only generated a maximum of 15 words per minute, he was able to communicate better than he could before the tracheostomy.[543] As his biographer Joel Levy observes, Hawking's synthesized voice became one of his trademarks and he even copyrighted it.[544]

Even once he mastered his voice synthesizer, he still found other, sometimes more direct, methods of communication. Hawking, who was famous for not suffering fools lightly, simply drove his wheelchair over his interlocutor's toes whenever they said something that annoyed him. And if he felt that someone was wasting his time, he would abruptly steer his wheelchair out of the room.[545]

The fact that Hawking became famous did not happen without and certainly not against his will. On the contrary. Even when it came to his earliest books, which he wrote for a scientific readership and not – as was the case with his later publications – as popular scientific works, he refused to behave like a typical scientist. Ahead of the publication of his third book, *Superspace and Supergravity,* Hawking had a series of heated arguments with his publisher about the book's cover. He wanted the publisher to use a color photograph of a drawing from the blackboard in his office for the dust jacket of both the hardback and paperback editions of the book.[546] His publisher refused. They said they had never had a color cover on a book like Hawking's. They insisted that the costs could not be justified given the scientific nature of the book and its expected sales figures and claimed that the cover itself would have no impact on the number of copies they would sell. Hawking threatened to withdraw his book completely if the publisher did not agree to use his cover. In the end, Hawking prevailed.[547]

After having written a handful of scientific publications, Hawking decided to turn his hand to popular science books. Allegedly, financial motives, including the high cost of his day-to-day care, played an important role in his decision.[548] This is probably true, but an even greater motivation for Hawking was that he wanted to become world famous – not only in scientific circles, but far beyond: "If I was going to spend the time and effort to write a book, I wanted it to get to as many people as possible."[549]

Hawking decided to write a bestseller. He explained to his agent that he wanted to write a book that would sell well in airport bookstores. The agent replied that there was no chance of that. It might sell respectable numbers to academics and students, but a book like Hawking's could never succeed in Jeffrey Archer territory.[550]

Unlike many other scientists, Hawking listened carefully to the advice of his editors. In one of their earliest discussions about Hawking's new book for the popular market, his editor explained: "It's still far too technical, Stephen. Look at it this way, Steve – every equation will halve your sales." Hawking, who spent the entire day working with mathematical formulae, did not understand the objection and wanted to know why his editor would say something like that. His editor responded, "Well, when people look at a book in a shop, they just flick through it to decide if they want to read it. You've got equations on practically every page. When they look at this, they'll say, 'This book's got sums in it,' and put it back on the shelf."[551]

Hawking followed his editor's advice, but he ultimately decided not to publish the new book with his previous publishing house – the academic publisher Cambridge University Press – but with a larger publisher which could reach a wider audience and pay a higher advance and more lucrative royalties on book sales. Hawking and his agent negotiated with several major publishers and finally reached an agreement with the American publisher Bantam. One of the things that clinched the deal was the publisher's assurance that the book would be available at every airport bookstore in America. "Hawking loved the idea. The fact that his book was with one of the world's biggest publishers gave him a real thrill."[552]

Most authors don't like editors who demand lots of changes to their books, and certainly not editors who call for almost a complete rewrite of the entire book. And for Hawking, who was not able to write at the same speed as other authors, these extensive rewrites were particularly laborious and time-consuming. But Hawking was determined to write a bestseller and made every effort to write the best book he possibly could. His new editor convinced him to rewrite the book so that even non-scientists could understand it.

"Each time I sent him a rewritten chapter," recalled Hawking, "he sent back a long list of objections and questions he wanted me to clarify. At times I thought the process would never end. But he was right: it is a much better book as a result."[553]

His former editor at his previous academic publisher made sure to warn Hawking: "Do ensure that you are quite certain that, if the aim is to make money and sell lots of books, you don't mind the marketing techniques." When Hawking asked him what he meant, the editor answered: "Well, I wouldn't put it past them to market it as 'Aren't cripples marvelous?' You've got to go into it with your eyes open."[554]

The book was published in the United States as *A Brief History of Time* and didn't need any such primitive marketing techniques to become a bestseller and far exceed the publisher's expectations. It spent 147 weeks on *The New York Times* bestseller list, a record-breaking 237 weeks on the London *Times* bestseller list[555] and, in Germany, 41 weeks on the *Spiegel* bestseller list. The book has since been translated into 40 languages and has sold more than 10 million copies worldwide.

Why was the book so successful? Hawking wasn't entirely sure and thought that most of the reviews, although favorable, were not particularly illuminating. As a rule, they all followed the same formula. They started by highlighting the fact that Stephen Hawking suffers from a serious illness, is in a wheelchair and can hardly move his fingers. Then they pointed out that, despite all this, he has written a book about the biggest question of all time: Where do we come from and where are we going? Their conclusions also followed the same pattern: If Hawking is right and we do find a complete unified theory, we shall know the mind of God. What they couldn't know is that Hawking had almost robbed them of this conclusion. At the last stage of the writing process, Hawking admits that he almost cut the last sentence of the book, which said that we would know the mind of God. He was glad he didn't. "Had I done so, the sales might have been halved."[556]

By deciding not to cut the final sentence, Hawking demonstrated his keen sense of sales and marketing. He also recognized that "undoubtedly, the human interest story of how I have managed to be a theoretical physicist despite my disability has helped."[557] In his autobiography, Hawking explicitly addresses the accusation that his publisher shamelessly exploited his illness and that Hawking was complicit because he had allowed a photograph—which he himself described as "miserable"[558] —of himself in a wheelchair set against a starry sky to be used on the book's front cover. He rejects this allegation outright and explains that his contract with the publisher gave him no control over the design of the cover. I think this explanation does not sound convincing. After all, if Hawking objected to the proposed cover, he would certainly have fought against it. Hawking's dealings with his former editor demonstrate that he was willing to threaten the complete cancellation of a book if his choice of cover was not used.

Hawking's editor also commented on the accusations that the wheelchair photo on the cover in any way took advantage of Hawking. "It was obvious the reviewer didn't know Stephen, to think that he could be exploited. No one could exploit Stephen Hawking. He is quite capable of looking after himself." On another occasion, the editor commented, "It was a triumph for a man in Hawking's physical condition to be on the cover of his own book."[559]

Hawking also refutes the suggestion that many people bought the book without actually ever reading it. He refers to the piles of letters he received from readers, full of questions and detailed comments indicating "that they have read it, even if they do not understand all of it." He also mentions that strangers stopped him on the street to tell him how much they enjoyed the book. As a result, Hawking concluded "that at least a proportion of those who buy the book actually do read it."[560] Well, for a scientist, this is not an entirely convincing argument. Like every author, Hawking naturally wanted his books not only to be bought, but also to be read and understood. Above all, the entire story surrounding the publication and incredible success of Hawking's *Brief History of Time* provides ample confirmation of Hawking's exquisite feeling for self-marketing.

Hawking also made sure he was actively involved in the book's marketing campaign. Within the book trade, some were amazed that he was willing to talk to tabloid newspapers such as the *Sunday Mirror*.[561] Shortly after the British publication of *A Brief History of Time*, people began to stop Hawking on the street to proclaim their admiration, which Hawking reveled in.[562] "I am pleased a book on science competes with the memoirs of pop stars," he explained.[563]

After *A Brief History of Time*, Hawking published a further 12 popular science books—including a children's book he co-wrote with his daughter. Many became bestsellers, but none could match the runaway success of his first mass-market book.[564]

The hype surrounding Hawking and the book also had a flip side. Several physicists said that Hawking was wrong to mix accepted and established scientific conclusions with his own controversial speculations without informing lay readers of the distinction between the two. Others said it was pretentious of him to end the book with potted biographies of Galileo, Newton, and Einstein. They felt that Hawking, by implication, was being arrogant by elevating himself in such illustrious company.[565]

Hawking's tendency to integrate scientific conclusions with his own speculations and opinions, combined with his inclination to express his personal thoughts on topics of general interest, created the model of success for his later books. In *Brief Answers to the Big Questions*, for example, Hawking explores the following topics at some length:

- Is there a God?
- Is there other intelligent life in the universe?
- Is time travel possible?
- Will we survive on Earth?
- Should we colonize space?
- How do we shape the future?

His answers to many of these questions have very little to do with scientific conclusions. His argument that we will not be able to survive on Earth forever because, for example, an asteroid collision could eventually end life on our planet, is by no means new. In fact, it is more or less common knowledge. On the basis of the risks our planet faces, Hawking describes it as inevitable that the human race will need to colonize other heavenly bodies.

Hawking also speculates that some researchers will use genetic engineering to breed a race of "superhumans." As a result, Hawking predicted that there would be major political problems with the "unimproved" humans, who would no longer be able to compete. "Presumably, they will die out, or become unimportant. Instead, there will be a race of self-designing beings, who are improving themselves at an ever-increasing rate."[566] This blend of science and science fiction contributed significantly to Hawking's popularity – and got him and his books onto the front pages of newspapers and magazines all over the world.

Hawking often weighed in on political topics, expressing opinions that were generally in line with the left-wing, environmentalist zeitgeist: "The Earth is becoming too small for us. Our physical resources are being drained at an alarming rate. We have presented our planet with the disastrous gift of climate change."[567] Convinced that the threat of climate change was worsening, Hawking issued ever-diminishing timescales for the imminent apocalypse. In 2016, he declared that a disaster to planet Earth was a near certainty in the next thousand or ten thousand years. In 2017, he warned that climate change could turn the earth into a fireball with a temperature of 250°C and sulfuric acid rain within the next 600 years. The following year, he slashed the countdown to just one century – the human race had no more than 100 years before it would need to colonize another planet.[568] As early as the 1990s, Hawking began to develop doomsday scenarios, although the focus of his apocalyptic warnings changed over the years – sometimes it was computer viruses or genetic engineering, then it was nuclear war or an asteroid collision before, finally, he settled on rogue artificial intelligence.

Hawking had never actually researched any of these topics, but when stark warnings are issued by the world's highest profile scientist, people tend to sit up and listen. Hawking always came up with new marketing ideas to draw attention to his scientific theories. Other scientists might have turned their noses up at addressing topics such as time travel—and if they ever did, they would have done so in scientific articles in academic journals. But Hawking had different ideas. On June 28, 2009, he organized a party for time travelers in his college, Gonville & Caius in Cambridge, to show a film about time travel. The room was decorated with balloons and "Welcome, Time Travelers" banners. To make sure that only genuine time travelers would come, he decided to send out invitations after the party and announce it on his 2010 TV show. "On the day of the party, I sat in college hoping, but no one came. I was disappointed, but not surprised, because I had shown that if general relativity is correct and energy density is positive, time travel is not possible. I would have been delighted if one of my assumptions had turned out to be wrong."[569]

On another occasion he made headlines for a scientific wager with the physicist Kip Thorne. They bet on whether or not the Cygnus X-1 system contained a black hole. The wager itself was nothing unusual, but the prize certainly was. If Thorne won their bet, Hawking promised him a year's subscription to the men's magazine *Penthouse*. "In the years following the bet, the evidence for black holes became so strong that I conceded and gave Kip a subscription to *Penthouse*, much to the displeasure of his wife."[570]

Even when he was wrong, Hawking still managed to stage the admission of a mistake as a major media appearance that increased his popularity. During a conference in 2003, his scientific adversary Leonard Susskind compared Hawking to a soldier lost in the jungle who does not yet realize that the war he has been fighting is over. This was an allusion to the dispute between the two physicists about the fate of information that falls into a black hole, a disagreement that had been rumbling on for more than 20 years. "By the following year, he [Hawking] was ready to make a pronouncement, widely heralded as likely to be a public about-face. With characteristic showmanship, Hawking let it be known that his proclamation would be forthcoming at a conference in Dublin, and the global media descended on the venue to the bemusement of many scientists."[571]

He essentially conceded that his scientific opponents had been right and presented the physicist with whom he had concluded a scientific wager with a baseball encyclopedia. However, given the fact that Hawking qualified his concession with a major "but," some of his colleagues adjudged his performance to be "puzzling at best, and at worst a stunt in which Hawking hijacked the conference to boost his media profile."[572] Hawking, as this episode demonstrates, was even able to transform a scientific error into a media event with him at the center.

Hawking became more and more a jet-setting media super-star. He no longer devoted a majority of his time to his scientific work, but to popular projects and appearances around the world. Hawking died on March 14, 2018, and was laid to rest between the tombs of Sir Isaac Newton and Charles Darwin. A grave in West-minster Abbey is the highest honor that can be bestowed upon a scientist in Great Britain and 25,000 people entered a lottery to win one of the 1,000 places at the funeral in Westminster Abbey. Hawking had led an incredible life. In his autobiography, Hawking looks back on his life: "I have also visited Japan six times, China three times, and every continent, including Antarctica, with the exception of Australia. I have met the presidents of South Korea, China, India, Ireland, Chile, and the United States. I have lectured in the Great Hall of the People in Beijing and in the White House. I have been under the sea in a submarine and up in a hot air bal-loon and a zero-gravity flight...My early work showed that classical general relativity broke down at singularities in the Big Bang and black holes. My later work has shown how quantum theory can predict what happens at the beginning and end of time. It has been a glorious time to be alive and doing research in theoretical physics. I'm happy if I have added something to our understanding of the universe."[573]

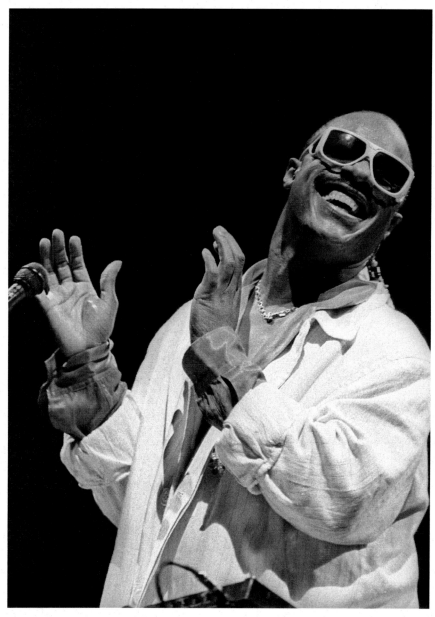

Stevie Wonder in Oakland, California, 1985: "People who do not want to change ideas, who are safe, usually get left behind."

Credits: Redferns / Getty Images

# 12. Stevie Wonder
## The Superstar

As Elton John said in an interview with *Rolling Stone*: "Let me put it this way: Wherever I go in the world, I always take a copy of *Songs in the Key of Life*. For me, it's the best album ever made, and I'm always left in awe after I listen to it. When people in decades and centuries to come talk about the history of music, they will talk about Louis Armstrong, Duke Ellington, Ray Charles, and Stevie Wonder [...] he [Wonder] evolved into an amazing songwriter and a genuine musical force of nature. He's so multitalented that it's hard to pinpoint exactly what it is that makes him one of the greatest ever. But first, there's that voice. Along with Ray Charles, he's the greatest R&B singer who ever lived!"[574]

Wonder has sold over 100 million albums worldwide, making him one of the best-selling musicians of all time. He has won 25 Grammy Awards—only one musician, classical conductor Sir Georg Solti, has won more, with 31 (both also received the Lifetime Achievement Award). Wonder's albums *Innervisions* (1973), *Fulfillingness' First Finale* (1974) and *Songs in the Key of Life* (1976) each won the Grammy Award for Album of the Year, making him the record holder of this major award. He is also the only artist to win the award three times in a row. Wonder was inducted into the Rhythm and Blues Music Hall of Fame, Rock and Roll Hall of Fame and Songwriters Hall of Fame and received a star on the Hollywood Walk of Fame. And he led the campaign to have Martin Luther King Jr.'s birthday declared a national holiday in the United States.

Stevie Wonder grew up in a grim environment. His father Calvin Judkins was chronically unemployed and 'earned' his money by sending his girlfriend Lula Mae Hardaway to walk the streets.

After handing all of her money over to Judkins, she received only a modest allowance. She was often beaten, by Judkins or by johns, one of whom nearly broke her jaw.[575] On May 13, 1950, Lula, who was 20 years old at the time, gave birth to Stevie, the third of six children. She had gone into labor two months before the scheduled due date and her baby weighed only four pounds. Stevie spent the first 40 days of his life in an incubator, clinging to life. It was only after 54 days that his mother was actually able to take him home.[576] Paradoxically, what saved his life as a baby also led to his blindness: he was given supplemental oxygen in the incubator, resulting in what is known as retinopathy of prematurity (ROP), a rare retinal disease that affects premature infants whose retinal vessels have not yet matured. Back then, nobody knew that excessive oxygenation could lead to this disease and even blindness. Stevie was one of 12,000 children affected at that time.[577]

Judkins was an abusive person and showed no regard for his wife or Stevie and soon forced Lula back onto the streets. One night in 1953, Judkins ordered her out to get him cigarettes. She refused, and he slapped her so hard across the face that she fell to the floor, not far from her sleeping baby. Judkins picked her up off the floor and flung her across the apartment, causing her to crash into a table, leaving her nose gushing blood. The three children woke up and screamed. Lula fought back, took a switchblade, and held it to Judkins' neck. He tried to knock the knife away, but severely injured his forearm. Judkins, a coward, feared for his life and fled the house bleeding. When he came crawling back hoping to reconcile with her, Lula made two conditions: She wanted to leave town and move to Detroit, and she would no longer work as a prostitute.[578]

In trying to find a cure for Stevie's blindness, Lula consulted several doctors and even a faith healer, but no one could help. Stevie recalls: "There are things that they said they could do, but I went to more doctors that said if there was any way they could return my sight they would try. It's one thing when you're blind from birth, you don't know what it's like to see, so it's just like seeing anyway... The sensation of seeing is not one I have, so I don't worry about it."[579]

Nine of the people profiled in this book were or are blind— James Holman, William Hickling Prescott, Helen Keller, Ray Charles, Andrea Bocelli, Marla Runyan, Johann König, and Erik Weihenmayer—but none of them were blind from birth. It seems that Stevie Wonder dealt with blindness more easily than some others because he never knew what it was like to see. That's why the subject of his blindness hardly ever crops up in this chapter—because it didn't play an important role in Stevie Wonder's life.

He became interested in music as a child, learned to play several instruments and sang in the church choir. One of Stevie's friends knew Ronnie White, a member of Smokey Robinson's band The Miracles, who had become a big hit for the newly founded record label Motown. This label was to play a pivotal role in Stevie's life. Motown's founder Berry Gordy Jr, an ex-boxer, record dealer and songwriter, had originally founded the music publishing company Jobete in 1958, before setting up his own record label Tammy a year later, and Motown (named after the Motor Town Detroit) a year after that.

Ronnie offered to introduce Stevie to Motown, and at his first audition, an employee asked the then-eleven-year-old if he could sing. "Yes sir. I can sing real good." And he added, "I can sing badder than Smokey." The Motown employee later recalled: "I never saw a kid as confident as Stevie was. Usually kids were in awe of us, they'd swallow their tongues. But Stevie had no fear. You couldn't help but like him. He was a funny little kid. But we had no idea he had so much talent."[580]

For Stevie, Motown soon became his second home. He often spent all day there, arriving at 3 p.m. after school and staying long into the night. He stood out because he often told the experienced musicians how they should do their job, how they should sing or play an instrument. It might have come across as pretentious at first, but they recognized that what he was saying made sense. However, there were still a few obstacles to overcome before Stevie could get a job at Motown. Berry Gordy, Motown's founder, believed kids should finish school before he would sign them to his label. In addition, Stevie was blind, and Gordy was not sure how any collaboration between them could work.

But when they heard him sing and play with his bongos, they were thrilled and soon realized that Stevie's blindness was not a hindrance. One remembered: "The funny thing is, I didn't even realize he was blind! Not right away...when he came in, he didn't act blind, didn't bump into things. He was wearing those dark glasses, but a lot of guys did because it was the cool look, and he looked at me when I was talking, he knew where I was."[581]

One day, a co-worker came storming into the Motown founder's office and told him to drop everything because he needed to hear Stevie for himself. Gordy rushed into the studio and saw Stevie there: "He was singing, playing the bongos and blowing on a harmonica. His voice didn't knock me out, but his harmonica playing did. Something about him was infectious...he was only eleven years old and people were already saying he could be another Ray Charles."[582]

Ray Charles had already proved that blindness was not an impediment to making great music and achieving success. But with Stevie, there was another problem—his age and the provisions of American child labor laws. But even these problems were not insurmountable. The record company had to guarantee that his schooling would not suffer, even when he was on tour. So, Motown assigned a supervisor to take care of Stevie and organize regular lessons for the boy.

Stevie would also not be allowed to collect the proceeds from record sales or concert performances himself; instead, the money was placed in a trust account that he would not be able to access until he was 21. His mother legitimately questioned why she should not manage her son's money, but she had not hired a lawyer to represent her and her son's interests, and eventually she signed the contract with the trust account. Stevie received only $200 a month, which was paid to his mother.[583]

At the age of eleven, Stevie got his first record deal. His first two singles were never released, but the third, in June 1962 ("I Call It Pretty Music But the Old People Call It the Blues"), almost made the top 100 in the U.S., and peaked at number 101. Soon, Little Stevie Wonder, as his record company named him at the time, went on tour with other Motown musicians. Throughout his life, Stevie was known for sleeping little—or sleeping at different times than other people, because it was always dark for him anyway. When he was on the road with the other Motown artists, he was sometimes still playing harmonica on the tour bus at two or three o'clock in the morning. Stevie soon got used to the others nagging him to shut up because they wanted to sleep.

At live events, he electrified the audience with his spontaneity. If you watch the live recording of the track "Fingertips" on YouTube, you will witness Stevie's first, great success. Stevie is led on stage after a performance by Marvin Gaye and introduced as a 12-year-old genius. He starts playing the bongo and asks the audience to "Clap your hands, stamp your feet." Then he starts playing harmonica and shouts, "Say yeaaah! Say yeah! Yeah! Yeah!" He kept playing and his enthusiasm spread to the audience. After he was led off stage, he came back, playing for a total of eight minutes.

Although they didn't normally do so, Motown decided to release the live recording as a single. And the decision was spot on: the single shot to #1 on both the Billboard charts and the R&B charts in August 1963. "Fingertips" was also included on Stevie's first album, *Recorded Live: The 12 Year Old Genius*. It became the first No. 1 album for Motown—and it was the first time a singer so young had a No. 1 album and a No. 1 single. According to Motown, the single sold over a million copies.

The early success thrilled Stevie as much as it did his record company, but they were also worried: soon his voice would break. What would his voice sound like then? In any case, Motown first released another single ("Workout, Stevie, Workout"), which reached No. 33 in the charts. Another nice success, but measured against the sensational earlier No. 1, not quite as impressive. At the beginning of 1964, Stevie's next single made it to No. 52.

One can imagine how much patience and perseverance are necessary for a young artist who, at the age of twelve, was catapulted to the top of the charts with a massive hit and then worked tirelessly to repeat this success. But after three years, the results were mixed. Out of seven singles, two had made the Top 30. Would Stevie find his niche at Motown and in the music business? Would the investment in him pay off? Stevie himself was frustrated at times. Motown dictated which songs he should sing, but he was convinced that he could do much better and be more successful if he sang his own songs. He hadn't got to that point yet. "But at Motown, you couldn't make those decisions yourself. You just had to wait it out. Motown was a big machine, man. You can't fight the machine. You're only one part of the machine."[584]

The way he describes it, it almost sounds as if Wonder, like other Motown artists before him, had been given "inferior material and lazy ideas," a situation that could end an artist's career. "Many believed this was Stevie Wonder's destiny."[585]

On a tour of England, the British tabloids, known for their sensationalist reporting, ran a story that Wonder wanted to undergo eye surgery that would restore his sight, but that his company, Motown, was preventing it. Apparently, so the story went, Motown was worried that if Stevie was no longer blind, they would lose a valuable marketing USP for the young artist. The story was fictitious but Wonder and some of his colleagues at Motown began to have doubts that there might be something to it.[586] However, this episode indirectly confirms that, at least from a marketing point of view, Wonder's blindness was not a disadvantage, but actually an advantage.

His contract would expire in May 1966, and doubts arose as to whether Motown would renew it. After all, Gordy didn't really need Wonder; his other musicians were much more successful. Some of Motown's other artists were jealous because they thought anyone else with a comparable track record would have had their contract terminated—Wonder apparently enjoyed special treatment.[587]

Gordy denied that he had thought about ending his collaboration with Stevie Wonder: "That was my job: to find the right combination. And you just keep releasing records to keep an act alive, keep the name alive, knowing you won't get a big hit out of it. That's what we did with Stevie. We didn't put a lot behind some of those records, but we kept him out there until it happened for him. Sometimes it's a matter of coming up with the right writer and producer. Sometimes the artists themselves come up with the right idea. With Stevie, it was both."[588]

Stevie Wonder did not rely on others, but demonstrated the combination of perseverance and willingness to experiment that is so crucial to achieving success. He was extremely eager to learn, including from everyone around him. Another Motown employee who spent time with Wonder recalls, "He was always askin' me, 'Hey, how do you do this, how do you that?' He did that with everybody. He was a real pain in the ass—I say that with love, but I'm still sayin' he was a pain in the ass. That's how he learned all he did."[589]

At the end of 1965, Wonder landed his next big hit "Uptight (Everything's Alright)," which made it to No. 3 on the *Billboard* Pop Singles chart and No. 1 on the R&B chart. In 1966, more singles followed, the best of which reached No. 9 and the least successful, No. 131. Then, in May 1967, he came close to making the big breakthrough with "I Was Made to Love Her," which climbed to No. 1 on the R&B chart and No. 2 on the pop chart. All the while, he continued to work on his music. "With his career on course, Stevie Wonder privately worked away studying voice techniques, learning Braille notations to assist with music arrangements, and of course, composing prolifically."[590]

In the 1960s, however, the big breakthrough continued to elude him. After his debut success in 1963, he released nine more albums, none of which performed better than *Up-Tight*, which reached No. 33 in May 1966. He also released 20 more singles after his 1963 hit "Fingertips," and two of them made it to No. 2 in the charts. Step by step, he started climbing the rung of the pop ladder. He went on tour for two months, supporting the Rolling Stones, although he didn't earn that much and was only allowed to play for 15 minutes. But still, even the legendary Rolling Stones became a little jealous when they saw how audiences responded to Wonder's performances and went as far as cutting his name from their concert marquees.

Then in late 1972, almost a decade after his first hit, he released "Superstition" and it shot to No. 1 on both the R&B chart and the pop chart—an even greater success than his first taste of chart glory! 1972 was also the year Motown moved its headquarters from Detroit to Los Angeles. Many Motown artists were devastated by the move, just like so many people who obstinately refuse to embrace change. It was typical of Stevie Wonder that he reacted differently and defended Berry Gordy's decision: "He had to change with the times. I think the move is a very good thing...People who do not want to change ideas, who are safe, usually get left behind."[591]

Like all successful people, Wonder was always open to new experiences, curious about change. And he had learned a lot in the years since he signed his first record contract, which expired on his 21st birthday. His earnings were now no longer deposited into a trust account. Based on records sold and other income, Wonder had estimated that the account should have a balance of about $3.5 million. But then came the shock: the check he received for his nearly ten years of work was for just $100,000![592]

Stevie Wonder had not been aware that, according to the contract, all of the record company's expenses were deducted from his income. For example, Gordy had "generously" given his mother a house—but had not said that he had taken the money from Wonder's account. The singer was shocked and canceled the contract. He hired a savvy lawyer who rejected Motown's 240-page new contract offer and presented his own draft, which called for an advance payment of $1 million (today that would be $6 million to $7 million), plus the kind of compensation only superstars get, and would tie Stevie to Motown for the next five years.[593]

Motown agreed. As his career flourished over the next few years, he was able to negotiate an even more lucrative contract that guaranteed him an advance of $13 million (in today's terms, that would be almost $60 million). On top of that, he was paid royalties of 20 percent. By comparison, superstars such as Paul McCartney and Elton John at the time received advance payments of $8 million and royalties of 12 and 15 percent, respectively.[594]

In addition, the new contract gave him far greater artistic freedom—and this was at least as important to Wonder as the royalties. He was now able to produce his own records. Stevie used his new-found freedom to experiment with modern technology, such as the Moog synthesizer. In an interview with the *Guardian* in 1972, he said: "A lot of people don't consider the Moog an instrument, in a sense, and they feel it's gonna take a lot of work away from musicians and all that. But I feel it is an instrument and is a way to directly express what comes from your mind. It gives you so much of a sound in the broader sense. What you're actually doing with an oscillator is taking a sound and shaping it into whatever form you want."[595]

After the success of "Superstition" in late 1972, his next No. 1 hit in the pop chart "You Are the Sunshine of My Life" followed just a few months later. Between 1974 and 1977, he achieved something he had not managed in almost ten years. And he did it three times: His singles "You Haven't Done Nothin," "I Wish" and "Sir Duke" all shot to No. 1 in the pop charts. In 1974 and 1976, he also scored No. 1 albums with the releases of *Fulfillingness' First Finale* and *Songs in the Key of Life*.

In November 1974, the mayor of Los Angeles even proclaimed a Stevie Wonder Day and the leading U.S. news magazine, *Newsweek*, featured him on the cover with the headline "Stevie, The Wonder Man."[596] The article said Wonder was "the most creative—

and popular—pop musician of his generation" and "with 40 million records [sold], Stevie is the favorite of young, old, black, white, the hip and the square... [As] an innovator admired by musicians from Paul McCartney to Henry Mancini...[His] success symbolizes the vaulting new prestige and popularity of black musicians in America."[597] *Time* magazine ran a major feature about him called "Black, Blind and on Top of the Pop."[598]

Although the period from the early 1970s to the mid-1980s was Wonder's most successful, there were also setbacks. This was related to the fact that he was always experimenting with new ideas. For example, he wrote the score for the film *The Secret Life of Plants*, which was challenging because he had never seen any of the plants and colors in his entire life. However, Wonder wanted to prove that a blind man was capable of writing music for a visual medium: "It shows that a blind person can come up with music that can work in a film. You don't have to see a film to do a good score and it's important for people to realise this. I can 'see' there are certain shapes and colours that I am able to perceive because at some point I have been given a verbal understanding of what they're about. I get a certain feeling in my head when a person says red, blue, green and so on."[599] Sales of the film score failed to meet expectations. Nevertheless, the album was an innovative breakthrough because it was one of the first to be recorded digitally rather than analog.

Wonder was no longer just a singer, he also wrote songs for other stars such as George Benson, the Pointer Sisters, and Michael Jackson.[600] He composed hits for Aretha Franklin,[601] sang duets with Michael Jackson, Julio Iglesias[602] and Ray Charles,[603] played harmonica on the Eurythmics' superhit "There Must be An Angel."[604] Together with ex-Beatle Paul McCartney, he landed a megahit in the spring of 1982: "Ebony and Ivory." The song, which used the image of ebony and ivory keys on the piano to evoke a vision of harmony between black and white people, climbed to No.1 on the pop charts.

Stevie Wonder worked tirelessly. He always had at least 1,000 half-finished songs in the pipeline and composed music every day. "He turns out five songs some days, others he writes one or two," reported his ex-wife, Syreeta. "He has to write at least one a day because he feels incomplete if by the evening he hasn't written a tune and got it down on tape."[605] The famous soul singer Jean Carn describes working with Stevie Wonder: "He never gets sleepy and I've been in a studio with him where he has been for three days and nights. In fact, he brought engineers to the studio in shifts and they would literally fall out of their chairs...He would only allow me to leave the studio to go to the hotel to change and eat."[606] Bassist Nate Watts reports that after an exhausting day in the recording studio, he had just come home and gone to bed when the phone rang. It was Stevie on the line, telling him to come back to the studio because he really wanted to record a song. It was three in the morning.[607]

Again, Jean Carn: "The amazing thing is that Stevie will work all night—we are falling asleep at the control board and at 7 a.m. he'll want you to lead vocals. He'll go in and do a reference vocal at that time of the morning and sound like an angel." Another employee reported: "He plays his instruments all night. He eats when he wants and he sleeps when he wants. It's always dark to him, so he don't know breakfast from lunch and dinner."[608]

Unlike many other artists, Wonder stayed away from drugs all his life. He tried marijuana once, but never touched any other substances. This does not mean that he led an ascetic life—on the contrary, even as a teenager he was very sexually active—and this was to remain so. Throughout his life, he had numerous girlfriends, even when he was married. In 1972, he divorced his first wife Syreeta Wright, but both remained close friends until her death in 2004; he even supported her in her artistic career and recorded songs together with her. In 2001, he married Kai Milliard, but the couple divorced in 2015. He got married for the third time two years later, this time to Tomeeka Robyn Bracy. Stevie Wonder's nine children have five different mothers.

In the United States, Wonder is also well known for his political activism. On several occasions, he even announced that he wanted to run for mayor of Detroit, although he never actually did. He also led the campaign to have the birthday of civil rights activist Martin Luther King declared a public holiday in the United States. The campaign collected six million signatures, making it the largest petition of its kind in American history. The campaign's demands were initially rejected, but in November 1983, a bill creating a federal holiday won a two-thirds majority in Congress. Today, civil servants and public sector employees, plus around a third of private sector employees, take the day off work and the stock exchanges are closed.

From the perspective of radical black activists, Wonder was not radical enough. He despised both black racism directed against whites—in line with his role model Martin Luther King—as well as racism directed against blacks. At that time, it was not yet common for whites to play in "black" bands. Once, when Wonder was playing a slow number at a concert, someone in the audience screamed at a white band member, "Motherfucker, what are you doing up there?" Wonder stopped, looked at the heckler, and shouted angrily: "Hey, motherfucker, get up there and stand toe to toe with my boy and say that to his face. Otherwise, shut the fuck up."[609]

The mid-1980s saw a second peak in Stevie Wonder's musical career with No. 1 hits including "I Just Called to Say I Love You," "Part-Time Lover" and "That's What Friends Are For." In October 1985, he made the top ten for the last time with the track "Go Home." In the years that followed, life became quieter for him, but every now and then he made spectacular appearances. In 2007 and 2008, he went on his first world tour in a decade. During the 2008 Presidential campaign, he enthusiastically supported Barack Obama and performed at the Democratic National Convention, where Obama was officially nominated as the presidential candidate. He sang at a concert in Washington, D.C. in January 2009, kicking off the celebrations for the inauguration of the new president, and marked the occasion by releasing the song "All About the Love Again." Obama honored Stevie Wonder by awarding him the Library of Congress' Gershwin Prize in 2009. In June 2012, Wonder was invited to perform at Buckingham Palace to celebrate the diamond jubilee of the reign of Queen Elizabeth II, and over the holiday season in 2015, he sang "Someday at Christmas" with the soul singer Andra Day in an Apple commercial.

Wonder's success is based on his professional discipline, combined with an openness to constantly reinvent himself and experiment with new technologies and stylistic elements. His fans might want to hear his classic hits and pigeonhole him in one musical category, but he is only willing to do this to a certain extent. What drives him is a productive dissatisfaction, which he once expressed in these words: "In every album that I have and shall do, it is not my goal for that to be better than that and the next to succeed others, but only that I do and give the best I can at the time of my doing and giving, and that only happens because of the dis- or satisfaction that made me want to be a better someone."[610]

Andrea Bocelli in Rome, March 2019: "Everything in this world is hard; every type of objective that we achieve is hard. Where there is competition, there is work. This doesn't frighten me; the main point is to try to improve day by day."

Credits: Independent Photo Agency Srl / Alamy Stock Photo

# 13. Andrea Bocelli
## Breaking the Barriers

Andrea Bocelli is not only one of the most successful Italian singers of all time, he is also one of the few who have been able to establish themselves on a global stage in both pop and classical music. He has performed in front of presidents of the United States and several popes, filled concert halls around the world, sung duets with the most famous singers of his time and broken one record after another.

His first album *Il Mare Calmo della Sera* reached the upper echelons of the charts after its release and received multiple platinum awards just a few weeks later. His album *Romanza*, released in 1997, sold over twelve million copies. His albums climbed high in the charts, achieved multiple platinum sales and won major music awards such as the World Music Award, ECHO, Classic Brit Awards, a Bambi in the field of classical music and a Billboard Award. Bocelli was also nominated for Grammys several times.

Andrea Bocelli was born on September 22, 1958, in Lajatico, a small town in northwestern Tuscany, Italy. His parents were self-employed and earned their money selling tractors and other farming equipment. They noticed shortly after birth that something was wrong with Andrea: his eyes were often inflamed and red. As their son continued to suffer, they consulted a specialist in Turin. His diagnosis: Andrea was suffering from glaucoma and the condition would gradually make him completely blind.[611] According to his doctor, surgery could not cure him, but it could slow down the process. Andrea underwent a total of 27 operations as a child, the first of which took place when he was only six months old.[612]

Andrea's parents did the right thing. They knew that there was no hope for Andrea, and they did not want to deceive him, so they decided to prepare him for the fact that one day he would not be able to see anything at all. His mother said: "I had to rule out pity; I had to force such strength within myself. It was terrible because it was almost impossible not to feel pity in front of that vivacious young boy who was like quicksilver, alive."[613] She watched Andrea's eyes grow emptier every day and forced herself to not break down in tears or tenderly pity the child: "I would have made him a victim, I kept telling myself."[614]

At the age of 12, Andrea suffered a momentous accident: He was attending a boarding school for the blind at the time, and, during a soccer game, a ball struck him in the right eye—the eye with which he could at least still perceive color and light. He felt a sharp pain, but the school nurse did not send him to hospital right away and decided to notify his parents instead. Andrea's mother came the next day and took him straight to hospital. The doctor said that it might be possible to save some eyesight, but he did not hide his doubts.[615] The doctor bandaged his head and sent him back to school. When the bandage was removed a few days later, Andrea realized that his sight was almost completely gone—he could barely make out the lightbulb of a lamp. One morning he opened his eyes and felt the warmth of the sun on his face, but realized he could no longer see the sun. He called for his mother. When she saw his anguish, she quickly burst into tears. He was distraught: He had just finished elementary school and soon the summer vacation would begin: What would he do at the beach? How could he play with his friends? And how would his friends behave toward him?[616]

His mother asked him if he now only saw darkness. He answered in the negative. What did he see then? "Everything and nothing," he answered. "I see that which I want to see. I see my room, the cupboard, the beds, but I see them because I know they are there." His mother did not understand what he was trying to say. Then she remembered the words of the director of the school for the blind, who himself was blind. He explained to her that only sighted people could experience the visual sensation of darkness. "The blind cannot see darkness, just like the deaf cannot hear silence, which is an auditory sensation, the antithesis of sound. That's all."[617]

Bocelli rarely talks about his blindness today. Before interviews, journalists are given a printed statement from his manager indicating that he will not answer any questions about his blindness. He has long taken his condition for granted. "The tragedy is that people continue to make a fuss about something *they* consider to be tragic, not I."[618]

In his autobiography, he writes that he hated being treated differently than sighted people. He felt himself capable of doing everything that other boys his own age did and insisted on being judged by the same standards as everyone else. Remarks like "'Be careful there'; 'That's too dangerous for you'; 'Wait for me to help you'" made him angry and brought tears to his eyes. In the face of such concern, he would throw himself into whatever it was that others considered especially dangerous just to show them. He wanted to prove that a blind man could achieve anything if he really wanted to. "Nothing that he ardently desired seemed impossible, and if people judged that something was beyond his capabilities, he felt obliged to prove them wrong."[619] A key phrase in his autobiography is that he was convinced he had to be "the best simply in order to be considered equal."[620]

Even as a young child, he was passionate about music. "When I was a child," he said, "everyone asked me to sing. Step by step I was understanding that that was my destiny, to sing."[621] After he graduated from elementary school, his parents looked around the country for a middle school that offered music courses. He had been taking piano lessons since the age of seven, and now wanted to explore other instruments as well. In Bologna, his parents enrolled him in the Instituto Francesco Cavazza, a school for the blind that allowed students, alongside their regular academic classes, to study music and singing. "I always had an extraordinary fascination with musical instruments when I was a child," he reported. "I spent a lot of money to buy all sorts of instruments, but more than playing them, I mistreated them."[622]

He soon discovered that his true talent was for singing. In his autobiography, he describes a particular experience when he was asked to sing at his school's year-end celebration. He was very excited but, as he took to the stage, the audience was whispering. This upset him—and gave him courage at the same time. He took a deep breath and his clear voice resounded throughout the room, *"Che bella cosa 'na iurata e sole."*

When reflecting on this early interpretation of the Italian folk song, "O sole mio," Bocelli remembers: "He had sung that first phrase all in one breath; when he breathed, he noticed, with surprise, that a great hush had fallen across the room. For a moment he thought he had forgotten the words. He breathed deeply and continued. When he reached the first high, *'ma n'atu sole,'* there was thunderous applause. Amos felt himself reinvigorated. His heart, which until a few moments before was hammering with fear, now was swelling with joy. It was the first time in his life he had been applauded. Amos attacked the finale in full voice and sustained it with all his might, and the entire duration of his breath. Before fading away, his voice overwhelmed by voices, cries, and hands clapping."[623]

Although his musical talent had become apparent at an early age, his parents wanted him to have a serious education, with real professional opportunities. "They said I could try to sing but they reminded me that people cannot live just with their dreams. You must have something more concrete." He agreed: "I wanted to learn a civil job. Love for the art does not guarantee a proper income."[624]

Bocelli decided to study law, but admits he also followed "pressure from my family" in doing so.[625] He enrolled at the University of Pisa, one of the most prestigious schools in Italy. With the help of a braille computer and translation software, he completed his studies and earned his doctorate with a dissertation project on the French philosopher Charles von Montesquieu. At the defense of his thesis, his examiners awarded him a score of 99 out of a possible 110 points.[626] That was good for Bocelli's self-confidence: "I haven't really accomplished anything yet, true, but the law degree represents an important achievement, especially for those who worried about seeing me lost, a man of no consequence in a society full of over-achievers...they have seen me catch up with the rest, compete head to head with the best-trained competitors; earn a position; they have learned to have confidence in me and I will show them that it is not misplaced. There will come a day when they will forget their worries and be proud of their son."[627]

After graduating and working as a public defender for a year, Bocelli started playing piano in bars a few evening a week, recording songs, and sending them to record companies—always without success. What helped him was the ability to be self-critical and work on his weaknesses. In his book *Talent is Overestimated*, Geoff Colvin profiles successful people—including outstanding musicians—to show that the main reason for their success was not talent, but 'deliberate practice' over years and decades with unrelenting self-discipline. The length of time spent practicing and the intensity and methods of practicing vary considerably between top performers and average experts in their field.

A host of scientific studies have confirmed what is commonly referred to as the 'ten-year rule': Whether in mathematics, natural sciences, music, or sports—it is very rare that anyone can become the very vest in their chosen field without at least ten years of intensive study or practice. And it's not only the length of time and the intensity of the practice that count, but also the type of practice. What many people understand by 'practice' has nothing to do with the 'deliberate practice' of which Colvin speaks. Performing a particular activity in the same or similar way over and over again does not, of course, lead to the kind of dramatic improvements necessary to achieve excellence. Rather, a key feature of 'deliberate practice' is that great performers concentrate on a very specific aspect of what they do and focus on just those things until they make significant progress. They identify very specific sub-areas that need improvement and approach them systematically. If this is the path to success, why don't more success-hungry people take it? Because it is tremendously mentally exhausting. The constant search for those specific sub-areas that need improvement, and the subsequent hard and often monotonous work on these weaknesses is more exhausting than most can possibly imagine. Most people prefer to keep doing the things that they are already good at anyway, simply because that is more enjoyable and offers them a quicker path to recognition. The trick, however, is to identify those sub-areas within the area in which you are good, and to optimize them to achieve greatness.

That's exactly what Bocelli did. Although he had always received recognition for his singing from those around him, he remained self-critical. In his autobiography, he writes that he subjected his songs to critical analysis and concluded, "that they did lack a certain originality and, probably, even strength...His singing could be judged pleasant, for the tone and timbre, but in it there were evident tensions, something forced, that in the end didn't leave anyone satisfied, even him."[628]

One day a piano tuner said to him: "Forgive my frankness, but I feel it is my duty to tell you that, with your voice, you could go a long way if only you entrusted yourself to a good singing teacher."[629] Bocelli was very surprised. For years, no one had spoken to him about studying singing. The piano tuner recommended an exceptional teacher, Luciano Bettarini, who had trained numerous opera singers including Franco Corelli. Other singers might have been offended to have a piano tuner recommend that they take singing lessons. Bocelli, however, listened to the advice and contacted Bettarini. Before auditioning for him, he took it upon himself to accept his judgment: "If that opinion had been negative, he had decided to put his mind at peace; for someone was finally going to tell him the truth."[630]

After Bettarini had heard him sing, he said: "You have a voice of *gold*, my son!" But, he added after a pause: "But you do the exact opposite of what you *should* do when singing. Proper study would not only improve your interpretative qualities, but it would really strengthen your voice; in short, it would put you in a new league. What I mean, to be frank, is that to the ear of the uninitiated what you do may sound surprising, but to the ear of an expert the defects of your voice are egregious."[631]

Nobody had ever spoken to Bocelli this way before, but he was eager to learn and from that day on he took lessons with the maestro. He now committed himself to improving the quality of his singing with all his strength—"the study of singing imposed a new discipline." He stopped drinking wine and followed a strict diet, "similar to that of athletes, so that, in addition to everything else, he felt better: more energetic and fitter, as much in body as in mind."[632]

In 1992, Bocelli got a surprising call. The famous Italian rock star Zucchero needed an operatic tenor to appear on an important demo tape he wanted to record. He had set his sights on getting the great opera star Pavarotti to sing a duet. Zucchero invited some singers to audition, among them Bocelli, who won the audition and recorded the demo together with the megastar.[633]

When the demo tape was played to Pavarotti, the maestro was convinced that Zucchero was trying to play a trick on him. Pavarotti had been led to believe that the guy singing the duet with Zucchero was an unknown piano bar singer from Pisa. That may have been true, but Pavarotti still couldn't believe it. After all, as Pavarotti explained, this was the voice of a great tenor. So, why were they trying to persuade him that this man was just a lounge singer? "Thank you for writing such a wonderful song," Pavarotti said, "Yet you do not need me to sing it—let Andrea sing 'Miserere' with you, for there is no one finer."[634]

When Bocelli was told what Pavarotti had said, he could hardly believe it. He suspected that Pavarotti had only wanted to find an elegant way to avoid singing with Zucchero.

The music manager Michele Torpedine also heard about Pavarotti's assessment of Bocelli's singing, so he called and asked him if he was already under contract. Bocelli replied that he wasn't, so Torpedine told him not to sign a contract with anyone else under any circumstances.[635]

Bocelli took this as a signal that Torpedine wanted to make him an offer, but his patience was put to the test. After the promising initial call, the busy manager didn't get back to him. Whenever Bocelli called to ask how things were going, he was told Torpedine was in a meeting. When he called Torpedine on his cell phone, Torpedine hung up or promised to call back right away, but never did.[636]

Bocelli was desperate and one day he decided to ambush Torpedine outside his office. However, Torpedine's secretary once again said that he was in a meeting and, when Torpedine finally came out, he explained to Bocelli that he was incredibly busy with another project. But, Torpedine continued, Bocelli shouldn't worry, everything would be fine, only right now he had absolutely no time because he had to rush to the airport.[637] On the way home, Bocelli was deeply disappointed and sad.

Time passed, and Bocelli was no longer expecting a call when one day the phone rang and, to his surprise, he heard Torpedine's voice: "I have some good news for you. This time, I think I did it; prepare yourself to leave toward the end of May for a tour of Italy, in the most important soccer stadiums."[638] Bocelli was speechless and could hardly believe his ears. The time had finally come, and the big day soon arrived. Bocelli sang the duet with Zucchero in a large soccer stadium. "At the end of the piece, the crowd seemed literally crazed. Fifteen thousand deafening voices were crying out, drowning even the sound from the enormous amplifiers." And he not only sang the song 'Miserere' as a duet, but was also given the opportunity to sing other songs. Bocelli, he writes in his autobiography, "had finally won his first, real battle."[639]

The tour of Italy turned into a triumph—for Zucchero, but also for Bocelli himself. He enjoyed the audience's tremendous applause and enthusiasm. He saw the success as a reward for his perseverance and for the fact that, despite all the doubts, he had never completely lost his optimism. But his success was not only the result of his perseverance or optimism, but the fact that he combined these qualities with a tremendous eagerness to learn. Just a few days after the tour, the famous tenor Franco Corelli was to lead a singing course for a small, select group of musicians.[640] After a great tour and a rapturous response from fans, other singers might have thought that they had 'made it' and didn't have anything left to learn. But Bocelli was eager for nothing more than to continue improving.

Out of 100 applicants for the course, 12 were chosen, and he was one of them. Corelli was tough. After the first participant had auditioned, he asked her: "You have a singing teacher?" She nodded and replied, "Yes." "And you *pay* such a teacher?", Corelli continued, his gaze fixed on the floor, as if he were talking to himself.[641] The singer ran back to her seat in tears. Then it was Bocelli's turn. As if in a dream, he now found himself singing in front of his idol. After he finished, a few seconds passed that felt like hours to him. Then Corelli came up to him, put a hand on his shoulder and said: "The voice is very beautiful; I believe I can give you some useful suggestions."[642] Bocelli gathered his courage and asked Corelli if he could visit him at home to take private lessons.[643] The next day, Corelli gave an interview to a daily newspaper in Turin and mentioned that he had been particularly impressed by Bocelli. When a friend read the interview to Andrea, he snatched the newspaper from his friend's hand, clutched it to his chest and vowed that he would keep it forever.[644]

Shortly after, Bocelli received a call from Torpedine: he should come to Milan the next day for a meeting with a record company. It was the same company to which he had often sent his tapes, without success. Now, following his successful tour with Zucchero, the company had demonstrated a genuine interest in him. The president of the record company sang his praises and told him how she got goose bumps the first time she heard his warm and expressive voice. She asked him if he wanted to present a song at the

San Remo Festival, the most popular Italian song contest. Bocelli was overcome with emotion: "...how many disappointed hopes, how many humiliations had he suffered; and now, all of a sudden, someone had turned the page." He could not wait for the moment to "show everyone who had ever closed a door in his face that he had been right all along."[645] The San Remo Festival (officially: Festival della Canzone Italiana) is a major televised event and is watched by one in three Italians. More than any marketing strategy, record contract, publicity event or talent contest, this festival is the biggest opportunity for a new pop singer to be seen and heard in Italy.[646]

In the three months before the festival, Bocelli recorded his first album. And then, finally, the big day arrived: 20 million Italians heard him sing "Il mare calmo delle sera," which Zucchero had written especially for him. His performance brought the audience to their feet: "The applause and the cries were deafening; many members of the audience had tears in their eyes and the emcee wasn't able to restore order for some time."[647] Bocelli had won, and this was the big breakthrough he had been waiting so long for.

After his victory, he received a late-night call from Pavarotti, who invited Bocelli to join him and a lineup of stars for his next "Pavarotti and Friends" concert—the show would be televised live throughout Europe from a magnificent amphitheater in Modena.[648] Just a few years before, Bocelli had tried to shake hands with the opera legend and had been swatted away by the maestro's security detail—and now Pavarotti was calling him personally. Bocelli spent a week with Pavarotti before the concert. That was the beginning of a great friendship.

This, again, demonstrates a key factor in Bocelli's success: he was always aware of the importance of making influential friends who were better and more famous than himself, who encouraged and criticized him. Bocelli easily managed to make friends with such people—he did nothing to hide his boundless admiration and everything to cultivate close relationships with them, not only on a professional but also on a human level.

Although Bocelli became famous after his performances with Zucchero and his victory in San Remo, wowing crowds all over Italy—and eventually in other European countries and the U.S.—he wasn't satisfied. He not only wanted to be a successful pop singer, but to become a respected opera singer. Just a few weeks after his victory in San Remo, he appeared on stage in Verdi's *Macbeth* in Pisa. Bocelli was always looking for new challenges, "it appeared to him… as a sign of destiny, and above all an authentic challenge to the skeptics who had repeatedly affirmed that it would be absolutely impossible for a blind man to tread the boards of the stage." He also recalled the words of Goethe, which were to become Bocelli's motto: "To live in the idea means to consider the impossible as possible."[649]

In 1998, one of Bocelli's longstanding dreams came true. He was offered the role of Rodolfo in Puccini's opera *La Bohème*. The opportunity came from an influential patron, Mario Dradi, who was an opera agent and one of the world's most successful classical music producers. It was Dradi who televised the first Three Tenors concert with Plácido Domingo, Luciano Pavarotti and José Carreras in Rome in 1990 to an audience of 1.5 billion viewers. And now Dradi was asking Bocelli to play the lead role in *La Bohème*, Puccini's masterpiece and one of the most performed operas in the world. "My legs were trembling just at the idea of singing the most beautiful opera in the world to me," Bocelli said. "But this was big for me; this *Bohème* was the appointment with destiny. It was something that I could not miss, even if it scared me to the extreme. If I had pulled back, what kind of artist could I call myself? How can I call myself an artist and not face this challenge? I had to face it and be brave against this and conquer my fears continuously. This also serves me for my own condition, to demonstrate to myself that I can do these things even with my handicap."[650]

His mind was drawn back to the words of an old high school teacher: "You cannot follow the conductor, you cannot go onstage, you cannot do that. Direct yourself elsewhere."[651] The weeks of preparation exhausted him. His contract stated that he had to rehearse eight hours a day for four weeks. He suffered from insomnia, was overcome with anxiety, and lost fifteen pounds.[652] "Being onstage means pulling down barriers seemingly insurmountable," he said during the third week of rehearsals.[653]

Movements had to be repeated again and again until they were graceful and spontaneous, including dancing, jumping, running toward Mimì, placing her down and picking her up from a bed, turning on cue, ripping up a manuscript and throwing it in a stove, lighting the stove, sticking a cigar in someone's mouth, and more.[654] Of course, his performance as a novice was not as professional as that of an established opera star—but that was not what he was aiming for anyway. What mattered to him was that he had mastered a new challenge. In the next day's *Corriere della Sera*, he was quoted as saying, "I'm emotional, but happy and above all satisfied. I demonstrated my knowledge of how to move onstage. I demolished a barrier."[655]

He followed *La Bohème* with appearances in numerous operas around the world. In 2001, he sang the lead in the opera *L'amico Fritz* by Pietro Mascagni in Verona and the tenor part in Verdi's *Messa da Requiem*. Bocelli became famous in both pop and classical music. In 2003, Universal Music Group, the world's largest classical music label, announced that Bocelli had taken first place in the Classic category, ahead of Anne-Sophie Mutter and Anna Netrebko. During his career, he has achieved so much in both pop and classical music and received so many awards and prizes that it is impossible to list them all here. On December 28, 2008, the asteroid 21891, discovered by an Italian astronomer in 1999, was even named after him—it is called Andreabocelli.[656]

What is it that drives this megastar? It's a productive dissatisfaction that he shares with many successful people, who are characterized by a specific combination of satisfaction and dissatisfaction. Past successes give them a core confidence that can also be called satisfaction. At the same time, they are always dissatisfied with what they have achieved. They live by the motto that there is nothing good enough that it cannot be improved. "Everything in this world is hard; every type of objective that we achieve is hard. Where there is competition, there is work. This doesn't frighten me; the main point is to try to improve day by day," Bocelli said.[657] The key to his success has always been his immense self-confidence, combined with the modesty of a student, who is always striving to recognize his weaknesses and learn new things—no matter how much success he has already achieved. In 2009, he said in an interview: "I am totally critical of myself. In the world of classical music in particular, it's extremely difficult ever to be fully satisfied with yourself."[658]

Soprano Ana Maria Martinez, who has sung extensively with Bocelli on his concert tours, said of him: "He works so hard. On the tours he worked every day on his voice. He's always doing exercises. Sometimes we even vocalized together. He's always curious to see what someone else is doing vocally and technique-wise...One day he told a group of us, 'I had a chance to become known doing my recordings, but what really interests me is every day to learn more, to polish my craft, to do things of real artistic value and integrity.'"[659]

Thomas Quasthoff at the ECHO Award Ceremony, Berlin, February 2008: "If I suggest 'I'm a sensitive soul, don't you dare insult me, don't you dare bring up my disability,' then I communicate fear and insecurity to my non-disabled counterpart. I approach people very normally, and they actually realize after two minutes that you can talk to me the same way you talk to your mates down the pub."

# 14. Thomas Quasthoff
## His voice has moved millions

*The Dreamer* is the title of an impressive documentary film about a man who dreamed of one day performing at Carnegie Hall and on the world's greatest stages. He dreamed of singing at the Salzburg Opera Festival, the Vienna State Opera and La Scala in Milan. His dreams may have been big, but Thomas Quasthoff made them all come true. Born in Germany, his unmistakable and incomparable bass-baritone voice has thrilled audiences all around the globe and secured him world-wide acclaim, especially in the United States.

In the spring of 1959, Thomas's mother took the tranquilizer thalidomide; she was pregnant at the time. And, just like thousands of women at that time, she gave birth to a child with severe birth defects. In his autobiography, Thomas describes the little Quasthoff as follows: "He just looks like a little seal, with crippled hands and feet that arch backwards at a ninety-degree angle instead of facing front."[660] His hands start just below his shoulders, and he is missing two fingers on his left hand and one on his right. His legs are so incompletely developed that he will later only reach a height of 1.32 meters (4' 4"). Before letting the little baby go home with his mother, the head of the clinic observed, "He'll never be able to walk, but with a plaster cast we should be able to correct it, at least the way it looks."[661]

Thomas spent the first eighteen months of his life in a plaster cast. He was only allowed to see his parents and his brother Michael at weekends and only from behind a protective glass partition—his doctors had put him in quarantine because they were worried that his condition would prevent his immune system from fighting infections. In order to get him into a vertical position, he was "strapped in" a clumsy prosthesis consisting of metal rails and fastened with leather straps and steel clamps. In the clinic, he recalls, he was "often leaned against the wall, or put in places where I cannot do too much damage if I fall. Of course, I fall repeatedly, and since I have no arms and legs to catch myself, I slam down each time like a broomstick. The bumps on my forehead grow as large as eggs."[662]

Thomas's parents refused to accept it when his doctors told them that their son would never walk. In their quest to teach him to walk upright, they became increasingly inventive. His father built a wooden rack that Thomas could hold on to and would be caught by when he lost his balance. In order to give him some exercise, Thomas's mother would set up the wooden rack six feet from a big plate of sweets on the kitchen table: "Come, little guy, come. Just put one leg in front of the other and get it."[663] Thanks in large part to his love of sweets, he was soon able to make it to the kitchen table without his wooden rack, and after a week could walk without the lure of chocolate. His orthopedist was amazed when Thomas's parents showed him how much progress Thomas had made. The orthopedist shook his head unbelievingly and confessed that he never would have thought it possible.

Thomas now learned to walk properly, an achievement that prompted his parents to decide to try and enroll him in a regular primary school. They visited every single elementary school in the city, and even some on the fringes of the city, only to face rejection everywhere. They were left with no choice but to enroll Thomas in a boarding school for the disabled. "My new comrades were either thalidomide cases like me, spastically paralyzed, or suffering from muscle atrophy. There were also some demented children, Down syndromes, epileptics and autistic kids."[664]

Thomas Quasthoff describes the ward matron as a sadist; his brother Michael calls her a "savage brute who ran her ward like a children's concentration camp."[665] Anyone who disobeyed her was locked in the storage closet or strapped into their bed, rolled out of the room and deposited in the bright hallway for the night. Many of the mentally ill children were shaken regularly by screaming fits, and others had trouble making it to the bathroom. Driven by panic attacks, they would climb out of their beds to smear themselves and others with excrement.[666]

Thomas's parents threatened the ward matron with a lawsuit—and never gave up looking for a normal school for their son. In the end, their persistence and perseverance paid off. But the new school was not easy for Thomas either. He was sometimes subjected to ugly remarks from other children, but his father nipped any bouts of self-pity in the bud: "Boy, the world is rude and dumb, and most of what stomps around on it is, too. It could be worse for you: you could be blind and mute. But stupid people are worse off yet, for they never realize how much stupidity they've been struck with."[667]

As he got older and his classmates started to see their first girlfriends, he became increasingly desperate: "You fooled yourself. You are not like the others. You are ugly. You are small. You are a crippled gnome."[668] As he was coming to puberty, Quasthoff remembers: "My friends were suddenly more interested in women. Me, too, but not them in me...I was lying in my bed and feeling sad, listening to music. Stevie Wonder helped a lot."[669]

He started to skip classes and his grades deteriorated, but he was determined to maintain the pretense to his parents that he was still a stellar student because they had fought so hard to get him into a normal school. Not happy at school and unwilling to share his feelings with his parents, Thomas decided to run away from home and, at around midnight and half-frozen, an old man found him shivering in a ditch.

Thomas recovered from his temporary crisis of confidence and soon discovered a talent that he most likely inherited from his musical father, a former contestant on a television casting show. Thomas discovered that he could sing and his parents, who wanted to encourage his talent, took him to see a successful pianist who was now head of the department of Chamber Music and Song at *NDR*, one of Germany's regional public broadcasters. But the radio boss was not interested and would not even give Thomas an audition. As the department's secretary explained: "Every three days they present a new wunderkind to us." But Thomas's father wouldn't let up and, after two dozen letters and telephone calls, he did manage to secure an audition. But the radio manager remained skeptical. When he saw Thomas, the first thing he said to Thomas's parents was "Why do you want to do this to him? Have you ever considered how the public will react to such a severely disabled person?"[670]

He soon changed his mind when he heard Thomas sing. The radio manager enthusiastically arranged an appointment with a soprano and experienced singing teacher, Charlotte Lehmann. She was equally convinced of Thomas's talent and agreed to give him lessons. In fact, she ended up teaching him for the next 17 years. At one point during their lessons, she recommended that Quasthoff study at the Music Academy in Hanover. Despite her support, he was turned down because he could not play the piano, which was one of the conditions of gaining admission to a conservatoire. He was not even allowed to attend as a guest student. At the time, Quasthoff was devastated; the Academy's rejection meant abandoning a lifelong dream. In retrospect, however, it turned out to be a stroke of luck. Quasthoff's intensive private lessons with Charlotte Lehmann built his voice much more solidly than would have been possible in the routine of academia.

However, he was still not sure whether he would ever be able to make a living from music. Like Andrea Bocelli, he decided to study law, which—unlike Bocelli—he never finished, dropping out as he did after six semesters. His inner voice told him that music was his true calling, not law. Quasthoff left university and came "to a decision." "One day," he promised himself, he would "earn money as a singer, come what may."[671]

The way he formulates his decision reveals a great deal about the reasons for Quasthoff's later success. Many people have vague wishes and say things like, "Wouldn't it be nice if I could maybe achieve this or that someday?" Exceptionally successful people do not abide by vague wishes, they make irrevocable and firm resolutions. And they combine high levels of patience and perseverance with equal levels of impatience and productive dissatisfaction.

This was also the case with Quasthoff. He toured community halls, churches and schools, his fees slowly increasing, his voice becoming ever stronger thanks to disciplined training. In 1984, Quasthoff's teacher entered him in a competition for the first time. He sang a Mozart aria at the annual Union of German Music Educators and Concert Artists' competition and was awarded the Walter Kaminski Memorial Prize, which he was told was equivalent to the first prize. He entered the same competition two years later and, although he was, according to all the jurors, the best, he was only given second prize, and first prize was not awarded to anyone.

But it was impossible for him to earn enough money to live off from competitions and performances alone. So, he began an apprenticeship at a bank in Hildesheim and ended up working in the bank's marketing department for six years. Fortunately, the bank's director was also a lover of classical music and allowed Quasthoff time off work to pursue his musical career.[672] Quasthoff eventually left the bank to work as a radio voice-over artist, where he was also allowed to host music programs and even act in radio plays. However, this was only a part-time position, which meant he was still able to devote most of his energy to his dream of becoming a famous singer.

In 1988, Charlotte Lehmann suggested that he participate in the renowned ARD International Music Competition, one of the most famous forums for young musicians in the world. There were sixty-two vocalists among the 229 competitors from 31 countries. Quasthoff had to prepare "eighteen songs, six arias from oratorios or concert arias, or arias from preclassical operas suitable for a concert repertoire"—and he had to know them all by heart.[673] On top of that, they had to come from three different style epochs and include at least three languages.[674]

Quasthoff won the competition and one of Germany's leading newspapers, *Süddeutsche Zeitung*, raved: "When it came to impressiveness none of the soloists could compare with Thomas Quasthoff. He communicated seriousness and humor as if singing was the easiest thing in the world. There are no seams there between intelligence, emotion, and vocal ability. One might even say that there has not been a comparable discovery in singing since Jessye Norman."[675] In contrast, the tabloids and gossip magazines tended to focus on Quasthoff's disability. The headline above one article in *Bunte* proclaimed: "Thalidomide, case 1600: Singing His Way to the Top of the World." The article summarized that Quasthoff "sings as if God wanted to make up for a workman's accident."[676]

After the *ARD* competition, the organizers were all over him; Quasthoff's brother Michael wrote that he "could easily have given 200 concerts."[677] For Quasthoff, winning the competition provided another surge of motivation—he practiced and practiced and practiced. The first major work he undertook with his teacher was Schubert's *Winterreise*, a twenty-four-part cycle for voice and piano, composed in fall 1827, a year before the composer's death. "I sang it in 1999 when, in the company of Charles Spencer, I made my debut in Lincoln Center, New York. How often have I sung these songs? I cannot say, but one thing I know for sure: I'll never be through with them."[678]

For Quasthoff, understanding a piece of music involves working through secondary literature, studying the history and context of a work, and comparing earlier interpretations. But these are only a starting point and are not enough on their own: "When a singer steps onto the stage," Quasthoff observes, "he must present his own musical interpretation."[679] On tour, although Quasthoff performed the same program every day, he was determined that it should not become pure routine. He not only wanted to surprise his audiences, but he also wanted to surprise himself, to create space for spontaneous ideas and to add variable accents because, as Quasthoff explains, "I don't *feel* the same every night."[680] As Quasthoff saw it, the artist's task is to strike the right balance between technique, reflection, inspiration, and experience.

According to Quasthoff, his voice possesses not only genetically determined properties such as circumference and force, but also a "velvety ground coat," which he has worked hard to develop. This allows him to use what in jazz would be called a 'cool' and supple phrasing. Whenever he rehearsed a new song, he first thought about which colorations he could use to bring out the best in the composition, but "without losing my own singing style, my personal 'sound.'"[681]

Quasthoff became an expert at using his voice and charisma to connect with his audiences. The *New York Times Magazine* wrote: "Without the freedom to move about the stage or to make dramatic gestures, he channels all of his feeling into his expressive face and subtly shaded voice."[682] Quasthoff was convinced that only singers who are able to show their emotions, even to perform a "psychic striptease" on stage, truly qualify as artists: "For people who are a little bit more expressive in their basic character, it is much easier to reach other people with their emotions and singing than it is for those people who are closed up or have a wall in their personality," he told the magazine. And added: "If as a singer you are not able to make a psychic striptease, you should do something else."[683]

In addition to classical music, Quasthoff developed a deep love of jazz. He appreciated the freedom of jazz because, although it has its own traditions, its governing principles are less binding. The only things that count in the jazz world are creativity, artistic freedom, and individual expression. The way he makes his music, Quasthoff explains, has been influenced just as much by soul singers like Stevie Wonder, Ray Charles, Aretha Franklin, and Al Green as it has by the most important interpreters of classical music.[684]

Quasthoff put together his own jazz trio and, on their very first attempt, won first prize in an *NDR* competition, before embarking on a concert tour of north German jazz clubs. But his singing teacher, Frau Lehmann, considered this kind of music "highly toxic" and his parents gave him an ultimatum: they would only continue paying for his singing lessons if he gave up his jazz.[685] Later in life, however, he did return to jazz—very successfully—and it did not harm his voice or his career in classical and opera music whatsoever.

Quasthoff does not regard being an artist, a musician, as a normal profession; it is a calling. Most singers, he realized, do not have enough talent for their voices to sustain them for thirty or forty years so that they can live off their music. That's why today, as a Music Academy teacher, he prefers to reject students who obviously don't make the grade.[686]

Added to this is the attitude to the profession that distinguishes him from many other artists. It is no wonder that he is, after all, even more successful in the United States than in his home country, Germany. After all, he has a pragmatic attitude toward art and music. In Germany, he notes, theaters, concert halls and the like are financed by the state, creating a situation that allows many artists to adopt the attitude: "This is my art, if people don't like it, that's their hard luck." After all, the state is always there with a pay check. Unsuccessful artists deceive themselves when they take their lack of success as proof of the public's stupidity and at the same time as infallible proof of their own genius. In the United States, artists inevitably have to focus more on their audiences—which does not, however, mean slavishly following every whim and fashion. Quasthoff sums up his attitude, which differs from that of many unsuccessful artists, precisely as follows: "What matters is the art. Whether it is pop or classical, whether Fritz Wunderlich or Stevie Wonder is on stage, in the end we are always entertainers."[687]

He is also skeptical about music that requires a lot of explanation: "Music I don't understand and I have to explain constantly to the audience is a problem. I think, the purpose of music is to entertain people, which has a very serious meaning. I mean high-level intellectual entertainment. That is what music is for. I don't think it is for intellectual contemplation and figuring out."[688] In his autobiography, he writes that classical music has always been "big business," just like rock and pop, "and there is nothing wrong with that—after all, people need to earn a living."[689]

These insights, combined with Quasthoff's attitude, were certainly also a prerequisite for his success in the United States. The door to America was opened for him by the musician Helmuth Rilling, who was also known as "Mister Bach," the authority on all matters relating to Johann Sebastian Bach. In 1995, Rilling took Quasthoff to Eugene, Oregon, where he had founded the Oregon Bach Festival in 1970.

Two conductors who had a great influence on Quasthoff were Claudio Abbado, chief conductor of the Berlin State Opera from 1989 to 2002, and his successor Simon Rattle, who wielded the baton there until 2018. At Abbado's side, and just ten days after the terrorist attack of September 11, 2001, Quasthoff traveled to perform at Manhattan's legendary Carnegie Hall, perhaps the most famous venue in the world. He had made his Carnegie Hall debut back in 1998 with Mahler's *Des Knaben Wunderhorn*, before going on to perform in almost all of the greatest concert halls in the world.

In 2003, Quasthoff took to the opera stage for the first time at the Salzburger Osterfestspiele under Simon Rattle. Until that moment, Quasthoff had always refused to perform opera because he didn't want his disability to be used as a stage effect. After a concert, Rattle had approached him and said: "My friend, I believe, now is the time, we have to work in opera." Quasthoff trusted Rattle: "O.K., Simon, what shall we do?" "Beethoven," replied Rattle. "*Fidelio* in 2003 in the Salzburg Festival House and Wagner's *Parsifal* in the Vienna Staatsoper."[690]

Quasthoff made his opera debut as Fernando in Ludwig van Beethoven's *Fidelio*, conducted by Simon Rattle. The next step in his career took him to the Vienna State Opera, where he played the maimed King Amfortas in a new production of Richard Wagner's *Parsifal*. The well-known music critic Eleonore Büning of the *Frankfurter Allgemeine* newspaper wrote: "Neither the direction nor Quasthoff left the slightest room for sensationalist effects. He sang his narration of crime, punishment and deliverance like a lied singer capable of packing the entire world's suffering into a few notes... Parsifal heard the call of the heart and had to cry, and it was the same for all those who listened."[691]

But of course, not everyone was so benevolent. Successful people always have to contend with envy from the less successful. Quasthoff once said, when asked by a British journalist what Berliners thought of Simon Rattle: "Generally they love him here. But in Germany, too, there is a tradition: if a head is going up through the clouds, there is always an animal which will try to push it back down."[692]

The mediocre and the unsuccessful attempt to put the achievements of the successful into perspective. They do not blame their own deficits for their mediocrity, and instead claim that the more successful have benefited from unfair advantages. Quasthoff recalls how, when he won his first Grammy, a disqualified colleague hissed at him, "You owe this victory to your disability, nothing else." Quasthoff comments on the episode in his autobiography: "This person's career went nowhere fast, and I can't say I am sorry."[693] And again in a newspaper interview in 2018: "They didn't give me this prize because I wobbled across the stage, but simply because I sang better than the others. I've been in this profession for 43 years. I got paid for my first concert when I was 15. I'm sure you don't last that long simply because you are granted some kind of 'cripple bonus,' but because you can really do something."[694]

He admits that he spent a lot of time trying to put talk of a 'cripple bonus' into some kind of perspective. It is also an issue that his parents knew that he was troubled by. He came to realize that compassion is free, but envy must be earned. And, of course, he is right: "Someone who looks like the hunchback of Notre Dame may pass for a season as a curiosity, but in the long run the audience will accept an artist only if he has quality and has something to communicate."[695]

Quasthoff conquered the stages of the world and was honored with numerous awards, including Grammys for Best Classical Vocal Performance in 2000 and 2006. He was awarded his third Grammy in 2008 for Best Choral Performance. In 2009, he received the Gold Medal of the Royal Philharmonic Society and, in 2011, the ECHO Jazz prize as German Singer of the Year.

Having achieved everything a singer could possibly dream of, he turned to teaching, from 1996 at the Detmold Hochschule and from 2004 as Professor of Singing at the Hanns Eisler Academy for Music in Berlin. He has developed a reputation as a very strict professor, refers to himself as a "poltergeist," and has even thrown students out of class because he didn't think they had what it would take: "I would be a pretty poor teacher if I created an oasis of bliss for my students and they had no idea what was in store for them after university."[696] He wanted to make sure, his brother Michael wrote, that his students learned enough to put them in a position to earn a half-decent living from their music. If Thomas was convinced that a student would not make the grade, he would take them aside and recommend that they look for another profession.[697] The old adage that the best way to learn something is to teach it to someone else proved true for Quasthoff: "My own singing has also developed a lot through teaching. You have to explain so many things that it forces you to rethink them for yourself."[698]

Quasthoff initially combined his teaching role with his career as a concert performer. For a while he also tried his hand at cabaret and enjoyed it. But after two years, he realized "that telling jokes on stage is not something that will satisfy me for years to come. My audiences didn't really buy it either. But jazz? Now that is a passion that will abide."[699]

In 2006, Quasthoff recorded his first jazz album and simultaneously announced his retirement from the opera stage. He simply wanted to devote more time to his concerts and his teaching. In the same year, he married his wife, Claudia. Four years later, in 2010, they announced their separation. In the same year, he was dealt a crushing blow when his brother Michael, with whom he had a very close relationship, died of cancer. Suddenly, Quasthoff found that he could no longer sing. Physically, everything was fine. "There was nothing wrong with my vocal cords. It was my soul that was damaged. My mother had just died. My marriage had fallen apart. Other people get depressed in those kinds of situations. With me, it was my voice. It didn't want to cooperate."[700] He became afraid that he would never be capable of performing again. His agent kept badgering him, asking him when he would be able to sing again, and he could only answer "I don't know." As Quasthoff knew well, his performances were planned three to four years in advance. He didn't feel comfortable making such long-term commitments so far in advance, so, in October 2011, he announced that he was stepping down from the jazz stage.

And then, in January 2012, he went one step further and issued a press release: "After almost 40 years, I have decided to retire from concert life. My health no longer allows me to live up to the high standard that I have always set for my art and myself."[701] His announcement triggered rampant speculation: "Could the issue with his health be laryngitis, which troubled him so much last year? Or is it his disability forcing him to resign?"[702] Quasthoff was adamant: "I really didn't have laryngitis...No, I just couldn't sing any more after the death of my brother. My vocal cords were fine. I saw one ENT specialist after the other and none of them could find anything wrong. It was in my head. It was my soul that was damaged."[703] But Quasthoff was able to overcome even this crisis. He reconciled with his wife and sought professional help to get past his psychological block. "Even though I had lived with a severe disability for 50 years, I realized I still had some issues to work through."[704]

Since 2015, Quasthoff has increasingly appeared as a jazz singer at international festivals. He has performed in numerous cities—Budapest, St. Petersburg, Novosibirsk, Madrid, Graz, Hamburg, and countless others. Nevertheless, he has ruled out any kind of comeback as a classical singer: "No, I've turned my back on classical music, that's over. When you leave something, like I left that world, it's better to stick with your decision. I've enjoyed such incredible moments in my life as a classical singer, been nominated for several Grammys and won three. In the end though, my decision to quit classical music was the right one, the best decision of my life."[705]

Toward the end of his autobiography, Quasthoff writes that he is "not a role model or life counselor."[706] In Germany, most of the disabled population is left to stagnate on welfare or packed away in homes and exploited as cheap labor. "Thank God," he writes, "I was able to flee this ghetto after my ninth birthday—thanks to the loving care of my parents, my musical talent, the tolerance of a select few, and a lot of luck."[707]

Such explanations are not atypical for successful people, who tend to talk down their own merits and emphasize what other people have done for them—and above all stress that they have been extremely lucky. Of course, in any life, it is true that other people play a role. In Thomas Quasthoff's case, for example, his parents did so much for him. And a healthy sprinkling of luck also comes into play. But no one is either always lucky or always unlucky. Across a whole lifetime, the positive and negative will usually balance each other out, and even talent is of no use if the talented person lacks the right inner attitude.

In his book *Envy: A Theory of Social Behaviour*, the sociologist Helmut Schoeck developed the thesis that the concepts of "good and bad luck, chance and opportunity" play a "crucial role in controlling the problem of envy." Man can come to terms with the "evident inequality of the individual human lot, without succumbing to envy that is destructive for both himself and others, only if he can put the responsibility on some impersonal power—blind chance or fortune, which neither he himself nor the man favoured is able to monopolize."[708]

When successful people point to luck, they are employing an unconscious defense against envy: "A sportsman, a schoolboy or a businessman who has scored an unusually brilliant success, thus becoming a possible object of envy, will simply shrug his shoulders and say: 'I suppose I was just lucky.' In this way, though usually unconsciously, he seeks to disarm possible envy."[709] This is what makes some successful people fall back on an "aimless, unpredictable and uncontrollable power which shapes events either favourably or unfavourably," or to a random combination of factors that results in an advantage or disadvantage for the individual.[710] When a very successful person says that they have "just been lucky," they also come across as far more sympathetic, human and pleasant than if they were to point out, for example, that their success is due to their outstanding abilities or the fact that they have worked harder than everyone else.

Despite their protestations, the successful know that they owe their success to their unique creativity, industriousness, and disciplined approach to organizing their day. Before two of his biggest performances in the United States, Quasthoff's mind was buzzing: within the next three weeks, he would be singing two of the most important concerts of his life, on stage with the best orchestras in the United States. "It was exactly what I had always wanted, and I knew I was up to it."[711]

This self-confidence to achieve great goals and to think and act on a global scale was undoubtedly more important for Quasthoff's career than luck or natural talent. The most important qualities Thomas learned from his parents were perseverance, tolerance for frustration and tenacity. Early in his life, his parents had refused to accept his doctor's insistence that Thomas would never be able to walk. They refused to give up when one elementary school after another rejected Thomas and kept trying until they finally found what they were looking for. Even the categorical disinterest of the radio manager at *NDR*, whom they approached to arrange singing lessons for their son, was no reason for them to give up. They were determined to persevere until their son got an audition.

Quasthoff's inner attitude has played a pivotal role in all that he has achieved. It has also helped him to deal with his disability. In an interview in 2015, he explained that he had met many Thalidomide victims who had died in bitterness. "I noticed that by maintaining a positive distance to oneself, you can cope much better with a disability." He also explained that the approach people with disabilities adopt toward others also has a major impact: "If I suggest 'I'm a sensitive soul, don't you dare insult me, don't you dare bring up my disability,' then I communicate fear and insecurity to my non-disabled counterpart. I approach people very normally, and I think they realize after about two minutes that you can talk to me the same way you would talk to your mates down the pub."[712] And although he has occasionally resisted being portrayed as a role model or source of inspiration for others, he has acknowledged: "Maybe it's a good life example, to have this kind of fate and make the best of it, not to look always on the gloomy side of life."[713]

Michael J. Fox describes Parkinson's: "Part of the disease's 'gift' is a certain stark clarity about the rest of your life. P.D.'s brutal assumption of authority over more and more aspects of life makes you appreciate all those areas where you can still have sovereignty. P.D. teaches you, perforce, to distinguish between the two and defend whatever you still can."

Credits: Trevor Collens / Alamy Stock Photo

# 15. Michael J. Fox
## Parkinson's couldn't stop him

There are probably few people who have not seen Michael J. Fox on television or in the cinema. From 1982 to 1989, the TV series *Family Ties* was one of the most popular in the USA. At the height of its success, a third of American households watched this sitcom, in which Fox played the conservative son of a left-wing father. It is reported to have been the favorite series of then President Ronald Reagan. Fox achieved global success with the *Back to the Future* trilogy, which launched in 1985. Produced for $99 million, the three films grossed a combined billion dollars at the box office. At the beginning of the first film, teenager Marty McFly (Michael J. Fox) arrives in 1955 from the present with the help of a time machine designed by Dr. Emmett L. Brown.

Fox was born in Canada in 1961. His father worked for the Royal Canadian Army Signal Corps and was responsible for encrypting and decoding messages.[714] Fox writes in his autobiography that his father had been a dreamer in his youth, but had come to see his first duty as protecting his family from any threat, "including the disappointment that would inevitably result from the pursuit of romantic fantasy."[715] His father never said it in so many words, but Fox clearly felt that "he expected me to be more like him in this way."[716] Fox instinctively resisted "any effort to fit me into the work-a-day mold embraced by my parents and their parents before them."[717]

His mother later told him: "You weren't going to be a laborer. You weren't going to be a union guy. That wouldn't have suited your personality, never mind your physique. You were the dreamer and the artistic type."[718] Fox was physically small (even as an adult he only reached 5' 5"), but he had great self-confidence. He promised his father and mother that one day he would buy each of them a new car and the whole family a big house. His parents just shook their heads, smiling.

Fox was stubborn. If his mother asked him to clean his room and he took too long for her liking, she would admonish him, "You don't think someone's going to be doing this for you the rest of your life, do you?" Fox replied that that was exactly what he expected, because he would later pay someone to do things like that for him.[719]

Just like many other people who achieve success later in life, Fox felt early on that he "was destined for a bright future."[720] As a child, he didn't know what field he would be successful in, but he knew "there were a lot of fun things to do in the world, and a few of those things I was pretty good at."[721]

In junior high school, he began taking acting classes. He noticed that he could memorize the texts effortlessly and slip into any role without much effort. His acting teacher said this could be his future, but Fox replied that he would rather make his living as a rock 'n' roll star. In the summer of 1977, his teacher told him about an audition for a new series on Canadian television. The show's producers were looking for a twelve-year-old. Fox was already 16, but looked much younger—also because of his height—and applied. He learned then that a supposed disadvantage can be a great advantage. Fox was hired. He was paid $6,000 for the eight episodes. In today's money, that would be about $27,000, a lot of money for a teenager. In addition, Fox was also given the lead role in a television movie. His father admitted that Michael was making more in a year as a part-time actor than he was in his full-time job. Fox kept getting new jobs, as an actor, in commercials and on the radio.

He had always been a good student, but his acting meant that he neglected his lessons and his grades deteriorated. Finally, much to the consternation of his parents, he decided to drop out of school. He packed his bags, left Canada, and headed for Hollywood to start an acting career. "Obviously, people in my life, my parents most of all, questioned my decision to leave school, home, and country for an acting career. It seemed like an insane proposition. They considered me naive, overconfident, short-sighted, and reckless; a cautionary tale waiting to happen."[722] In retrospect, Fox admits his parents and the other people who warned him against the move weren't entirely wrong. But he had a different attitude: "If you don't take risks, there's no room for luck. I took a chance. I got lucky."[723]

In his new home in Beverly Hills everything was much more expensive. At first, he lived in a seventeen by twelve-foot apartment. As a fish out of water in California, he met many "eccentrics, risk takers, and freethinkers" and "The logic of this mecca of nonconformity was this: not fitting in meant that I truly belonged."[724] But starting out in Hollywood is not easy for anyone. He once auditioned for the well-known ex-actor and producer Robert Redford, who didn't seem too impressed by Fox's reading and spent the audition flossing his teeth.

Fox got the odd role, nothing spectacular, but such that he could have made a living if only he hadn't signed contracts with agents that ate up a third of his income. And since he also had no money set aside for taxes, it wasn't long before he was perilously broke. He even resorted to selling his few belongings, such as furniture, to pay his bills. Temporarily, Fox toyed with the idea of returning to Canada, but the prospect of perhaps working as a construction worker on one of the sites his brother supervised seemed less than enticing. In addition, he still owed money to the IRS, and if he left the U.S. without paying it off, he would be barred from ever re-entering the country.

Fox's big break came when he auditioned for a role in the series *Family Ties*. Originally, the actor Matthew Broderick was the first choice for the role, and the decision-makers were initially skeptical as to whether Fox was the right man. But Broderick declined the role and finally Fox was able to win them over. The decision to hire him turned out to be the right one. According to the original concept, Fox's left-wing parents were to play the main role in the series, but it was their conservative son who soon became the real attraction. Michael J. Fox won three Emmy Awards with his performances in *Family Ties* in 1986, 1987 and 1988, and the Golden Globe in 1989. From September 1982 to May 1989, a total of 176 episodes of 25 minutes each were broadcast and Fox became a star.

With the series already on the air, he received an offer to star in the upcoming *Back to the Future*. He accepted. For more than three and a half months, his typical day started at 9:30 a.m., when a car picked him up and took him to Paramount, where they spent the day filming that week's episode of *Family Ties*. Then at 6 p.m., another driver would pick him up and take him to Universal Studios, or to an outdoor location, where filming for *Back to the Future* went on until just before sunrise. "At that point, I'd climb into the back of a production van with a pillow and a blanket, and yet another teamster driver would take me home again—sometimes literally carrying me into my apartment and dropping me onto my bed. I'd catch two or three hours of sleep."[725] The next morning, the first driver would reappear, open the door to Fox's apartment, make coffee, and wake up the young star to drive him to the next day of rehearsals for *Family Ties*. "Each production operated completely independent of the other. The onus of coordinating between the two fell squarely on my shoulders."[726]

*Back to the Future* was a huge success. It hit theaters on July 3, 1985, cost $19 million and grossed $380 million. Film reviews were also very positive. A sequel followed in November 1989, grossing $332 million, and a third installment, released in May 1990, grossed another $244 million.

The media were buzzing about Hollywood's latest star. There was a story in *People* about "The Secret of His Success," *Rolling Stone* ran the headline: "The Hot Issue—Michael J. Fox,"[727] and millions of teenagers adored him, especially girls. He confessed: If someone asked him the question, "Does it bother you that maybe she just wants to sleep with you because you're a celebrity?" he answered, "Ah...nope."[728] Fox now had plenty of money, and because he loved cool cars, the driveway of his house soon resembled a luxury car lot, including a Ferrari. He met the rich, beautiful and influential of this world; at the royal premiere for *Back to the Future* in London, Princess Diana took a seat next to him. Sometimes his success seemed so unreal that he thought he was dreaming—or was really just a gigantic impostor whose deception would soon be exposed.

In 1988, Fox married Tracy Pollan, a colleague who had played his girlfriend Ellen on *Family Ties*. The following year, the film *Casualties of War* was released, by far the best film starring Michael J. Fox in my opinion. It is based on a true story and deals with a crime committed during the Vietnam War: a unit of American soldiers kidnaps a young Vietnamese woman, rapes and kills her. Fox's character does not bow to the enormous peer pressure, denounces the crime, reports it to his superiors and finally brings the perpetrators to justice. A harrowing film, which unfortunately

failed to become a box office success. The film's score was composed by the best composer for me, Ennio Morricone, and it was
nominated for a Golden Globe Award.

It was during the filming of the movie that Fox began to experience the first symptoms of Parkinson's disease. In his autobiography he dates the event, which he describes as a divorce of the
brain from his mind, to November 13, 1990, when he felt a slight
twitch in the little finger of his left hand. At first, none of the doctors thought it was Parkinson's, since the disease usually affects
older people and it's not very common for a person to develop it in
his late 20s. Only one in about 100,000 North Americans starts
experiencing such symptoms at such a young age; it is called Young
Onset Parkinson's.

In October 1991, Fox, by then the father of a son (who would
later be followed by three more daughters), consulted one of the
leading specialists in the field, whose diagnosis gave him certainty:
yes, he had Parkinson's disease. His initial reaction was similar to
that of many people who are told they have a serious and—as with
Parkinson's—incurable disease: They go into denial. "Stubbornly, I
clung to fantasies of escape, hoping against hope that somehow my
diagnosis would turn out to be a mistake. Or, better yet, having de-
fied the odds by being one of a tiny population of young adults with
Parkinson's, I would further defy the odds by being the only reported case of the condition magically disappearing."[729] At least he
didn't fall into the trap that some people fall into when bad things
happen to them: Apportioning blame. "I never once found myself
resorting to blame."[730]

The doctor told Fox that if he received the right treatment, he
could probably continue his work as an actor for another ten years.
This prediction changed his strategy: he would now have to do everything in those ten years to provide for his young family. But Par-

kinson's was not his only problem. He had another problem, which he—like most people affected by it—had previously denied and repressed. He was an alcoholic. At dinner, he would ask his wife, Tracy, if she wanted some wine. When she said yes, he would choose a bottle, pour each of them a glass, and then take the bottle back to the kitchen—ostensibly to put it in the refrigerator. In the kitchen, he quickly polished off the bottle, tossed it in the trash can and took an identical bottle from the wine rack. "I'd open it and swill enough to lower the level of liquid in the second bottle so it matched that of the first when I'd left the living room. Returning from the kitchen, as if I'd spent the last five minutes checking on the pot roast."[731] He would then ask his wife if she wanted him to freshen up her glass, and would fill his again, too. Sometimes he would get out of bed at night after his wife had fallen asleep and continue drinking.

But increasingly he was unable to hide his addiction from Tracy. When he tried to justify and make excuses to his wife after a night of heavy drinking, she replied calmly and emotionlessly, "I don't want to hear it." She walked to the door and looked back: "Is this what you want?" she asked, "*This* is what you want to be?"[732]

Fox realized he had hit rock bottom—and he was lucky enough to realize it sooner than most alcoholics. As paradoxical as it sounds, his Parkinson's actually helped him: "Part of the disease's 'gift' is a certain stark clarity about the rest of your life. P.D.'s brutal assumption of authority over more and more aspects of life makes you appreciate all those areas where you can still have sovereignty. P.D. teaches you, perforce, to distinguish between the two and defend whatever you still can. Which meant the alcohol had to go."[733]

Fox conquered alcohol the way millions of other people around the world do: by regularly attending Alcoholics Anonymous meetings. I was very moved by his description, because it was the same for me. I, too, had an alcohol problem in my 20s and stopped earlier than the vast majority of alcoholics. And I, too, am sure that I would not have made it without regular support from AA meetings. I haven't had a drop for 35 years.

In Alcoholics Anonymous, a phrase is always recited at the end of every session that, as Fox writes, became the guiding principle of his life—and, of course, can help people who don't have problems with alcohol:

"God, grant me the serenity to accept the things I cannot change

Courage to change the things I can

And the wisdom to know the difference."

Parkinson's is an incurable disease, but it is possible to temporarily control some symptoms with medication. However, these drugs do not work all day, but only for a few hours at a time. When the effect wears off, the symptoms, such as violent trembling of the arms and legs or the whole body, reappear. Fox faced the daily challenge of timing the intake of the medication for filming, interviews and other public appearances in such a way that the outwardly visible symptoms were likely to be suppressed at the right time. However, this was not always successful, and there was also the problem that too strong a dosage of the medication led to other symptoms.

About three to four times a day, Fox alternated between 'on' periods when the medication worked and 'off' periods when the disease had complete authority over his physical being and he was at the mercy of the full spectrum of symptoms: "rigidity, shuffling, tremors, lack of balance, diminished small motor control, and the insidious cluster of symptoms that makes communication—written as well as spoken—difficult and sometimes impossible."[734]

He continued his acting career, but was exhausted by the strain of trying to stave off the return of his symptoms. The effort to hide his illness became, as he writes, his "acting."[735] On some nights during filming of his TV show, the studio audience had to wait, unknowingly, until his symptoms subsided. "I'd be backstage, lying on my dressing room rug, twisting and rolling around, trying to cajole my neuroreceptors into accepting and processing the L-dopa I had so graciously provided."[736] He kept his illness a secret because he feared that otherwise it would have a negative impact on his career and his relationship to his audience. In the end, that was no longer possible, and he had to let a close circle—colleagues, producers and others—in on the truth.

There was another treatment that, while also not curing the disease, could suppress some symptoms for a time and involved an operation on a deep part of the brain to turn off the brain cells responsible for the tremor. The surgery was risky, but Fox decided to go ahead with it anyway. Fox needed to be awake throughout the surgery because the doctors have to observe the patient's responses as certain areas of the brain are targeted. His head was fixed in place with a metal frame and a small hole was drilled through the top of his skull. The operation was successful, but because it was only on the right hemisphere of his brain, it was clear from the outset that only the left side of his body would be stilled. It did not take long until Fox noticed a trembling on the hitherto quiet right side of his body.

Increasingly, rumors spread that Fox was suffering from Parkinson's disease. In late November 1998, he decided to go public about his illness. He planned to give two interviews, one on television and one in a print medium, and then return to living his life as before. But the public reaction was tremendous and his revelations grabbed all the headlines. He was contacted by other people with Parkinson's, including Muhammad Ali, who called his house and whispered into the phone, "I'm sorry you have this, but with both of us in this fight, we're going to win now."[737]

Although Fox didn't plan it that way, going public launched a new phase of his life as an activist in the fight against Parkinson's. In particular, he championed stem cell research, which is regarded as often the best hope of curing Parkinson's and other degenerative neurological diseases, although the method is controversial because the cells are derived from embryonic tissue. In the United States in particular, opinions on stem cell research are divided and opposition to this form of therapy is strong among religious and conservative groups.

In a major and widely publicized appearance, Fox spoke at a Senate hearing on September 28, 1999 on the subject of funding for Parkinson's research. He had decided not to take any medication beforehand. He wanted people not only to hear his testimony but also to see what Parkinson's meant: "I looked as though an invisible bully were harassing me while I read my statement. My head jerked, skewing my reading glasses as if the back of my skull were being slapped. I was fighting to control the pages of my speech, my arms bouncing as if someone were trying to knock the paper out of my hands." But his words were resolute: "The time for quietly soldiering on is through. The war against Parkinson's is a winnable war, and I have resolved to play a role in that victory."[738]

Fox continued to act even after he had made his illness public, for example in the series *Spin City*. Although everyone now knew that he had Parkinson's, he still did everything he could to hide his illness when acting—and this became increasingly strenuous. In his book *Always Looking Up. The Adventures of an Incurable Optimist*, he reports that on the last day of 1999, the cusp of a new millennium, he decided to stop acting. Officially, he was only retiring from *Spin City*, but for him this was tantamount to saying goodbye to acting.[739] Artistically, he had always evolved, so he felt it was unfortunately ironic "that at a time, when I felt in full possession of the emotional and intellectual dimensions of my performing identity, I could no longer count on my body to play along."[740]

At this point, he did not know what he would do after retiring from acting. He had no particular plan, but began to think about setting up a foundation.[741] He wanted to actively support people who suffered from Parkinson's disease. His role models included the actor Christopher Reeve, who was paralyzed after an accident, and the cyclist Lance Armstrong, who suffered from testicular cancer and campaigned for cancer research.

In May 2000, he established the Michael J. Fox Foundation, whose stated goal was to make itself obsolete by supporting research to cure Parkinson's. "Less than a year earlier, I had stepped away from my acting career with no specific direction in mind. And now, here I was, stepping into an entirely new career—with a very specific direction, indeed."[742]

Successful people always have big goals. Once they have achieved a goal, it is only a matter of time before they fill the vacuum by setting themselves new, even more ambitious goals. What helped Fox as an activist was, above all, the immense trust people had in him. Gaining the trust of others is one of the most important characteristics of successful people—in my book *Dare to Be Different*, I devoted an entire chapter to the topic of winning trust. In a 2006 ranking of the celebrities Americans trust most, Fox came in fourth, behind Tom Hanks, Oprah Winfrey, and Bill Cosby.[743]

Fox saw trust as his greatest asset and decided to become more politically engaged. He writes that he had always been "a political junkie"[744] but few people knew this at the time. After all, an actor who wants to build a rapport with the largest possible audience will usually refrain from political statements and activism.

Now, because of his commitment to stem cell research, he found himself caught up in the maelstrom of a political battlefield. He decided to actively throw his celebrity clout behind those candidates in congressional elections who also supported stem cell research. It didn't matter whether the candidates were Republicans or Democrats, but in practice they were mostly Democrats, who were in any case more closely aligned to Fox's personal political beliefs.

The battle was sometimes fought below the belt, as when conservative radio host Rush Limbaugh (who had up to 20 million listeners a week at the time) accused him of deliberately exaggerating his symptoms during a television appearance. At first, Fox was shocked by this attack, especially since Limbaugh had stooped so low as to imitate Fox's symptoms on television.[745] But in the end, he proved to be a PR professional who recognized the opportunity that lay in this attack and used it to communicate his own messages. "By neither appearing defensive nor firing back with inflammatory rhetoric, we were taking the high road, effectively a passive resistance sort of approach."[746]

Here, once again, one of the characteristics that distinguished Fox—just like all other successful people—was evident, namely turning bad into good. "He [Limbaugh] had given us a significant push, and we were ready to take to the road. Let's face it, the whole episode, unpleasant though it may have been, was a gift in the same way I have described Parkinson's as a gift."[747]

Fox also used the illness as an opportunity to develop as an actor. A few years after he officially ended his career, he returned to primetime TV—but now he took on roles in which he no longer had to hide his illness. In the series *Boston Legal*, he played a terminally ill businessman in several episodes. In the series *Scrubs*, he appeared as a doctor suffering from obsessive-compulsive disorder, and in the series *The Good Wife* he had numerous guest appearances as a manipulative lawyer who also suffered from a neurological disease. "The array of characters I embodied in my second career all had something in common: all were over-achievers...All were passionate; all had a flaw that was relatable to my own. Each had a vulnerability, and a corresponding point of damage."[748] He was nominated for a total of eight Emmys for his appearances in these series. "Somewhere, somehow, between *Spin City* and *Boston Legal*, I had become a character actor. I can think of no higher calling for a thespian," he wrote in his 2020 book, *No Time Like the Future.*[749]

Fox later had to cope with further setbacks. For example, a malignant tumor was discovered on his spine, and his doctors told him that the risks involved in surgery would be even greater than those associated with the brain operation he had undergone for Parkinson's disease. But the risk of not having surgery seemed even greater. After the operation, he had to learn to walk again, and this was particularly difficult for him as a Parkinson's patient. After all, a simple fall could have been disastrous after the spinal surgery. He needed 24-hour supervision—for example, when he had to go to the bathroom during the night. He was temporarily confined to a wheelchair and hired a therapist who slowly taught him to use his legs again.

Even this didn't stop him from actively running his foundation, which has, to date, been exceptionally successful and funded research into Parkinson's disease to the tune of one billion dollars. Michael J. Fox has not lost his sense of humor. In 2020, when the coronavirus pandemic began, and people were forced to social distance, he jokingly remarked: "I never thought in this way, but for years I've been practicing my own version of social distancing—in my case, the length of an arm plus a cane between myself and others, as a means to protect people from the dangers of *me*."[750] In his own light-hearted way, Fox is alluding to the fact that he has been forced to keep a certain safe distance from other people for fear of injuring them due to an uncontrolled spasm as a result of his illness. In his own words an "incurable optimist," Fox also had this to say about the coronavirus crisis: "We can all take something positive from the class of 2020; to accept what has happened in the past, to embrace the present, and to remain open to the probability that it will get better in the future."[751]

Erik Weihenmayer on the summit of Mount Everest, 2001: "I spend like 15 minutes just every day, envisioning myself standing on the summit ... And, when I summitted Everest, I had summitted it 100 times in my mind already. So, I think that kind of belief system and that kind of programming it into your subconscious is hugely important so that you can truly be there."

Credits: Didrik Johnck / Corbis Sygma

# 16.  Erik Weihenmayer
## A blind man conquers the world's seven highest mountains

Very ambitious mountaineers all share a single goal. They aspire to climb Mount Everest—at 29,031 feet the highest mountain in the world. Since the first man summited Everest in 1953, many others have followed—and at least 300 people have died in the attempt. And for those who even this is not enough, men and women for whom even Everest is not enough, take on the Seven Summits challenge to climb the highest mountains on each of the seven continents of the Earth. Depending on the precise definition, the Seven Summits list typically includes Denali (known as Mount McKinley until 2015) for North America, Aconcagua in Argentina for South America, Puncak Jaya in Indonesia or Mount Kosciuszko in Australia for Australasia, Kilimanjaro in Tanzania for Africa, Mount Vinson for Antarctica, Mont Blanc in the European Alps, or Elbrus in Russia for Europe in addition to Everest. In 1985, the American mountaineer Dick Bass was the first person ever to achieve the incredible feat of conquering all Seven Summits.

When the blind American Erik Weihenmayer set his mind on achieving the Seven Summits' challenge and climbed Mount Rainier (a 14,411-foot mountain near Seattle) as training for Mount McKinley, a worried guide told him: "There's no way you can climb it safely, and as far as McKinley goes...well, that's ten times harder than Rainier." Even after Weihenmayer had climbed McKinley and started to plan his attempt at the almost 23,000-foot Aconcagua in the Andes, experts told him: "I can understand how you got up McKinley. It's all snow, you don't really have to see where you're stepping, but Aconcagua, that's a different story. It's way too rocky and inconsistent. You'd have a lot of trouble finding your footing."[752] Despite their skepticism, the athlete from New Jersey climbed Aconcagua the following winter.

After conquering Aconcagua, Weihenmayer announced that he also wanted to climb the world's highest mountain, Everest. Almost everyone told him he would never manage it. When I interviewed Weihenmayer, he recalled: "You know, a couple of other people said things like I didn't belong on the mountain or like–or anybody could get to the top of the mountain with 13 seeing guide dogs. I heard one guy say he was going to follow me to the summit and take a picture of my dead body just to make some money with the media. So, yeah, there are assholes out there. I call them naysayers. And sure, there are naysayers and I feel sorry for naysayers because they're people who go around with the door in their mind shut and it's really more tragic for them."[753]

On May 25, 2001, Weihenmayer climbed to the summit of Mount Everest. And on June 18 of that same year, he was featured on the cover of *Time*, which used the same photo that I chose for the opening page of this chapter. The *Time* story ran under the headline "Blind Faith: The Inside Tale of Blind Climber Erik Weihenmayer's Daring Conquest of Everest."[754] President George W. Bush invited Weihenmayer and his team to the Oval Office and his photo towered fifty feet tall in Time Square.[755]

But the most important words at the time were said to him by his expedition leader Pasquale—or "PV" for short—right after he had summited Everest: "Your life's about to change. Don't make Everest the greatest thing you ever do," PV cautioned. As Weihenmayer later confessed, "Those words sank into my brain and rattled around."[756] During our interview, I asked him what those words meant to him today. He responded by referring to research by Dr. Paul Stoltz: "Stoltz studied people around the world and teams around the world and came away with the understanding that people fall into three categories: quitters, campers or climbers. Quitters are sort of self-explanatory. Campers are people that have some degree of success but then they kind of just fall off the map, they lose belief in themselves, they get cynical, maybe they, you know, try something and they fall short or get beat down, and, they kind of get—they just get exhausted, their momentum dies, they get shoved to the sidelines, and they stagnate and all their potential is lost. So, I think about that. I think about, okay, for me, what does it mean to be a climber, which means always growing and evolving, and trying to discover new things. They are not all physical things either. I've been going to counseling and learning about myself, trying to understand my own psyche, trying to illuminate the depths of my own character, through that, through counseling, and through meditation."[757]

Erik Weihenmayer is a man who always sets himself new, ever more ambitious goals. He regards every goal he achieves as little more than the launchpad for his next new endeavor. But that was not always the case. Weihenmayer has also been through terrible crises and phases of despair. But let's tell his story from the beginning: Erik Weihenmayer was born in 1968 in Princeton in the U.S. state of New Jersey. When he was just a few months old, his father took him to a football game. After the game, his dad was playing with Erik, trying to make him laugh by pulling funny faces and then getting him to focus on a small football as he moved it from side to side. As Erik's dad did this, he noticed Erik's eyes shaking as they tried to follow the ball. Erik's dad was worried and asked Erik's mom if this was normal for a baby. Erik's mother called the pediatrician and made an appointment. "That call began a two-year nightmare of doctor visits around the country as specialists tried to diagnose my strange disease."[758]

When Erik was three years old, doctors at the famed Boston eye clinic, Retina Associates, finally declared that he was suffering from an extremely rare disease, retinoschisis. His retinas were already detached in the center of his pupils, so he couldn't see straight ahead, but he did still have limited peripheral vision.[759] Over time, however, the pressure in his eyes would gradually increase, eventually causing both retinas to split. When Erik's parents asked how long their son would be able to see, the doctor haltingly admitted that Erik would be blind by his early teens.

Although Erik could only see with the aid of special thick magnifying glasses, his parents were adamant that they did not want to send Erik to a school for the blind; they wanted their son to attend a normal school. They also refused to allow their son to be treated any differently from other children of his age group. Once, in first grade, he came home from school bragging that he had gotten all the words right on a spelling quiz. He proudly showed his mother the paper, but when she looked closer, all she could see was the pictures of animals whose names her son was supposed to spell, and a series of illegible marks scribbled all across the page in yellow crayon. A smiley face sat at the top of the page in recognition of his 'achievement.' The next day his mother showed up in class and approached the teacher, quiz in hand: "...when a child hands in a paper full of yellow scribbles, surely it doesn't deserve a smiley face... Draw a pitchfork and horns next time. Anything but a smiley face." The teacher justified herself, saying she had only wanted to boost Erik's self-esteem. "He doesn't need self-esteem," Erik's mother replied, "He needs to know how to spell."[760]

Erik was lucky to have the parents he had. His father, a Vietnam veteran, read him his favorite poem, "Don't Quit":

*When things go wrong, as they sometimes will,*
*When the road you're trudging seems all uphill,*

*When the funds are low and the debts are high,*
*And you want to smile, but have to sigh,*
*When care is pressing you down a bit—*
*Rest if you must, but don't you quit.*
*Life is queer with its twists and turns,*
*As every one of us sometimes learns,*
*And many a fellow turns about*
*When we might have won, had he stuck it out.*
*Don't give up though the pace seems slow—*
*You may succeed with another blow.*
*Often the goal is nearer than*
*It seems to a faint and faltering man;*
*Often the struggler has given up*
*When he might have captured the victor's cup;*
*And he learned too late when the night came down,*
*How close he was to the golden crown.*
*Success is failure turned inside out—*
*The silver tint of the clouds of doubt,*
*And you never can tell how close you are,*
*It may be near when it seems afar;*
*So stick to the fight when you're hardest hit—*
*It's when things seem worst that you mustn't quit.*[761]

Erik gradually relinquished his grip on sight. At first, he refused to face the truth, especially as his ability to see tended to vary
anyway. At the best of times, he clung to a vague hope, convincing
himself that the doctor was wrong and that he wouldn't go blind by
the age of thirteen. Summoning all of his willpower, Erik was determined to prove everyone wrong. But one day, struck by the realization that he could hardly see anything, his hopes and illusions were
destroyed. Looking to escape, he went into a new house that was
being constructed on his road, picked up a handful of heavy metal

nails from a wooden box and hurled them toward the hazy light of a window. Pieces of glass exploded outward, spraying the ground. "Then I walked around the entire house, aiming and shattering, not wanting one window to be spared."[762]

When his sight completely disappeared, Erik sank into what he describes as "bitter relief."[763] Trying to live as a sighted person had become more painful than blindness could ever be. Nevertheless, he was not yet ready to accept himself as being totally blind. Early one summer, his mother gave him a cane to help him get around. The cane became symbolic of Erik's battle to accept his blindness: he destroyed one cane after the other by bending them until they snapped. When he started high school, the state assigned him a teacher for the blind to assist him and help him learn Braille so that he could keep up with his classes. Erik purposely tried to obstruct his teacher and her Braille lessons.

Erik refused to acknowledge that he was now blind. He even got into an argument with the driver of the special car the state sent to take students with disabilities to and from school. The driver stopped the car, ordered Erik out and threw a basketball at his head:

"You're blind," the driver yelled.

"Bullshit!" Erik yelled back.

"You're blind," the driver repeated. "Get used to it."

"I'm not," replied Erik a little more weakly.

"Well! You can't catch a basketball...Erik, you may not want to be blind, but you are. The answer isn't always to fight. Let people in. Let 'em help you for a while."[764]

Little by little, Weihenmayer adjusted to the situation and managed to find a sport he could become good at: wrestling. Unlike basketball or football, blindness was much less of an obstacle, and Weihenmayer became increasingly successful as a wrestler.

Weihenmayer also signed up for a climbing course for the blind. He quickly found that he liked the training and started going on climbing trips with a friend. It was as though his senses had awakened! "Never again would I thunder down a basketball court on a fast break or jump a dirt bike over a ramp; the past was dead, and no matter how much I fought, there was no reclaiming the dead. But one hundred feet above tree line with the sun in my face and a sound of openness all around me, none of that seemed to matter as much, because, I had just discovered, I could climb."[765] Weihenmayer and his climbing partner embarked on increasingly difficult climbs. One day they were climbing a craggy volcanic peak that jutted sharply from the smooth desert floor. Near the top, his partner turned to him and said, "Hey, what do you say we go try something a little bigger?" "Like what?" Weihenmayer asked cautiously. "How about Mount McKinley?"[766]

They started training by getting permission to run the back stairway of the tallest building in downtown Phoenix: fifty floors with seventy-pound packs on their backs. "My training regimen wasn't very scientific; each night I only allowed myself to quit when, after four or five times to the top, I felt so nauseous and dehydrated that I thought I was going to throw up."[767]

The big day came in 1995. Mount McKinley (known by its original Alaskan name of Denali since 2015) is the highest peak in the Alaska range and is the mountain with the largest base to peak rise of any mountain that lies entirely above sea level. Denali is famous for its inhospitable climate, severe weather, strong winds and extremely low temperatures, which can be minus 60 degrees Celsius at high altitudes and feel like minus 83 Celsius with wind chill.

The ascent was harder than Weihenmayer could ever have imagined, even in his worst dreams. At times, he came close to turning back. And yet: "Every few moments, when I had thought

I was at my absolute limit, I was able to push through it...Some limits were real, like the inability to climb a twenty-thousand-foot peak before acclimatizing to the thin oxygen. But many more limits were conceived and imposed in my mind, and there was a torturous beauty in crossing through them."[768] During the 19 days Weihenmayer and his team spent climbing Denali, three other climbers died trying to reach the summit. By a twist of fate, Weihenmayer and his team reached the summit on Helen Keller's birthday, June 27.

After conquering the highest mountain in North America, Weihenmayer immediately started to forge his next plans. "I had a tendency," he writes, "to live in the future, to make a long list of goals and then scheme and conspire about how I would get there..."[769] Two years later, he climbed Mount Kilimanjaro in Tanzania—another of the Seven Summits. There, at thirteen thousand feet on the Shira Plateau on Mount Kilimanjaro, he married Ellen "Ellie" Reeve, who, like Weihenmayer, was a middle-school teacher.

Before attempting any of the remaining Seven Summits, Weihenmayer ventured to the infamous El Capitan rock face in California's Yosemite Valley, whose vertically sloping flanks rise up to 3,300 feet above the valley floor. Climbing presents particular challenges for a blind person. As a result of being blind, Weihenmayer was unable to glance up a crack in the rock to find the next suitable placement for their climbing gear. Being blind, Weihenmayer had to scan the crack with his hand and then try to find the right piece of gear to use and hope it was the right size.

During his ascents, Weihenmayer's hearing replaces his sight, and his partners use trekking poles to tap on rocks they think he should avoid. Weihenmayer also uses the poles himself to test the terrain around him. In the films about his climbs, you often see him tapping the ground around him with his telescopic poles.

"I use my trekking poles to feel my way forward, just like a regular blind man uses a cane. I listen for the footsteps of the men in front of me, who have large bells attached to their packs so that I can follow their movements."[770] On some climbs, though, he realized that the wind would blow so loudly that he couldn't hear the bells jingling in front of him. At such moments, he had to find his own way, his own rhythm, all by himself.

The next one of the Seven Summits that Weihenmayer had set his sights on was Aconcagua in the Andes. He was forced to abandon his first ascent due to bad weather conditions and, reluctantly, Weihenmayer and his team realized that pressing on would be suicidal. Books about successful people often claim that they never gave up and always kept going, even in the face of the most adverse conditions. On the one hand this is true, but on the other hand it is quite wrong: successful people also know when to back down, gather their strength and go again another day. In the mountains, knowing when to press on and when to head for home can easily mean the difference between life and death.

After Weihenmayer and his team had decided to turn back, he escaped outside the tent, pretending to organize his pack so that his two partners wouldn't see the tears spilling from his eyes. One of his partners, Jeff, nevertheless understood exactly how he was feeling and followed him out into the whipping wind. "When you try big things," he said, "you gotta expect to fail sometimes."[771] Weihenmayer knew Jeff was right. Jeff's words took the edge off Weihenmayer's disappointment and helped give him the strength he needed for the descent.

People who claim to have succeeded in everything in life are either liars or have always set themselves unambitious goals that are far too easy to achieve. In contrast, people who think big and set ambitious goals will fail from time to time—just like Weihenmayer and his team on their first attempt to conquer Aconcagua.

A year later, he returned to Aconcagua. The previous year's failure had gnawed at him so much that he was now absolutely determined to finish the job. Unfortunately, the second attempt wasn't any easier than the first had been. One of his three teammates was forced to abandon the climb because he got high-altitude pulmonary edema. This left Weihenmayer alone with his other partner, Chris. Both men were very aware that if one of them got sick or injured, they would have no safety net. They both had to trust each other blindly—in the truest sense of the word.

When I interviewed Weihenmayer, he told me: "The weather, it's just pouring rain, and you're just like, 'What the heck?' You know, everything is going wrong. And then things turn around. I've also had great expeditions until the very last second and then the shit hits the fan and you don't summit. Aconcagua was one of those funny ones where, right from the start, everything was really bad. One guy was sick on the team. Do not arrive sick on an expedition. He passed it all around, and it was really ugly, my teammates were all sick and throwing up. And then in the Vacas Valley there was an avalanche and so it was filled with snow so we couldn't get our donkeys, our mules up to Vacas so our whole route had to change. And then there was tons of snow. And these penitentes (ice formations) that we had to navigate through, they were like these big pointy tentacles of ice and there were whole fields of them that we had to weave and bolt through. We couldn't get our mules up to the base camp. I don't know. It just seemed like one disaster after the next. We had mostly wind and snow and terrible weather. But one sunny day, we were in position. I learned a lot on that trip. That you have to be aggressive. You can't just kind of go through the motions, you've got to be really aggressive and strategic, you've got to push hard, get in position, be ready for that weather window."[772]

At one point, the only way to get to the other side of a river was by jumping over it. "It's about nine feet across, and there's not much to land on, just a sixty-degree slope of ice and scree," Chris told him. "You're just gonna have to trust it. When you land, your front points will stick and you'll forward with your palms." If he didn't make it, he would either drown immediately or the river would suck him back under the glacier after about 100 feet. Weihenmayer stretched his pole as far forward as he could, but Chris said, "You can't reach the other side. You just have to trust it. You have to jump."[773] Weihenmayer later admitted: "To this day, I cannot explain how I triggered the circuits that enabled my legs to crouch, my body to lean forward out over the abyss, and then my legs to spring, so that I launched across, through the roar of the river and the mist that rose up like cold frost."[774]

Weihenmayer started to panic. He was experiencing a terrible stabbing pain in his eye. Plus, there were just the two of them now. He thought he might be going insane and confided in Chris. Weihenmayer was worried they would have to go back down the mountain if they didn't make it to the summit soon. "It's the thin oxygen talking," Chris warned. "You'll get down and be disappointed in yourself because you'll know you didn't give it your best shot."[775]

They eventually reached the summit. Weihenmayer says that he doesn't believe it when people say they summit mountains for the beautiful view. He couldn't enjoy the view anyway, only have his partner describe it to him. But he thinks that a summit is not just a place on a mountain, it is something that exists, above all, in our hearts and minds. "A summit is a symbol that with the force of our will and the power of our legs, our back, and our two hands, we can transform our lives into whatever we choose them to be, whatever our hands are strong enough to create."[776]

Having conquered Aconcagua gave him the confidence to tackle the world's highest peak—Mount Everest—in 2001. He spent two years preparing for the ascent and one year in intense physical training. Weihenmayer's team had immense trouble recruiting the Sherpas they would need for the climb because the Sherpas were worried about Weihenmayer's blindness. When they saw how confidently he moved, they had a different suspicion and thought he was lying about his blindness. Weihenmayer resorted to drastic measures to convince them of his inability to see by pulling down his left lower eyelid and plopping out his artificial eye: "I can take the other out if you want."[777] Now the Sherpas believed him.

In the films about the climb, you frequently see Weihenmayer crossing ladders. Even many sighted climbers crawl over these ladders, but he always walks upright. Your breath catches in your throat when you see him, balanced on a ladder over an icy abyss, blindly putting one foot in front of the other. I asked him why he had chosen to walk upright over the ladders in this way: "Sherpas, they are the leaders on the mountain and they walk over the ladders. I heard a Sherpa one time and he was talking about this guy and the guy was crawling over the ladder and he said, 'He'll be going home in a few days.' And sure enough, that guy went home. So, yeah, there's almost like a superstition, right, like you've got to walk across those ladders, that's what you do. You don't crawl across, you've got to walk. And it's sort of a symbol that like I'm going to own this situation. Even though it was really scary and I had to learn how to lean on the ropes and put my crampons just over the rungs in certain ways that I could lean back."[778]

Again, he had to jump, this time over a crevasse, and managed to land right in the notched boot prints on the other side. He also had to climb fifty feet vertically to the top of a serac, a tower of glacial ice. He is often asked what it felt like to finally stand at the summit of the highest mountain in the world. In one interview he explained, "Language cannot describe it. It is something I had dreamed of all my life. I paid my dues climbing mountains all over the world. I suffered for it, tortured myself, endured pain and, suddenly, there I was at the finishing line. There's no higher place on Earth. It's the absolute peak. I was speechless, overcome by emotion, hard to say."[779]

Was he scared? Of course, he was. What sets courageous people apart is not that they don't experience fear, but that they learn to deal with it. And no one without fear will ever be able to conquer Mount Everest. As Weihenmayer explains: "Of course, there is fear, respect for the mountain. After only five minutes on the summit, I urged my team mates to leave, to go down, because there was a storm coming in. Jeff reassured me: 'Erik, we're all nervous about the storm, but you're only going to be here once in your life. Take your time and think about what you've accomplished.'"[780]

But Erik had not yet achieved his ultimate goal. He had climbed Mount Everest, yes, but he still needed two peaks to complete the Seven Summits challenge. The following year, he summited Europe's highest mountain, Mount Elbrus (18,510 feet) in the Russian Caucasus. Then, in Australia he scaled Mount Kosciuszko (7,310 feet above sea level).

In 2004, he returned to Tibet to lead an expedition called the Climbing Blind project. He took six children from a school for the blind in Lhasa and climbed a mountain near Mount Everest. The expedition was accompanied by an American film crew, who documented the adventure in the film *Blindsight*, which is well worth seeing.[781]

People like Erik Weihenmayer are always looking for the next challenge. After completing the Seven Summits challenge, he decided to take on the Colorado River, the largest river in the southwest of North America, 1,540 miles long. It is famous for its more than 200 white water rapids, which are rated for their speed and difficulty on a scale of one to ten. On September 7, 2014, eight years after getting his first taste of kayaking on this river, he embarked on his greatest adventure to date: as part of a team of ten kayakers, he set out to conquer the river's most extreme rapids.

Weihenmayer was connected by radio to one of the guides, who gave him instructions and helped, at least a little, to compensate for Weihenmayer's blindness. Unfortunately, the radio didn't always work and, even when it did, Erik couldn't always understand what was being said as he was buffeted by roaring waves, some of which were over twenty feet tall. "If we get separated for any reason," his guide told him, "Don't panic. Relax. Breathe. Be at peace with the river. You're here in this moment. Nothing else matters."[782]

The Colorado River's most formidable rapids are Lava Falls, which are rated ten out of ten for their velocity, turbulence and elevation drop. Weihenmayer had never been as scared in his life as he was when he took on Lava Falls. He leaned his upper body the wrong way and was instantly upside down in the river, not knowing which direction his boat was pointing: "...I felt a collision like hitting a solid wall. My boat was thrown up and backward as I flipped again. My kayak spun above me as I managed to roll up once more, now hyperventilating."[783] The waves pounded him, spun him around and shook him. He gulped water, gasping for air. At some point he heard a voice over the radio, "You're done, buddy. No more big rapids."[784]

Yes, he had made it through Lava Falls, but "blind, frantic, bathed in fear, and emerging on the other end like a drowned rat." He was not satisfied with himself: "Don't let that be the culmination!" he admonished himself.[785] When he woke up the next morning, he went to the guide, "What do you say we...maybe...try it again?" The guide turned to him and replied: "You know. I've been thinking the same thing. In fact, I was hoping you'd say that."[786]

Weihenmayer co-founded No Barriers USA, an organization that empowers people with disabilities to break through barriers. The organization's motto is: "What's within you is stronger than what's in your way."[787] Throughout his life, Weihenmayer has taken a lot of risks, but he is by no means a risk junkie. Although he is blind, he doesn't take blind risks. As strange as it may sound, he is actually quite cautious and deliberate, a man who analyzes risks carefully, looks for the best partners, trainers, and guides, spends months or even years preparing for a new challenge and has a definite streak of perfectionism running through his core. Despite all this, he still finds the courage to act. I asked him about his attitude to risk: "Risk-averse. I mean, I'm a wimp, I'm a chicken. I don't want to die, you know. I want to be safe. You know, there are certain people, they write great books and because they are chaos seekers, they love chaos. They subconsciously don't plan properly so that they can have big epic climbs and they can have these great adventures. And I do believe it's almost subconscious. Or maybe it's the fact that they're trying insanely hard things and when you do that, you have a risk of disaster. So, maybe it's a combination of those two. But, no, I put myself on the risk-averse side. I'm trying to minimize wild cards. Like when I look at an adventure, I think, okay, I've got to minimize, I've got to eliminate or minimize as many wild cards as possible."[788]

It is impossible to achieve the extraordinary in life if you aren't willing to take risks. At the same time, if you don't want to hand control of your life over to fate and coincidence, you can't afford to trust blind optimism, especially when the stakes are high. No, you need to do everything you can to manage the risks.

If you want to think big and set yourself ambitious goals, like Erik Weihenmayer, you have to program them into your subconscious. I remember something the mountaineer Reinhold Messner said during a lecture a few years ago. He was describing how he had fallen into a crevasse and was almost certain that he would never get out again. With death a real possibility, he firmly resolved that if he did manage the improbable and somehow got out of the crevasse, he would turn back immediately. Once he was out, however, he continued on to the top of the mountain. "I couldn't help it, because I had woken up every morning and gone to sleep every night with that one goal, and I had programed it into my mind over and over again every day," Messner explained. His subconscious forced him to keep going and continue the climb to the summit.

I asked Weihenmayer if he took a similar approach, i.e. programed his goals into his subconscious. He answered, "I spend like 15 minutes just every day, envisioning myself standing on the summit—to the point where I'd hear the snow crunching under my crampons. I'd hear the slacks, I'd feel the sky, just feel the cold, and I'd feel the hearts of my teammates, I'd feel the tears, I'd literally start tearing up because I was there. So, yeah, no, I think that's what you're talking about. And, when I summitted Everest, I had summitted it 100 times in my mind already. So, I think that kind of belief system and that kind of programing it into your subconscious is hugely important so that you can truly be there."[789]

Visualizing goals and "programing" them into your subconscious are important techniques on the pathway to achieving your goals: "Envision yourself on the top and you're there. Yeah, then it gives you a kind of energy because you have this goal in your mind. Yeah. And I do find it's energizing."[790]

At the end of our interview, I asked Weihenmayer what he thought the secret of success was. His words reminded me of Napoleon Hill, who, in his book *Think and Grow Rich,* repeatedly stressed that every disadvantage contains the seed of an equally great advantage. Weihenmayer calls this, "the idea of alchemy, turning bad things into good things, trying to find the surprises, unexpected gifts in situations...Not just surviving it but really harnessing it, using the energy of that bad thing to propel you into a new place that you probably wouldn't have gone to in any other way. And you see that time and time again. And it's an art and a science. It's really almost magical to watch it appear because you see people just go through so much hell and pain and suffering. And through that pain and suffering and loss, sometimes it becomes the seed of creation and energy and discovery. And so, that translation [from bad to good, R.Z] is something I think we can spend a lifetime trying to achieve."[791]

Marla Runyan racing in 2003: "You can't control what happens to you, but you can control how you respond, and how you think about it. And how you feel about it." Marla Runyan's most important message is: "No matter what happens, you always have a choice in how to respond."

Credits: Getty Images North America / Getty Images

# 17. Marla Runyan
## "The future has not been written"

There are many athletes with disabilities who perform exceptionally well at the Paralympics, but Marla Runyan not only
won five gold medals at the international sports competition for
the disabled, but she also triumphed in the 1500 meters at the Pan
American Games in 1999 and became the first blind athlete in
history to compete in the Summer Olympics in Sydney in 2000
(finishing eighth in the 1500 meters). She won many other competitions, including three consecutive U.S. National Championships
in the 5000 meters between 2001 and 2003 and the U.S. National
Championship at 20 km in 2003 and 2006.

Runyan is 'legally blind,' meaning she sees almost nothing.
She can see the feet and the colors of her competitors' jerseys, the
red plastic surface of the track and the waving of flags – though she
can't make out which nations they represent. She can't see the finish line. "When I run a race, I don't always know whether I've won
or lost. I can't see the clocks, or the lap counters, or the scoreboards.
I only know that the finish is at the end of the straightaway."[792]

Her greatest difficulty is recognizing things directly in front
of her. A parking meter, a person standing alone, or anything sta-
tionary, seems to jump out at her. "It appears out of thin air and I
have to quickly dodge it ... I only run into objects that are perfectly
still."[793] What she sees is a permanent blot in front of her eyes, a
large oval that blinks and flickers like a strobe light. "It has no particular color or definition, but it moves across walls and ceilings
and blue skies like a gray stain. It is not something tangible, that's

really in *front* of me...But the blot moves just as quickly as my eyes, and blocks the view."[794] What she is 'seeing' is actually the scar tissue in her retinas.

If you read her autobiography and compare it with the biographies of completely blind people—such as James Holman, Ray Charles, Andrea Bocelli, and Erik Weihenmayer, all of whom feature in this book—you get the certain impression that it was much easier for the completely blind to get used to, accept, and live with their condition than for Runyan. But let us tell her story from the beginning.

At the age of eight, the previously healthy girl from Santa Maria, California, first noticed a blob in front of her eyes. Soon after, her teacher called Marla's mother and told her to have Marla's eyes checked because she could only read if she held her books no more than a few inches from her face. Once in class, Marla started crying because she saw the teacher writing something on the board but couldn't make out what it was. At first, she could still make out some of the words if she sat all the way forward, but soon she couldn't decipher them even up close. In addition, Marla's eyes were incredibly sensitive to bright light. Although nobody knew it at the time, she was suffering from a disease in which artificial light is perceived ten times brighter than normal.

Marla's mother first took her to an optometrist, who performed an eye test but could not find anything wrong with her eyes. Over the next few months, her mother took her from one doctor to the next. One said it must be psychosomatic and her parents stayed up all night desperately trying to work out whether it was their parenting that was causing the problem. They were not convinced by the doctor's diagnosis, so they went to see other experts. Marla was examined to see if she had a brain tumor, but fortunately the findings were negative.

They consulted a nutritionist, an advocate of the anti-sugar movement, who advised Marla to stop eating Rice Krispies and drinking 7-Up. Following the nutritionist's recommendations, Marla's mother put her on a strict diet. Marla wasn't even allowed to eat applesauce after her mother heard a nutritionist on TV proclaim, "Applesauce is like candy, and apple pie might as well be poison."[795] But changing her diet did not help either.

A retina specialist told her shocked parents that Marla was suffering from butterfly dystrophy and would eventually go completely blind. After further examinations, the doctor admitted he had made a mistake and that Marla was actually suffering from Stargardt's disease. At least, and this was the news her parents focused on in that moment, the disease would not lead to complete blindness. And she could read, albeit very awkwardly, with an apparatus consisting of a desktop monitor, a camera and a sliding tray.

At elementary school, she faced insurmountable difficulties. One day, when she visited a school for the visually impaired with her parents, she was immediately impressed: "What I liked best of all was that when I was in *this* room, no one expected me to be able to see fully. It was okay to be partially sighted, or even blind, and in fact, it was not a big deal. The realization hit me that this was where I belonged. I didn't even want to go home," she writes in her autobiography.[796] After graduating from that school, she attended a junior high school that also offered special classes for the visually impaired.

At school, Marla discovered the joys of sports. She was the fastest kid in her school. She hated being overtaken by anyone while running—whenever that happened, she felt helpless again. When she was outdoors and running, she no longer felt blind, she felt like the fastest girl in the world. She even tried her hand at high jumping, despite the fact that she couldn't see the bar. "It became a matter of pride with me to prove that I could do anything, to seek out those things that *ought* to be most difficult, and to show that I could master them."[797]

She began to play the violin and became first violinist at school. She could read the notes only with a magnifying visual aid, a bioptic, which looked like the device a jeweler would use to examine fine stones. It consisted of a heavy black frame with a small telescope lens about three inches long and one inch in diameter.[798] "With the three-inch-long bioptic in my eye, I would peer at five notes of music, my face pressed to the page, too close to the stand to hold my violin. After I had memorized the five notes, I'd set down the bioptic, pick up my violin, and play the notes." Then she would put the bioptic back on to study the next five notes. Using this method, it took an hour to learn just two lines of music.[799]

For Marla, her disability was an incentive. She was the top student in her school and was even invited to give a valedictory address during her school's graduation ceremony. She chose to speak about setting goals. Other people react to life's challenges with despair and frustration, and Marla Runyan, too, often felt despair. But for her, she harnessed her desperation and adopted the attitude: "I'm gonna show them."[800]

In an interview she recalled: "When I was diagnosed with Stargardt's, it felt like the expectations around me just fell. No one really expected me to do much. Before that time, I was expected to be a good student, to go to college, and so on. But after the diagnosis, it was like, 'Marla, just do your best.' This really angered me. My reaction was to push myself even harder, to hold higher expectations for myself than what others held for me, and to prove to others that I had value and that I could excel. While I was a straight 'A' student in high school, the track ultimately became my venue to prove myself. The track was everything I was about: challenge, accountability, determination and competition. My reaction to losing my sight was to run."[801]

She directed her willpower not only at sports, but also at other fields. "The more my eyes betrayed me, the more determined I was to become an academic overachiever, and an athletic one, and a musical one, all at the same time. I had to prove that I wasn't dumb, and that I could do all the things that came naturally to others."[802]

Marla Runyan had tremendous strength and worked incredibly hard, drawing on her unbending will to overcome all difficulties. As a result, she found it hard to understand her non-disabled classmates. She often wondered what they could accomplish if they had the same strength, energy and perseverance as she did—a fair question. "I could not understand how some of my fellow students could be so lackadaisical about their work; about assignments that were incredibly time-consuming for me. Why didn't they use their vision to the fullest? It seemed to me that they were wasting perfectly good eyes. At times, the felling was alienating."[803]

From the perspective of a person who expends so much energy on doing even the smallest things, it seems incomprehensible that people without disabilities do not make the most of their inherent skills. "If I had your eyes," she sometimes thought, "I would not only know what is on the board, I would get an A in this class."[804] She admits that she had no tolerance whatsoever for classmates who simply didn't try hard.[805]

If you, dear reader, are not living with a disability and are reading these stories of people who, with tremendous willpower and determination, have achieved the exceptional despite their disabilities, don't you also ask yourself, "What could I accomplish if I only exhibited the same persistence, determination, and willpower?"

It turned out that playing the violin at concert level would not have been possible anyway because of Marla's disability. All the more she now trained her focus to sports. She spent years trying to hide her disability from others. One reason she did so was that she didn't want to use her blindness as an excuse. Whenever she couldn't do something, she never said, "It's because I can't see."[806] This is what sets winners and losers apart: Losers always look to external conditions and unchangeable circumstances as the causes of their defeats. One the one hand, this provides them with a convenient excuse, but it also makes them helpless. Winners look inside themselves for the causes of their setbacks. As Runyan puts it, "If the cause of failure was not my eyesight, then it had to be a deficit in my effort or skill. I told myself to work harder, and I was intensely critical of the final product."[807]

But the fact that she hid her disability had another positive effect. Her mother called it the "Great Illusion," and Runyan explained, "I was becoming so good at hiding my disability that I almost convinced myself it didn't exist."[808] She thus used—probably unconsciously—the method of autosuggestion. And she had intuitively recognized: If you present yourself to others in a certain way, what starts as playing a role soon becomes the real you.

She probably overdid it, however, because she also tortured herself and made life unnecessarily difficult where it would have been better to seek help from the people around her. When she had to give a paper, she insisted on typing it herself and laboriously searched for keys on her typewriter instead of accepting her mother's offer of help. She refused to listen to tape recordings of books, instead asking the teacher to enlarge them with a photocopier so that she could read them word by word with a magnifying glass. She was worried that if she fell back on her visual impairment as an excuse for not being able to do the little things, she would end up doing the same for bigger things for the rest of her life. "I didn't want to get into the habit of humoring my blindness; I cultivated denial as a protection from the temptation to become a victim."[809] She later recognized that this approach to life served her well on the one hand, but on the other, it also made her life more difficult than it had to be.[810]

She performed well in the high jump. She got offers from several colleges and universities, including one from the track and field coach at San Diego State University. She decided to attend this prestigious university. Her new professors were amazed to find out that she was not only a gifted high jumper, but also had an excellent grade average of 3.98 in her academic subjects (the highest possible score was 4.0). However, she no longer had the luxury of trying to do things the same way everyone else did. She was forced to hire a paid "note taker" to help her during lectures.

Having followed the Seoul Olympics avidly on TV, Runyan was fascinated by the heptathlon and set herself the goal of becoming an elite heptathlete. The heptathlon is an a seven-event competition for women that has been held as a two-day competition and in its current form since 1981. The seven disciplines are 100-meter hurdles, high jump, shot put and 200-meter run on the first day, and long jump, javelin and 800-meter run on the second day. Her coaches initially had reservations about whether she would be able to compete in the hurdles because of her visual impairment. "Since I couldn't see a hurdle until it rose directly in front of me, I relied almost entirely on my rhythm."[811] Sometimes her trailing leg would catch the top of the hurdle and she would fall. "But I loved the hurdles, I loved the pace and beat of them and the feeling it gave me to conquer them so improbably."[812] And, strange as it may sound, it had never occurred to Runyan that her competitors could see the hurdles better than she could.

Runyan continued to set ambitious goals for herself in college. "I would rather struggle with lofty goals, I decided, than settle for more comfortable ones."[813] Intuitively, she applied insights from Goal Setting Theory, the central tenet of which is: "There is a linear relationship between the degree of goal difficulty and performance." The founders of this theory, Edwin K. Locke and Gary Latham, found that the performance of individuals with the highest goals was over 250 percent greater than that of individuals with the easiest goals.[814] "Specific, difficult goals lead to higher performance than no goals as well as vague, abstract goals such as 'do your best.'"[815] For Runyan, this mindset paid off: She graduated as a teacher for deaf and blind children magna cum laude in all subjects.

Perhaps this attitude was also the reason that Runyan was skeptical about the Paralympics. She did participate with great success, winning gold medals in various disciplines. "My performances as a post-collegiate athlete broke the existing world records for these events within my disability classification (B3). For the most part, I expected that I would win gold in those events, but you really never know for sure. Eventually, I set world records in the B3 classification for every distance from the 100m to the marathon, as well as the high jump, long jump, and pentathlon."[816]

However, Runyan wasn't only interested in measuring her performance in competition with people in her disability group, but against all athletes. "While the Paralympics were wonderful, I knew I didn't really belong there. I was determined to compete in the mainstream Olympics, and I felt that settling for anything less would have been using my disability as an excuse to be less of an athlete. I would be a better athlete if I made the commitment."[817]

She set herself the goal of qualifying for the 1996 U.S. Olympic Trials for the summer games in Atlanta. She writes that she devoted herself to the heptathlon with the "same fanatical work ethic" that she had applied throughout to graduate school.[818] But she made a mistake that many ambitious people make in thinking 'more is more.' Up to a certain point, that's true—your input is in direct proportion to the result you achieve. But at some point, the equation flips when the stress becomes too great. In sports, this is called overtraining.

Footballer Oliver Kahn, three times winner of the Best Goalkeeper in the world, put it this way: "It's essential to learn from experience at what point discipline becomes a compulsion and can then become counterproductive, destructive even." Without discipline, Kahn said, you can never be the best. But Kahn, after bitter experiences with overtraining and burnout, understood more clearly what discipline really meant: "It's the discipline of 'not too much.'"[819]

Ambitious people must take special care to ensure that, in addition to phases of maximum tension, they also make time to relax. Otherwise, they will end up like Oliver Kahn, who only learned this lesson after a dramatic burnout. Successful people often learn this the hard way. And that's precisely what happened to Runyan: "I trained relentlessly, and I couldn't understand it when I grew fatigued and my performances suffered. I didn't realize that rest was as essential to building a strong, efficient body as the work itself. If all you do is train, you don't build; you break."[820]

In 1995, Runyan won bronze at the U.S. Olympic Festival—a now-defunct tournament to select future Olympic athletes. But after her victory, five weeks before the Olympic trials, she felt herself getting weaker and weaker and her performances deteriorated as a result of overtraining. She didn't do as well in the first six disciplines in the heptathlon as she had hoped, so she focused all her energy into the final, most demanding event, the 800 meters. And her time of 2:04.70 was the fastest ever achieved by a U.S. heptathlete. Despite her elation, she soon realized that this American record in the heptathlon's 800 meters, while highly significant to herself, went virtually unnoticed by the public. Nevertheless, the victory opened her and her coach's eyes to something else: she was in the wrong sport. She was not a heptathlete, but a runner.

From then on, Runyan worked entirely toward one lofty goal: she wanted to compete as a runner in the 2000 Olympics. But the next few years were arduous, and it's a miracle she survived them intact. In October 1996, she was forced to have surgery on her left knee. One injury followed another, plus the symptoms of over-training: declining motivation, irritability, abnormal weight loss, increased morning heart rate. Sometimes she thought about giving up. But then she told herself that wasn't an option: could she sit in the stands as a spectator, squinting at the track through her monocular? "Could I sit there and wonder, *What if I hadn't given up?* No, I decided; I couldn't quit. Not and be a happy person."[821]

Over the years, she writes, she had disregarded the simple realization that training must be balanced by rest—sleep, in her eyes, was a waste of time. "After two surgeries, innumerable cortisone injections, acupuncture, chiropractic adjustments, four pairs of orthotics, and eight months of plantar fasciitis [an inflammation of the tendon plate of the sole of the foot, R.Z.], I finally realized I had to let go. When I did, I learned how to run a distance race."[822]

In addition to the physical challenges came the psychological ones. In 1999, she came a disappointing fourth in the 1500 meters at the U.S. Championships, and that meant she didn't qualify for the world championship squad. Runyan describes the intense pain she felt because she knew she simply hadn't run her best. "Had I finished fourth with an honest effort, after giving it my all, I could have lived with it. Had I been half-dragged off the track in utter exhaustion, I could have lived with that, too. But to walk off the track feeling that there was more inside me that I could have given—that was the greatest pain I've ever experienced."[823] She understood that she had fallen victim to her own self-doubt—and she vowed that she would never, ever let this happen to her again.

Then, in 1999, she achieved her first breakthrough when she won gold at the Pan American Championships in the 1500 meters. She was overjoyed, and the media and first sponsors began to take an interest in her. But what bugged her was that after her win, journalists didn't want to talk about the competition, but rather about her visual impairment. A year later, she won the national indoor championship in the 3000 meters. However, all these were only intermediate stages for her to reach her big goal: the 2000 Olympics in Sydney.

But again, she was plagued by new injuries, the deadline for qualification was fast approaching. She consulted more and more doctors, tried more and more new treatments. She became increasingly desperate and lost faith that she would make it to Sydney. She also sought psychological help. Sometimes it is just one sentence that changes something in our lives. That's what happened to Runyan when the sports psychologist she talked to about her fears of not being able to start said, "The fact is, we really don't know if you can make the Olympic team until the gun goes off. Right? *Marla, the future has not been written.*"[824] She repeated this sentence again and again, it gave her strength. Even when she was standing on the starting line at the Olympic trials, she remembered these very words: "The future has not been written." She came third and qualified for Sydney.

She had regained her confidence and come "to understand that injuries, and stress, and emotions that erupted in tears or anger were a part of this game. Unforeseen circumstances were as much a part of the sport as the rewards. You had to know this going in, and you have to be prepared to deal with it. No whining or excuses. No backing out when things got rough. You set a goal and make a commitment."[825]

Then, at the end of September 2000, the Olympic flame was lit in Sydney. Fifty female athletes took part in the preliminary heats of the 1500 meters, and twelve of them made it to the finals. Runyan was one of them—that in itself was a huge success. But in the days leading up to the final race, her self-doubt grew, she didn't really believe in herself. In the end, she managed eighth place, but that was a disappointment for her: "For me, my eighth place finish at the 2000 Olympics was a disappointment. I had hoped to run faster and place higher. Even though no other American female had finished higher in that event at that time, that didn't matter much to me. I still believe I could have run a smarter race, and I believe if I had done some things differently in my training, I could have performed much better at the Games."[826]

Marla Runyan was the 5000 meters U.S. champion each year from 2001 to 2003 and won the Freihofer's Run for Women over that distance on three consecutive occasions from 2002 to 2004. In 2002, she finished fourth at the New York City Marathon as the fastest U.S. woman in 2:27:10. She always remained self-critical: "While finishing fourth was a strong showing for my first marathon, I believe I could have run faster. The winner was only one minute ten seconds ahead of me. And, just like in the Olympics, I believe there were things I could have done differently in my preparation that would have allowed me to run faster. Elite athletes are rarely satisfied with their performances."[827]

She finished fifth in the Boston Marathon in 2003 and seventh in the Chicago Marathon in 2004. After becoming national marathon champion in 2006 by winning the Twin Cities Marathon, she ended her athletic career. Today, she is a teacher at the Perkins School for the Blind in Watertown, Massachusetts, where Helen Keller also taught. "I work with high school students and teach them to use technology to support their access to their education as well as develop their social communication skills and independence...Even though I am teaching 'technology' skills, there really isn't a day that goes by when I am not also teaching life skills—how to advocate for yourself, how to communicate with others, how to make good choices, and how to problem solve. I believe that self-determination is at the foundation of everything we do. You can learn skills and you can acquire technology, but you must determine how you will use your skills and tools to achieve your goals. You also must know how to deal with setbacks."[828]

In her autobiography, Marla Runyan writes that one of the most important lessons she learned from her mother is to not let things get you down. We know from psychological research that losers see themselves as victims of external circumstances and believe their lives are determined by factors beyond their own control. Winners, on the other hand, place much more emphasis on those things that they themselves can influence and change. They see themselves as the shapers of their own destinies. The first attitude leads to passivity and despondency, the second to activity, motivating you to ever greater efforts. As Marla's mother taught her: "You can't control what happens to you, but you can control how you respond, and how you think about it. And how you feel about it." And Marla Runyan's most important message is, "No matter what happens, you always have a choice in how to respond."[829] The future has not been written.

Johann König: "If you believe that your work is dependent on what other people say, you might as well give up right now."

Credits: Malte Metag

# 18. Johann König
## The blind man who opened an art gallery

Johann König is probably the only gallery owner in the world who was practically blind when he opened his first gallery. And he is not only one of the best-known art dealers in Germany, he is, according to one of Germany's leading newspapers, *FAZ*, "one of the most influential gallery owners in the world"[830] and "the rock star of German gallerists."[831] Germany's leading business newspaper, *Handelsblatt,* is equally effusive: "Dealing in art is an art in and of itself. There are hardly any gallery owners in Germany who can match the extent to which Johann König has mastered his trade."[832]

He is also an ingenious self-marketer—in the most positive sense of the word. Too many artists fail because they believe that good art speaks for itself and have no understanding of the importance of marketing. This applies all the more to gallery owners. *Kunstforum International,* a leading magazine for contemporary art, ran a portrait of König under the headline "The Rebel Gallerist." The article went on to say: "He seeks the limelight in the press and on Instagram. In the gallery world, however, there is still an unspoken rule: it's fine when a good artist creates a cult of personality around themselves, but not a gallery owner, who should never be more than the serious but shadowy figure steering the art world from behind the scenes. König takes center stage, but without stealing the show from his artists."[833] König has proved that he knows how to launch artists onto the global stage—and massively increase their market value. He profits from raising his artists' profiles—and they benefit from his fame in return.

Many other successful people with disabilities do not like to talk about their disabilities. For example, anyone who wants to interview the blind singer Andrea Bocelli, for example, is informed by his press people beforehand that he doesn't like to answer questions about his blindness. If you read biographies of successful people with disabilities, you will often find that they are annoyed whenever journalists turn to this topic because they have the impression that too much attention is devoted to their disability and too little to their achievements. König, however, is far more pragmatic. He understands the rules of the media game. If he didn't, he wouldn't be anywhere near as successful. The profile in *FAZ* goes on to say: "After all, every good brand needs a good story. König himself now also playfully discusses his visual impairment. As he explains: 'It is my unique selling point. I owe at least a portion of my success to it.'"[834]

König recognized the value of his USP very early in his career. When—as a student— he was designing the logo for his first gallery, he chose one that was so blurry it was almost impossible to work out what the gallery's name was, and placed his ad in the magazine *Texte zur Kunst*: "That was my first experience of life as a visually impaired gallery owner."[835] When I spoke with König in preparation for writing this book, however, he confessed that he doesn't like to be asked about his visual impairment so much today: "I've said and written everything about that, and there are so many other topics that are infinitely more important to me."[836]

As an established art dealer, König also knows that provocation is part and parcel of the art business—and in this respect he is happily following in Andy Warhol's footsteps. There is another trait that König and Warhol share: König is not easy to pin down, is determined not to be pigeonholed and loves surprising his audiences. He grew up in a decidedly leftwing home and anyone who reads his autobiography or interviews him will quickly realize that he still leans to the left today. But that doesn't stop him from writing sentences like this: "At the same time, it was important for the gallery to evolve again and become bigger. The essence of capitalism is that it does not tolerate stagnation. And nowhere do you see that as strongly as in the art market."[837]

When we spoke, he explained that artist are not just artists, they are also entrepreneurs.[838] And in an interview with *Handelsblatt* in January 2021, he explains: "I like to talk about the market and its mechanisms because I am convinced that newcomers to the market will only get involved in art if they also understand the financial ins and outs of it. Otherwise, everyone just thinks it's crazy because they are convinced art is overpriced."[839] He adds that, in many ways, art is "similar to the financial markets." What does he mean by that? Well, as far as buyers are concerned, artists with long careers and great reputations are the blue chips, perhaps comparable to companies on the Dow Jones. You can't go far wrong there. "And then there are the upstarts, artists with potential, that you could perhaps compare to angel investments." That's where the excitement lies, he says. Of course, he adds, the vast majority of collectors and buyers don't approach a piece of art as an investment, "but because they fall in love with the work."[840]

When König criticizes the overregulation of the art market, he certainly sounds more like a libertarian than a leftwinger. For example, during an interview in 2020, he denounced Germany's regulatory frenzy and its impact on the art market: "There is no country in the world where the art trade is so severely curtailed. The state has raised the sales tax for galleries to 19 percent and introduced a cultural protection law that requires private collectors to obtain an export license if they want to take valuable and historical works abroad. The artists' social security fund is also in desperate need of reform."[841] In another interview in 2021, he looks back 20 years to the time he founded his contemporary art gallery in the German capital and confesses he never thought back then that he would end up wanting a "strong, conservative and pro-business voice" for his adopted city of Berlin, a city that is governed by a coalition of three leftwing parties. He would now be happy "if we at least had a conservative opposition worthy of the name."[842]

Today, König also has a gallery in London. He even has a presence in Asia—he initially opened a gallery in Tokyo, but has decided to relocate to Seoul, where his latest gallery will soon be opening.[843] He may be an international success, but his base is still in Berlin, despite the issues he has with the city. After relocating a few times, in 2012 his gallery settled in the district of Berlin-Kreuzberg, where it has been housed in a typical, late-1960s building—a former church that looks more like a bunker than a house of worship and is so ugly it is considered cool. The building is all the more impressive for the contrast between its brutalist exterior (it is, by the way, a listed historical monument) and its aesthetically pleasing interiors.

Johann König was born on July 22, 1981, in Cologne. His father, Kasper König, was a museum director and art professor, his mother an illustrator and his older brother is an art dealer in New York. But Johann, who from the age of seven grew up in Frankfurt, probably never thought that he himself would one day earn a living with art: "Growing up in the art world pissed me off. My parents even chose our holiday destinations based on which studios or museums they wanted to see. We always ended up visiting some artists who were living in Ireland because they didn't have to pay taxes there."[844]

At the age of twelve, he had a serious accident that was to change his life forever. To this day, König's mother only ever talks about his life or that of the family in terms of the time before and the time after the accident. As a boy, Johann owned a starting pistol, the kind of gun that is normally used to give the starting signal at sports events. The pistol's cartridges contained small charges of gunpowder. One day, he decided to take small balls of gunpowder from the cartridges and put them all together in a box. The box exploded: "I had never heard such a loud noise. The bang seemed to reverberate for a small eternity, so long that I had the feeling of being shot from the earth. A huge jet of flame flared up in front of me, and suddenly I was enveloped in all the colors of the rainbow. Red. Yellow. Green. Violet. A giant rainbow, a phenomenon of light and sky." He knew immediately that something terrible had happened, even though he didn't feel any pain at first. Seconds later, however, the pain hit him, and he knew that his hands had been destroyed. "My face and upper body had also been hit, the right side of my face more than the left. The whole room must have been bathed in blood." He couldn't see anything. "Nothing but a dark rusty brown, a pulsating mix of red, brown and black."[845]

The explosion had almost completely destroyed his eyes. From that moment on, he had no pupil, no lens and no iris in either eye. His retinas were also severely damaged, but at least the central parts were still intact. His optic nerves were also spared.

Over the next few years, Johann underwent more than 30 operations—including skin grafts on both hands, laser surgery on his retinas, operations to stabilize his intraocular pressure and several corneal transplants. "My whole face had been hit by the explosion, my hands were damaged, I needed skin transplants. I was given cortisone, got fat and lay swollen in bed, my hands wrapped in bandages."[846] At the age of 14, Johann weighed over 220 pounds because of all the cortisone injections. He wasn't completely blind, but he could hardly see anything at first—even with his "insanely thick glasses" he was only able to make out strong colors, light, dark and the hazy, blurred outlines of large objects.[847] He resorted to audio books (which were nowhere near as common then as they are now) or read with the help of a reading machine that displayed hugely magnified letters on a screen. He had to decipher each word, syllable by syllable, unable to read any faster than a first grader.

Looking back, he acknowledges that going to an integrated school, where students with disabilities are taught together with students without disabilities, would not have been right for him. He was sent to a school for the blind in Marburg, where being around young people with similar problems helped him to process the accident. Above all, he learned that there was no point asking himself certain questions: "What if I hadn't messed around with the gunpowder? Why weren't my parents stricter? Couldn't they have watched over me more closely? Why didn't the accident happen to other boys who played with starting pistols?"[848]

Questions like these, aimed at past events that cannot be changed anyway, are of course futile—they focus on the past, not the present or future. And yet so many people fall into the trap of asking themselves meaningless questions about irreversible events. People like this, who focus on the past, end up dwelling on yesterday rather than moving forward and embracing tomorrow.

At school, one of Johann's teachers inspired his interest in contemporary art. Johann realized that he had met many of the artists the teacher was speaking about in class at his parents' house. He also had a few friends who were involved in the art scene and so it became clear to him that, despite his former aversion, he also wanted to carve out a career in the world of art. So, while he was still at school, he decided to open a gallery.

In retrospect, he says, he was incredibly naive and had no idea what problems lay in store. But, at the time, he was optimistic. He was convinced he could make it work—a trait he shares with all business founders. Still, he wasn't quite ready to share his plans with his father. In fact, he was pretty sure his father would advise against it. But he did let some of his friends and acquaintances in on the idea—most of whom told him he was crazy; very few were positive. "I decided to just listen to the voices of encouragement."[849] He was certainly right to do so. After all, if you listen to all of the small-minded naysayers when you are about to start a business, you will only end up reinforcing any doubts you may have and might even abandon your dreams of ever starting your own business altogether.

König eagerly approached other gallery owners and asked them to explain the ins and outs of the business. This is another attitude he shares with other successful entrepreneurs. Even one of the most successful entrepreneurs in history, the Walmart founder Sam Walton, confesses in his autobiography: "Most everything I've done I've copied from somebody else."[850] Lots of people are simply too proud to learn from others. They think something is only worth achieving if they have come up with the idea themselves. Walton thought and acted differently. He had no qualms about asking his competitors what had worked for them. He went to their stores, and even their head offices, asking as many questions as it took to find out everything he needed to know.

Before he opened his first gallery, König consulted the gallery owners he knew in Frankfurt for tips and advice. The art dealer Michael Neff, for example, "explained the precarious economic fundamentals of running a gallery and told me about his approach to the business."[851] Today, König believes that cultural industries can learn a lot from the start-up scene, where—unlike in the arts—companies do not shroud everything in secrecy: "In the startup scene, everyone is learning from each other, sharing trade secrets, which means they are not secrets any more. They all know that, ultimately, everyone benefits."[852]

His first exhibition was a total flop: not as many people as expected came, there were no sales and no press coverage. Afterwards, he collapsed in tears—but he quickly dusted himself off and got back on his feet: "I realized that I just didn't know enough about running a gallery. So I started to find out how the art business really works. I contacted other gallery owners, artists and curators and asked them every single question I could think of."[853] He kept at it, probing and persisting, until people were uncomfortable, probably often beyond.

But he did not imitate anyone. On the contrary, he threw a lot of their well-meant advice to the wind. From the very beginning, he understood that marketing is all about being different, about refusing to be the same as everybody else. This is known as "positioning" and König is a true positioning expert—he knows exactly what it takes to position artists, just as he also knows how to position himself.

He applied his determination to be different to choosing the site of his first gallery. At the time, all of the most influential art dealers in Germany were based in his hometown of Cologne. But König didn't want to set up shop in Cologne with all the others. One reason was that he wanted to escape out of his well-known father's shadow and, "in Cologne his shadow was bigger than anywhere else."[854] So, in 2002, König decided to open his gallery in Berlin. "Intuitively," he recognized, "Berlin in the early 2000s was a city that promised freedom, rebirth and change."[855]

Being almost blind, König decided, at least at first, not to exhibit paintings. His visual impairment proved to be an advantage because it pushed him to be all the more creative. He decided to go for broke with an exhibition that one of Berlin's biggest newspapers, *Tagesspiegel*, described as follows: "The young Danish upstart Jeppe Hein has placed a polished silver steel ball, about two feet in diameter, in the center of the almost empty gallery's floor. Just about visible on the windowsill, a motion detector is linked to the steel ball via radio signal. Whenever someone opens the door, the motion detector triggers a motor in the sphere, and it starts rolling around the gallery. At first, the massive ball rolls straight ahead—until it crashes, with some force, into one of the walls. The impact changes its direction, and it rolls toward the next wall. This 'impactful' process repeats itself as long as the visitor remains in the gallery, which is progressively destroyed by the steel ball. In effect, the visitor is complicit in the destruction of the gallery."[856]

König believed in the idea, scraped together all the money he could get his hands on and commissioned three of these balls. Visitors lined up outside on the night of the vernissage, and more came every day. Each ball had cost €7,000 to manufacture and he was able to sell all three, at a price of €25,000 per ball, half of which went to the artist. From this one exhibition, he made enough to keep the gallery running without worries, at least for a while. Incidentally, the same sphere installation still appears today in exhibitions all over the world. Clearly, being blind was no obstacle to exhibiting this kind of art. All that König needed was the ability to judge an idea, not the ability to see.

In 2003, just one year after opening his gallery, he was invited to attend Liste Art Fair Basel, the international fair for new discoveries in contemporary art that runs parallel to Art Basel, the world's largest and most important art fair. During the fair, he sold "really a lot of art" for the first time and was so happy that he hugged everyone in delight and danced around his exhibition stand in joy.[857] He acknowledges that this was when he developed a habit that "is essential if you want to get ahead in the art market. You need to be bold in communicating your successes and the successes of the artists you represent—you could even call it 'bragging.' It's one of the central pillars of the business. I have mastered the art of marketing and probably do it better than almost any other gallerist out there."[858] This is true, and you could go even further: Underestimating the importance of self-marketing, suffering from a reluctance to "sell" and naively believing that quality alone is a guarantee of success are probably the main reasons why so many artists never become successful. If you are interested in finding out more on this, I actually wrote an entire book on the importance of these self-promotion strategies, *The Art of Becoming Famous*. One thing is for sure: Johann König doesn't need to read my book, he has already mastered this art. "In Germany," he explains, "artists simply do not understand that you have to draw attention to yourself. It's very different in the U.S."[859] This is just one of many examples that confirm König is so successful because he does not follow the herd but does things differently.

There is another important factor behind König's success: he thinks big. He moved his gallery into new premises that were, based on the size of his gallery at the time, way too big. Incidentally, I did the same when I founded my own company and fully furnished and equipped lots of individual offices even though it wasn't entirely clear that I would ever employ so many people. When my only employee asked why I was getting so many offices ready, I told her that vacuums tend to fill up. Later, I needed even more space. I suspect König thought along similar lines.

As I have already mentioned, König underwent dozens of operations to treat his eye injuries. Then, in spring 2008, König's blindness was miraculously reversed by a revolutionary corneal transplant. He vividly remembers the moment his bandages were removed. He could not believe his good fortune. "It was indescribable. So much light seemed to fall into my eye. I put on my glasses and saw my doctor and the nurse who had removed the bandage. I saw the room I was in, the hospital bed, the medical equipment." His vision was still a bit distorted at first, but one thing was clear: "The operation had been an incredible success."[860] It still took a while for his brain to adjust to the new input, but he can now see between 30 and 40 percent again. Admittedly, that's not much compared to someone with full vision, but compared to his earlier condition—almost entirely blind—it was a tremendous sensation and changed his life.

His improved vision allowed him to start working with artists whose work had a stronger visual focus, such as Katharina Grosse. His gallery was developing an ever-stronger international reputation and it had also become clear that Berlin was exactly the right location for him. A growing number of young artists from all over the world were drawn to Berlin, and the German capital soon overtook Cologne as Germany's most influential art scene. In 2008, König's gallery was ranked the 14th most influential gallery in the world in a survey of artists conducted by the renowned Italian magazine *Flash International*. And in 2009, his name appeared on the British art magazine *Art Review's* annual list of the 100 most influential people in the world of contemporary art for the first time.

His gallery now attended all of the world's major art fairs and generated significant sales. Soon the new—initially too big—gallery in Berlin became too small and, in 2015, König moved to his current location, the former church mentioned at the beginning of this chapter. He rented the brutalist concrete block from the Archbishopric of Berlin on a 99-year lease. Two years later, he expanded to London, opening a branch of his gallery in an underground car park in Marylebone.

When it comes to technology, and especially on the internet, König has always been an early adopter: "Anyone who follows his Instagram stories will quickly realize that Johann König attends more museum tours, studio visits and parties in a single day than most people do in an entire year."[861] He also gives tours of his gallery's exhibitions on Instagram to explain what he thinks of the works.

When a journalist asked him how he deals with criticism of his "Instagram antics," he responded unequivocally: "It doesn't bother me in the slightest. I've been through so much in my life, there are certain things I've risen above. If you believe that your work is dependent on what other people say, you might as well give up right now."[862] When the coronavirus pandemic struck, having 200,000 followers on Instagram paid off and he launched a series of online talks. He uses the internet not only to showcase art, but also to facilitate a direct dialog between artists and art enthusiasts—he calls it "community building."[863] Last but not least, social media has also enabled him to sell artworks ahead of art fairs: "To the chagrin of my artists, I transport most of their art by ship because it's cheaper. If I want to exhibit an artist at Art Basel Hong Kong in March, everything has to be ready before Christmas. In the months in between, we can already sell the work."[864]

König never stops coming up with new ideas. Under the name König Souvenir, for example, he has launched a range of design articles that he insists are not art, but serve to gradually introduce young people (and anyone who can't actually afford a real work of art) to the world of art. His gallery's shop is not only full of books, it also stocks hoodies, leggings, towels and T-shirts. There's even a red baseball cap emblazoned with the word "Guilt" in bold letters—for anyone who wants to register their disapproval and the "guilt" associated with the ex-president of the United States, Donald Trump, whose baseball caps read Make America Great Again. König explains: "Art is still widely regarded as elitist. Too many people are afraid of art and rarely dare to enter a gallery or museum. From the very beginning, one of our key concerns has been to break down inhibitions."[865]

König understands what it means to turn a disadvantage—his visual impairment—into an advantage. "Paradoxically, my disability was probably key to my success." Because of his blindness, he found himself capable of an unusual degree of inner concentration and heightened perception, which helped him to "develop a distinctly personal idea of what makes good art."[866]

Today, he has a more evolved perspective: No one should romanticize disability. A disability is a disadvantage, that is a fact. But, König has come to believe, "You have to accept the things you cannot change and then see how you can make the most of them. Back then, I didn't see any alternative."[867]

Johann König's story confirms that what really counts in life is not what you see, but what you cannot see, namely ideas. "Vision is the gift of seeing invisible things," wrote the Irish essayist Jonathan Swift. And when König was asked in an interview how a blind person can possibly run a gallery, he answered: "As a gallery owner, you are not an art dealer; you represent the artists who create the works in the first place and you have to be there as a sparring partner, supporting them throughout the process of finding ideas. At the beginning there is nothing to see anyway."[868]

Nick Vujicic with his wife in 2019: "I believe if you create the life you want in your imagination, it is possible to create it in reality minute by minute, hour by hour, and day by day."

Credits: Kathy Hutchins / Alamy Stock Photo

# 19. Nick Vujicic
## Motivational speaker and evangelist

Nick Vujicic is one of the most sought-after motivational speakers in the world. He has spoken in sixty-three countries[869] and reached millions of people with his inspirational appearances. In Ukraine, he spoke in front of 9,000 people, in Colombia he thrilled an audience of 18,000 in a bullring, and in India he gave a talk to 120,000 people.[870] On a trip to Slovenia in 2016, his speech to 5,000 students was broadcast to every middle and high school in the country. Classes were interrupted everywhere as Vujicic was introduced by the Slovenian president.[871] He has had the honor to meet with a total of sixteen presidents, prime ministers, and other heads of state.[872] and if you Google his name, you'll see him side by side with prominent business leaders and politicians at the World Economic Summit in Davos.

If you watch one of the many videos of Vujicic on the internet, you can see for yourself how his crowds respond to him. They cry, they cheer. He touches them deep inside – and gives them hope for their own lives. In the first ten years of his career as a motivational speaker, he reached an estimated 600 million people around the world; by the second decade, he had reached 1.2 billion people across all platforms, including speaking, videos, webcasts, podcasts, livestream events, television appearances, and social media. His goal is to reach seven billion people.[873]

Nick was born on December 4, 1982, in Melbourne, Australia. His parents are both the grandchildren of Serbian immigrants. During her pregnancy, Nick's mother, Dushka, went to regular

check-ups, never smoked, and did not take any alcohol or medication. So, there were no indications or reasons to suggest that she
should not give birth to a healthy child.

Nick's father, Boris, was present at the birth and saw Nick's
head and neck come out. He immediately noticed, however, that
something was wrong with Nick's right shoulder: "The shoulder
first appeared to be unusually shaped, and then I saw that there
appeared to be no arm. It was difficult to tell for sure from my
poor vantage point. The medical team moved in and blocked my
view."[874] His mother, who was herself a midwife, had actually expected her baby to be placed in her arms, as normally happens.
When the midwife did not do so, Nick's mother became nervous:
"Is the baby okay?" she asked. The question was met with silence.
She asked again, this time in a more urgent tone, again there was
no response. Nick's father later recalled, "When the medical team
refused to respond to Dushka, I felt queasy and clutched my stomach. A staff member observed this and escorted me outside without
a word. As I left the delivery room, I heard a strange word uttered
by one of the nurses: *phocomelia*."[875]

"I need to talk to you about your baby," the doctor said.

"He's got no arm," the father blurted.

"Your child has no arms or legs."

"What? No arms and no legs at all?"

The doctor nodded. Later, the doctor explained that phocomelia was the medical term for missing or severely malformed limbs.
"I've never been punched hard in the head, but I imagine the jolt
to your brain would be similar...My brain was racing, yet my body
felt numb."[876]

Boris thought about how he could possibly break the news to
his wife, but someone had already told her. She did not want to see
the child. "Do you want me to bring him to you now?" Boris asked.

She shook her head and sobbed into her blankets. Nick's father later recalled, "I had no words to lighten her burden. Our lives had been cut adrift from the reality we'd known and expected."[877] He was surprised to find that his wife did not want to hold their son even after two days. When the hospital social worker saw how much she was suffering, she delicately suggested that they could put him up for adoption. "And then when Nick arrived, we were devastated and all our joy was gone because he had no limbs. Our faith was shaken. Our lives were thrown into turmoil," Nick's father recalls.[878]

But Boris' father made it clear that he saw no reason to even consider putting Nick up for adoption. His mindset was, "Why would you even talk about adoption? This is your child. You are accountable and responsible for raising him. You can handle it. If you can't, we will do it. If you don't have the strength, God will provide it."[879] Boris has vivid memories of the expression on his father's face: his jaw muscles were tense, his gaze penetrating. Nick's mother's parents felt the same way. And finally, they decided to keep and accept their child.

In the early years, his parents realized that Nick didn't miss his arms and legs at all, because he didn't know any different. "Nick was like most infants at that stage of development," his father recalls.[880] "As a child," Nick reports, "I just assumed I was a perfectly adorable baby, naturally charming and as lovable as any on earth. My blissful ignorance was a blessing at that age. I didn't know that I was different or that many challenges awaited me."[881]

Nick first learned to raise himself into an upright position, which is very difficult without arms and legs. He braced his forehead against a wall and slowly raised his body. He also learned to use his larger left foot to grasp things – it had two toes fused together, which were separated by surgery when he was four years old. Today, he makes great use of his foot. He can use it to steer his own special electric wheelchair, use a computer and cell phone, and operate a piano keyboard or digital drum kit. He can grasp a pen with it, although he mostly writes with a pen in his mouth. He can type with it and gets an impressive forty words per minute on his laptop.[882]

As a young child, Nick received a lot of support and donors financed a trip to Canada to see if Nick could be fitted with state-of-the-art prostheses. For a year, he struggled to get to grips with them, but for him, the artificial arms weren't right. "No matter how often he wore them and practiced using them," his father recalls, "there was escaping the fact that this particular model was very uncomfortable and awkward for our small boy to wear for any length of time."[883] Eventually, Nick's parents realized that prostheses weren't going to make a significant difference in Nick's quality of life. "Nick had already figured out ways to accomplish most tasks, and his methods usually were simpler and easier for him and felt more natural."[884] He had long since taught himself to pick things up with his foot, chin, or teeth.

But as Nick got older, he became increasingly aware of his disability: he couldn't eat or drink on his own and constantly had to ask other people for help, for example to go to the toilet. Even worse than these disabilities in everyday life were the worries he had: "I'll never get a girl to love me. I don't even have arms to hold a girlfriend. If I have children, I'll never be able to hold them either. What sort of job could I ever have? Who would hire me? For most jobs, they'd have to hire a second person just to help me do what I was supposed to do. Who would ever hire one for the price of two?"[885]

Nick became increasingly desperate. One day, he sat on the countertop in the kitchen and watched his mother cook. "It struck me that I didn't want to stick around and be a burden to her. I had the urge to throw myself off the counter. I looked down. I tried to work out what angle I should use to make sure I snapped my neck and killed myself."[886] When he was ten years old, he tried to drown himself in the bathtub. He couldn't bring himself to do it but kept thinking about suicide and told his brother that he would take his own life one day.

At about eleven years of age, he hit puberty. The other boys his age began to take an interest in girls, and he felt even more of an outsider than ever before. He was teased at school. He often just hid in some corner so that the other kids couldn't see him. As unbelievable as this sounds once he even got into a fight. Chucky, the school bully, teased him, "I bet you can't fight." Nick was determined not to back down and replied, "Bet ya I can." The two arranged a fight at lunchtime and half the school came to watch. Chucky demanded that Nick get out of his wheelchair, Nick retorted that the fight would only be fair if Chucky fought on his knees. Nick hoped a teacher would come and intervene or Chucky wouldn't get serious after all. "I was still thinking that he wouldn't possibly go through with it. Who would be so low as to hit a little kid with no arms and no legs?"[887]

The girls shouted that Nick should stop, but he did not want pity from girls. And Chucky started punching Nick until Nick got so angry that he went on the counterattack: "I flipped onto my stomach, planted my forehead, and raised myself up for a final charge." One can imagine that all the pent-up anger and frustration in him wanted to vent at that moment: "My adrenaline was pumping. This time I galloped at him as fast as I could go, which was a lot faster than Chucky had anticipated. He'd started to backpedal on his knees. I took a flying leap, using my left foot to launch myself like a human missile. My flying head butted Chucky smack in the nose."[888] Blood was leaking from Chucky's nose. Half the crowd was cheering, the other half was mortified – for Chucky. His days as the schoolyard bully were over. Nick never saw him again – he probably changed schools out of shame.

The situation was made more difficult for Nick by the fact that his parents decided to move from Australia to California in 1992. He was twelve years old at the time. He was terrified of having to start all over again without friends. And indeed, at first, he suffered a real 'culture shock' because so many things were different. And then there were the questions from his new classmates: "I could not believe how curious American middle-school kids were about how I managed in the restroom. I prayed for an earthquake, just to stop the endless interrogations about my toilet tactics."[889]

Until then, he had always been a good student, but the move caused him to fall behind. He hated his new life in America and at his new school. "During recess and lunch hours, I went off on my own, sometimes hiding behind the bushes near the playground."[890] His life had been altered in so many ways, he was simply overwhelmed. He lost all the confidence he had painstakingly built up over the years. "My Australian classmates had accepted me, but in America I was a stranger in a strange land with a strange accent and an even stranger body. Or at least that's how I felt."[891]

In addition, there were other problems: His parents had difficulty finding suitable health insurance for him in the USA. The high cost of living in California was also a problem. The family's lawyer explained that Nick's disability could prevent them from getting a residence permit because the authorities didn't believe they could pay Nick's substantial medical costs themselves in years to come. Boris and Dushka realized that the decision to move from Australia to California had been a mistake. After just four months, they moved back to Brisbane, Australia.

Nick came to a turning point in his life: At a small Christian discussion group, the leader asked the young people to talk about themselves. At previous meetings, Nick had always resisted. For months he had refused to tell the group anything about himself. Finally, he summoned up all his courage and talked for ten minutes about what it was like to live without arms and legs. He had even prepared index cards beforehand for his short speech. But there was one thing he was not at all prepared for: when he finished, he looked up and saw that many of the listeners were crying. He had touched them deeply with his life story. After the talk, one boy in the group asked him to tell his story again to another youth group.

Over the next two years, Nick received dozens more invitations from student and youth groups. He discovered something very important: He could talk, and people were willing to listen to him. At first, he gave his little talks with the aim of showing people that he was just like them.

Talking did him good, it gave him the chance to share his world and make connections. But then it became increasingly clear to him that as a speaker he could actually help other people – and that his disability just might help him contribute something special to the world: "I found that people were willing to listen to me speak because they had only to look at me to know I'd face and overcome my challenges."[892] He didn't lack credibility, because his listeners instinctively felt that he might have something to say that could help them with their own problems. Nick slowly realized that speaking was his calling: "Each of us has some gift – a talent, a skill, a craft, a knack – that gives us pleasure and engages us, and the path to our happiness often lies within that gift."[893]

For the first time he also heard a talk given by a professional motivational speaker, and this had strengthened his resolve to become a motivational speaker himself. The speaker was Reggie

Dabbs, who told nearly 1,400 students at Nick's high school about his mother, who as an 18-year-old prostitute lived in a chicken coop with her three children while pregnant with him. He had endured a terrible childhood and adolescence. One of Dabb's statements particularly spoke to Nick: "You can't change your past, but you can change your future."[894] It was now clear to Nick: motivating people by talking is what he wanted to do.

Nick no longer relied on the invitations that were spontaneously extended to him but started approaching schools and all kinds of organizations himself to offer himself as a speaker. He didn't even want a fee for doing so – he just enjoyed it and wanted to gain experience. "I must have rung up every school in Brisbane offering my services at no charge."[895] Most turned him down, but he didn't give up. His tolerance for frustration proved to be a great asset. In fact, this quality is one of the most important in life: Don't give up, even when things get tough. When you hear one no, ten no's, or even 100 no's, keep going anyway. Nick kept going. And he didn't give up even when a speech went wrong, which, early in his career, happened on more than one occasion.

During an appearance at a school in Brisbane, he got distracted and started badly. He was sweating through his shirt and kept repeating himself. "I wanted to crawl off in a hole and never be seen again. I did so poorly I thought word would spread and I'd never be asked to speak in public for the rest of my life."[896]

But even after this experience, he did not give up. He honed his presentation and delivery, gaining confidence the more often he spoke in public. He learned that he had a unique gift: his expressive eyes and face. He was unable to gesture with his hands, as other public speakers commonly do. Therefore, he increasingly used his facial expressions and his eyes to captivate his audiences.

Today, Nick Vujicic inspires thousands or even tens of thousands of people, but the beginnings of his speaking career were very difficult, as he candidly explains. In the beginning, he says, he made the mistake of putting himself in front of a large audience before he was ready: "...before I'd really prepared for such a thing. It wasn't that I had nothing to say, I just hadn't organized my material or honed my presentation...I stuttered and stammered through that speech...But I learned from the experience, recovered, and realized that I should seize only those moments that I am fully prepared to handle."[897]

His father initially objected when Nick first declared that he wanted to become a professional speaker. Boris was an accountant and wanted his son to follow in his footsteps. Nick went along with his father's plan and graduated from college with a degree in accounting and financial planning.[898] But he didn't give up on his original plan to become a world-renowned speaker. And he got better and better. But he realized that Australia was not the right base for his ambitious goal of developing a worldwide audience for his speaking career. "But Down Under was too remote a launching pad and didn't offer the options and the exposure that I've found in the United Sates."[899]

When he told his parents and friends about his decision to become a motivational speaker, they were more than skeptical. His parents had concerns about his health. "I respected my parents' concerns, but I felt God was calling me to be an evangelist. My mission then was to be obedient and patient and pray that they'd come to feel the same way. By God's grace, not only my parents but also the church accepted my calling."[900] In 2008, at the age of 26, he was officially ordained as a missionary pastor.

Christianity had always played a major role in his life, as he had grown up in a very Christian home; his father was a lay preacher. But for a long time, he had struggled with God. What kind of God was this who had made him without arms and legs? If God really loved him like all the other children, why didn't He give Nick arms and legs? Why did He make Nick so different from other children? As a child, he had prayed many nights that the good Lord would give him arms and legs; after falling asleep, he dreamed that he would wake up with arms and legs – or at least with an arm or a leg. "When they did not appear, I grew angry with God."[901]

The turning point came when he discovered that he could be an accomplished public speaker. He now felt God's love; indeed, that God had a plan for him, a special mission. He had never completely given up hope of God someday miraculously giving him arms and legs; in his talks he even confessed that he had a pair of shoes waiting at home. But he now began to see his missing limbs as an advantage: "Men, women, and children who can't speak my language only have to see me to know that I have overcome many challenges. My lessons, they know, did not come easily."[902] A friend once told him, "Nick, if you'd been born with arms and legs, I don't think you would be as successful as you will become without them one day. How many kids would listen to you if they couldn't see right away that you have turned what should have been an incredible negative into something so positive?"[903]

The title of the first chapter of his autobiography is "If You Can't Get a Miracle, Become One." Nick had a revelation that God wanted him to give hope and encouragement to other people who lived in bleak situations. "My joy would be to encourage and inspire others. Even if I didn't change this planet as much as I would like, I'd still know with certainty that my life was not wasted."[904]

From then on, this was the message he proclaimed in his speeches: If God can use someone without arms and legs, then He can use you, too. Vujicic had realized that concentrating only on his own problems was no good to himself or anyone else. The moment he started to see his task in helping other people, giving them strength and hope with his speeches, he felt better. He met people on his tours who had been desperate and to whom he had given hope. For example, he met a woman in Indonesia – a country where Vujicic is very well known. The woman, who worked 14 hours a day and was still destitute, had been contemplating suicide, but found new hope when she saw one of Nick Vujicic's DVDs. He got to know the woman personally, and later she went to college and became the director of youth ministry for one of Indonesia's largest churches.[905]

The more often he had the experience of helping other people, the more he was able to see the positive side of his disability. In 2009, he got a role in the short film *The Butterfly Circus*. Many millions of people watched the film online and Vujicic received the award for best actor at the Method Fest Independent Film Festival in California.

One of his biggest worries had always been that he would never find a wife. In his school days, he recalls, "I tended to like the same pretty girls as all the other guys."[906] But the girls told him they couldn't imagine anything more than friendship. He had his first serious girlfriend at the age of 19. He met her at a youth camp in the USA. But the girl's father made it clear that he wasn't on board with their relationship.[907] It took Vujicic years to come to terms with the break-up.

In 2010, at the age of 28, he met Kanae Miyahra.[908] That April, he had spoken in McKinney, a suburb of Dallas, and could hardly concentrate on his text because he was captivated by a beautiful girl in the audience. Kanae and her older sister Yoshie had come to hear him speak with a friend who knew Vujicic. After the lecture, Vujicic spoke with her briefly and offered her his email address. However, she said that they could stay in touch through their mutual acquaintance. For months, he waited in vain to hear from her.

Then he found out that his dream girl had a steady boyfriend and was completely distraught. Eventually Kanae broke up with her boyfriend, she and Nick became a couple and got married. At first glance, their story sounds no different to that of many other couples around the world. And yet it is different. Because Nick, given his lack of arms and legs, had doubted whether he would ever find his soulmate. Now, here he was, married to a truly beautiful woman, the daughter of a Japanese father and a Mexican mother.[909] Anyone who sees a photo of the happy couple cannot fail to be struck by Kanae's beauty. In every other respect, too, she matched his idea of a dream woman. Years earlier, he had made a list of ten points that he wanted in his dream woman – and she really fulfilled every single one of them.

His parents were very protective of their son, especially as he had been disappointed many times before. His father found fault with every acquaintance he made. "Whenever I talked to my father about girls I was interested in or showed him their photograph, he would express negative opinions about them."[910] After Kanae's first long conversation with his parents, she described it as an "interrogation."[911] His father admitted that they had "asked Kanae many probing questions."[912] And his mother asked her if she was really aware of the impact the disability had on his daily life, including help with eating as well as going to the bathroom. Kanae convinced Nick's parents that she was the right woman for their son. The two married in 2012.

Some readers may think that this is the classic story of a beautiful woman who is attracted to a successful man. And that might not be entirely wrong, because without his fame and success, their relationship probably wouldn't have happened. On the contrary, Vujicic was not at all rich at the time – in fact, he was experiencing serious financial difficulties, which he overcame only with the support of his father. In February 2013, Vujicic and Kanae had their first child, and two years later their second. Then, in August 2017, they had twins, completing their family of two boys and two girls.

Professionally, Vujicic has two major roles. He heads *Life Without Limbs*, a non-profit organization that coordinates charitable and spiritual engagement, and the motivational company *Attitude is Altitude*, which handles his corporate and educational speaking engagements.[913] Vujicic describes himself as working both sides of the fence. "Many have heard me speak about spiritual matters in churches, where I also make altar calls in my mission to bring as many people to God as I can. Yet even more people around the world know me as an inspirational speaker to secular audiences in schools, national education systems, corporations, business leadership conferences, and government agencies."[914]

He had already worked out and written down his strategy in 2002. It was clear to him that he could not achieve his goals only on faith-based platforms. "You can't save the lost by looking for them inside churches," he says.[915] Time and time again, he says, his corporate clients ask him to keep the spiritual content of his talks to a minimum or to nothing at all. Vujicic is always willing to appear in secular contexts, "...where I may not be able to preach but where I still can plant seeds of love and hope."[916]

Vujicic's advice to everyone is to think about the kind of person they want to be as they age and the kind of life they want to look back on, so that each step of their journey brings them closer to their destination. "I believe if you create the life you want in your imagination, it is possible to create it in reality minute by minute, hour by hour, and day by day."[917]

As Vujicic's father writes in his impressive book *Raising the Perfectly Imperfect Child*: "None of us are limited by our circumstances and...all of us can create meaningful, fulfilling, and joyful lives if we choose to focus on our gifts rather than on what we may lack."[918]

Felix Klieser: "Of course, I could have wasted my energy on feeling sorry for myself and telling the world how mean everything is. But anyone who has ever done that quickly realizes that it doesn't achieve anything."

Credits: Hasko Witte

# 20. Felix Klieser
## The horn player without arms

He was not even 30 years old by the time he had written his autobiography, recorded four CDs, and won numerous awards, including the ECHO Classic Award for the Young Artist of the Year in 2014. Born in 1991, this German horn player has performed with the British pop star Sting and given concerts across Europe, Asia, and the United States. Today, he is regarded as one of the very best horn players in the world.

There is probably one question Felix Klieser has been asked more than any other: How did he come to play the horn in the first place? His answer is not an artfully embellished anecdote, it is a simple "I just don't know."[919] Nevertheless, one thing he and his parents do know is that he first expressed a strong desire to play the horn when he was four years old. And his parents did everything they could to fulfil his wish.

It was an unusual desire because playing the horn normally requires two hands and Felix Klieser was born without arms. Yet even for someone with arms, the horn is a particularly difficult and highly sensitive instrument. Some say it is almost impossible to ever learn to play the instrument flawlessly. In one interview, Klieser explained: "Maybe I chose the horn because I thought: If I can do this, I can do anything."[920]

Klieser is one of those people who wants more from life than an average existence and a run-of-the-mill job. "I have always felt this massive urge to be the best," he confesses in his autobiography, which he published at the age of 23. He adds, "And when I am, I want to be a better best. I don't focus on my successes or strengths; I always look at the things that haven't turned out as I wanted them to."[921]

There are people who settle for being "satisfied." Successful people, however, are driven from one success to the next by a productive dissatisfaction that keeps them moving forward. Klieser is definitely one such person. He writes that he doesn't "strive for satisfaction. My need is to achieve what I want—even if I cannot always put my ideas into practice."[922] But that doesn't bother him. Music, he explains, is a bit like mathematics: "I use the math metaphor to describe an approximation, a striving towards infinity. And the first day I'm satisfied with myself will be the first day I stop being good."[923]

From the moment Felix was born, his mother lived by one credo: unconditional support. He never once heard her say "You can't do that" or "That's impossible." And when, at the age of four, he told his mother that he really wanted to learn to play the horn, she picked up the phone and made an appointment with their local music school. At such a young age, no child has the lung capacity or musculature to play the instrument properly. But at least, he was told, he could practice for five minutes a day. Unlike the flute, for example, the horn is not simply played by blowing into a mouthpiece; a hornist has to makes their lips vibrate and it is this vibration that is amplified and enhanced by the instrument. The horn player's art is in using muscular tension to hit just the right note among all the possible tones.

He is often asked how it is even possible for someone to learn to play the horn with their feet. His response is that he has never actually asked himself this question. "I don't usually think about arms."[924] Klieser has never had arms, which means that he naturally uses his feet to do the things other people do with their hands:

eating, writing, brushing his teeth, using his smartphone, and even driving a car. And, of course, playing the horn. He has never talked to his horn teacher about playing with his feet instead of his hands. His toes grip the horn's valves at shoulder height, while his heel rests on the stand and his left leg forms a right angle. He only uses his right foot now and then to move the mute into position. "For other people, this posture would be a major physical feat; for me, it's nothing more than well-developed dexterity."[925]

After his first public performance at the age of six, his audience responded with enthusiastic applause. Their obvious appreciation of his skills did him a lot of good. And he was determined that his first taste of success should not be his last. At the age of ten, he entered *Jugend Musiziert*, a competition for young musicians, and promptly won first prize in his age group at his very first attempt. After the competition, he was approached by the head of horn classes at Hanover's University for Music and Theater, who invited Felix to contact him if he ever needed advice or help. At first, the boy did not take up this generous offer. Three years later, however, he did remember the professor and contacted him. Felix was invited for a trial lesson, which went so well that he was immediately accepted for horn lessons, which would run parallel to his normal grammar school education.

He experienced his first tastes of success and was even featured in a number of newspaper articles. At the age of 16 he gave an interview, accompanied by his music teacher. The journalist asked if Felix could imagine a career as a horn player. Felix offered an evasive answer, but his teacher said: "From my point of view, it will be nothing more than a hobby."[926] The ambitious student didn't let on, but his teacher's words stung him deeply.

At that moment, he was worried that the journalist might include his teacher's comments in the article and inadvertently destroy any chances of the professional career Klieser was secretly striving for. Fortunately, the journalist did not refer to the teacher's comments. Other people might have been immeasurably frustrated and discouraged by such an assessment. They may even have given up entirely. The extent to which his teacher's throwaway remark had affected him is evident from the fact that he still brings it up in interviews ten years later. But for Klieser, this was no reason to abandon his secret dreams.

Klieser had other ideas, although he did realize that his teacher had been partially correct, because there was one important horn playing technique that Felix could never use because of his missing arms. Yes, he could play with his feet, but without hands he could never do what horn players call 'hand plugging,' which involves stopping the horn's bell with their right hand in order to create pitch variances that are not present in the instrument's natural tone series.

It was the fact that Klieser was unable to 'plug' because of his lack of arms that led to his teacher skeptically remarking that he would only ever be able to play the horn as a hobby, not professionally. "When something gets in my way or I notice that a plan doesn't work out, I withdraw completely. Not out of resignation, though, but out of aggression. I fight and struggle and grit my teeth."[927] Klieser, unlike most people would have done, did not give up. He was "driven by a kind of aggressiveness, by the unconditional will to wrestle the problem to its knees."[928] He didn't talk to anyone about it, not even his teacher. But he began to experiment.

This attitude is characteristic of all successful people. Perseverance is an important quality, but it only leads to success if it is paired with a willingness to experiment. No one who persistently does the same thing over and over again will succeed. Conversely, we know that successful people—whether athletes, musicians or businesspeople—practice and experiment, finely honing certain aspects of their performance over and over again.

"Finding the right sound was actually the greatest challenge," Klieser confessed in an interview in 2019. And it was something he worked on for many years. At first, he said, his sound was too high, almost like a trumpet. "But I wanted to sound like everyone else and I had to work on that. Honestly, I've been working on it for 20 years and I'm still nowhere near done. What audiences see at my concerts, how I play the horn and press the keys with my toes, I never had to practice that. That has always worked and is simply the right way for me. But the part that the audience doesn't see, the part they only hear, that's what I've had to work really hard on."[929]

For Klieser, trial and error meant playing a few notes and changing the position of his teeth, jaw and tongue in ever new variations and listening to how each sounded. Since he could not 'plug' with one hand, he had no choice but to regulate the pitch solely through his mouth and blowing technique.[930]

Klieser steadily improved and developed his own style. He played pieces by Richard Strauss, Ludwig van Beethoven, Michael and Joseph Haydn, Johannes Brahms, and Wolfgang Amadeus Mozart. After winning another competition, he was invited to join the acclaimed Federal Youth Orchestra in 2008, at the age of 17. Although he was still at school, he now spent most of the year touring Germany and abroad. Klieser had invitations from the Minister of Family Affairs and the Federal President, which he presented to his school principal, requesting that he be exempted from school as a member of the Federal Youth Orchestra.

Klieser only attended two months of his final year at school—
the rest of the time he spent on tour in Germany and overseas.
Klieser had set himself a goal—and put everything else on the back-
burner in order to achieve it: "For example, from tenth grade on, I
decided not to do any more homework. I wanted to invest the limited time I had outside school in the horn. I made a lot of decisions
like that as a teenager. Many people, especially the teachers, just
shook their heads in disbelief. Looking back, people would probably have said that I was completely insane. Or asked, 'Whatever will
become of him?' But today I know that if I had listened to those
people back then, I would certainly never have become what I am
today. And I am convinced that there is a fascination in all of us that
we just have to discover. The only option we have is to set ourselves
a goal and pursue it."[931] Focus is one of the most important factors
of all if you want to achieve something extraordinary in life.

Klieser noticed that his mindset changed completely: In his
new world, the only thing that counted was what happened on
stage. The audience and critics didn't care how hard or long he had
practiced. At school, however, his teachers were indeed skeptical as
to whether he had been putting in enough hours—even if he performed quite well in his exams. Balancing grammar school, music
lessons and concerts was a punishing burden. So, when he finally
left school and started university full-time, it is not surprising to
hear him describe the change as "hugely liberating."[932]

While he was at school, he had already worked with the Finn-
ish horn teacher, Professor Markus Maskuniitty. Klieser loved the
fact that that the professor gave him the freedom he needed to develop his own style. Some teachers train their students to be nothing
more than imitators. Maskuniitty, however, allowed his students a
greater degree of independence—and that suited Klieser down to
the ground. For Klieser, a teacher should be a sparring partner, a

source of inspiration and ideas that he would never have come up with on his own. Once the ideas are there, Klieser decides for himself whether to implement them or not. On the one hand, Klieser is open to new ideas: he listens to what conductors, colleagues, teachers and critics have to say. On the other, he alone decides which suggestions to take on board and which to reject. From his point of view, developing his own sound was the biggest challenge he ever faced: "You have to develop from a young person, someone who is told what to do and what not to do by everyone around them, into a person in your own right, someone with an opinion of their own. An opinion and, if possible, a style of their own."[933]

Developing this musical autonomy once again spurred on his already enormous ambition. Klieser says he has never been driven by external influences or circumstances. His ambition grew the more he developed his own personality.[934] In his book, he describes himself as a perfectionist. Depending on how you look at it, he has chosen either the best or the worst profession. After all, the chance of making a mistake is particularly high when playing the horn. "Every horn player makes mistakes and lets out the odd squeak during a concert. Anyone who chooses this instrument has to learn to deal with it and not let it drive them crazy." According to Klieser, no one plays the horn perfectly. It is an instrument that requires strong nerves, he explains, and as soon as you succumb to the fear of playing a wrong note, everyone in the hall will be able to tell.[935]

For a self-confessed perfectionist, this is of course a tremendous challenge. The first chapter in his autobiography is called "The Pursuit of Perfection." However, he is not quite so happy with the term today. "Perfectionism," he says in our interview, is linked to exaggerated expectations, "and we often fall short of those." He prefers the term "patient perseverance" and emphasizes the importance of a certain amount of patience. "Success is not a 100-meter sprint, it is a marathon with many ups and downs. If you don't understand that, there's no point in even starting the race."[936]

Klieser is also right when he says: "If you take a look at the biographies of people who have achieved something special in life—and I don't necessarily mean musicians, but also athletes and entrepreneurs—you will notice that they have done absolutely everything in their power to reach their goal...If you really want to achieve something, you have to work harder. Push yourself and your performance to the absolute limit. Think more. Do more. Push yourself harder, push yourself further. So far, that you can't do anymore."[937]

Talent, he says, is secondary and accounts for at most 30 to 40 percent of success. As he sees things, it is far more important to have a strong will to succeed and the right attitude. Talent is "simply there to ensure that if you work hard, it will pay off at some point. Hard work and perseverance are the most important factors."[938] That's why you can't just say you've played a particular piece a certain number of times, so "now I'll put it in the corner and won't have to look at it again." You always have to keep at it, practice every day—and never allow yourself any major breaks.[939]

So, does Klieser have any interests or passions besides the horn? In his book he writes that the life of a professional musician does not leave much time for anything else. He is either practicing, traveling, or playing in concerts. "There's not really much space in between. So, it's lucky that I'm so passionate about practicing, incredibly fond of travelling to new countries and, most of all, love playing concerts."[940]

He says that he always practices whenever he has some time off or nothing else to do, even if it's just for a couple of hours. He even practices in hotel rooms. But what if the people in the next room complain? Well, if he is asked to stop after five minutes, as far as he is concerned, he at least managed to squeeze in five minutes of practice. He often tries half an hour later, at least until someone tells him to stop again. "But I am very flexible. I even take the horn with me to the restroom when I have to."[941]

His attitude may seem strange, even off-putting, to other people—but it is no more than an expression of his "desire to become better."[942] Klieser admits that other music professionals—such as a sound engineer he worked on a CD with—sometimes find it hard to comprehend his all-consuming dedication: "If perfectionism is the line musicians walk between healthy passion and pathological compulsion, then maybe I already have one foot on the pathological side. I just can't help it, and I always feel that way, even during rehearsals."[943]

His perfectionism also includes striving to keep his body "under complete control," because that is the prerequisite for his profession. Outsiders may not fully appreciate it, but playing the horn is all about muscle work. The muscles in his upper body, which support the flow of air when he plays, combined with his facial muscles, have to "literally play along and manage even mammoth tasks like the second horn concerto by Richard Strauss—and do so seemingly effortlessly...If my body can't do something, I trim and bend it until it's where I want it to be." He loves to be in control, to prove himself in things that can be measured in some way—be it with the horn or in sports.[944]

In general, he lives his life in much the same way as a competitive athlete, including strict dietary discipline. It all starts with his breakfast. He can't eat kiwis because their acidity disrupts the receptors in his oral cavity and plays havoc with his physical sensations. "Most people don't mind the slight tingle on the tongue after a piece of pineapple, but it makes me feel incredibly uncomfortable—playing the horn afterwards is like going jogging with vertigo."[945] Alcohol doesn't really play well with his need for absolute control either—so he never takes a sip.

What can we learn from Klieser's path to success? One thing above all: that everything boils down to setting goals for your life. Many people either fail to set themselves goals, or they set goals that are nowhere near ambitious enough. In an interview, Klieser once said: "I think the problem is quite often that people lack a vision of the future...One of the most important things is to give people hope and show them a perspective and say: You can change and achieve a lot if only you believe in it and want it."[946]

He also understands how the media works. Of course, it sometimes annoys him when people spend so much time asking him about his disability, but he also understands: "That's less due to the disability itself than to the fact that it makes me so interesting. If I came from China, I would be the Chinese horn player Felix Klieser."[947] He became a polished media performer at a very young age. He comes across as casual and natural, nowhere near as aloof as some other classical musicians. On one occasion, he was interviewed after a concert and his interviewer said: "Yes, Mr. Klieser, you play the horn with your feet because you were born without arms..." Klieser leaned in close to the microphone and whispered conspiratorially, "...well I certainly wouldn't be doing that if I had been born with arms." He had the laughs on his side.[948]

He is also critical of the fact that many people with disabilities "reduce themselves to their disabilities to a far greater extent than the world around them does." For example, he does not think much of support groups for people with disabilities or self-help groups where people with disabilities talk about little but their disabilities.

"In my opinion, that's like ten women getting together to philosophize about having large busts. It doesn't change anything. Neither in their lives nor in the way other people see or perceive them."[949]

Just like all successful people, Klieser sees himself as a shaper of his own destiny—and not as a victim of adverse circumstances: "Of course, I could have wasted my energy on feeling sorry for myself and telling the world how mean everything is. But anyone who has ever done that quickly realizes that it doesn't achieve anything. Each of us has strengths and weaknesses. With some people, you see them immediately. With others, they are not quite so obvious. But that does not mean they are not there. We all have to come to terms with our weaknesses and make the best of them."[950]

In retrospect, he sacrificed almost every aspect of a normal teenager's life for his music: wild parties, getting tipsy with his friends, hanging out at the open-air swimming pool. He gave up these things for his passion—without knowing whether it would ever pay off. It was only later in life that he realized the risk he had taken. "My musical blinkers were actually the best thing that could have happened to me, because they pushed me forward without considering the risks and side effects. In any case, I didn't miss anything in my youth—I just wanted to play the horn to the best of my ability."[951]

Klieser is still on the road to success. Most recently, he recorded all four of Mozart's horn concertos with the Camerata Salzburg, one of the world's leading chamber orchestras. He spent four months in the top 10 of the classical music charts. And he continues to win awards, such as the Schleswig-Holstein Music Festival's Leonard Bernstein Award and the Usedom Music Festival prize. And Klieser is still young, so he has a lot ahead of him. What goals has he set for himself? "I have already more than achieved everything you can achieve with the horn," he says during our interview.

"But that doesn't mean I don't have other goals. In the future, I would also like to move into areas that don't necessarily have anything to do with music. For example, I am very interested in the topic of motivation. What drives people? Why do some people manage to achieve one goal after another, while others sit at their breakfast table every morning and just feel sorry for themselves?"[952]

# The Author

Rainer Zitelmann was born in Frankfurt am Main, Germany, in 1957. He studied history and political science from 1978 to 1983 and graduated with distinction. In 1986, he was awarded the title Dr. Phil for his thesis *Hitler. Selbstverständnis eines Revolutionärs* (English: *Hitler's National Socialism*) under the mentorship of Professor Freiherr von Aretin. The study, which was awarded the grade "summa cum laude," received worldwide attention and recognition.

From 1987 to 1992, Zitelmann worked at the Central Institute for Social Science Research at the Free University of Berlin. He then became editor-in-chief of Ullstein-Propyläen publishing house, at that time Germany's third-largest book publishing group and headed various departments of the leading German daily newspaper *Die Welt*. In 2000, he set up his own business, Dr. ZitelmannPB, GmbH, which has since become the market leader for positioning consulting for real estate companies in Germany. He sold the business in 2016.

In 2016, Zitelmann was awarded his second doctorate, this time in sociology, with his thesis on the psychology of the super-rich, under the mentorship of Professor Wolfgang Lauterbach at the University of Potsdam. His second doctoral dissertation was published in English as *The Wealth Elite*, as well as being published in China, South Korea and Vietnam.

Zitelmann has written and edited a total of 27 books, which have enjoyed substantial success in 30 languages around the world. He is a much sought-after guest speaker in Asia, the United States, South America and Europe. Over the last few years, he has written articles and given interviews to many of the world's leading media outlets, including *The Wall Street Journal, Newsweek, Forbes, The Daily Telegraph, The Times, Le Monde, Corriere de la Serra, Frankfurter Allgemeine Zeitung, Neue Zürcher Zeitung,* and numerous media in Latin America and Asia. Readers of this book are especially recommended to read his book *Dare to be Different and Grow Rich.* Detailed information about the life of Rainer Zitelmann can be found at rainer-zitelmann.com.

# Notes

# Bibliography

Beethoven, Ludwig van, *Beethoven's Letters*, J.M. Dent. London. 1909.

Berg, Marita. "Quasthoff nimmt Abschied." *DW*. January 27, 2012. https://www.dw.com/de/quasthoff-nimmt-abschied/a-15688214

Bernau, Patrick. Interview with John Forbes Nash, Jr. "Die Menschen sind nicht immer rational."(Original interview from 2010). In *Frankfurter Allgemeine Zeitung*. May 25, 2015.

Blochwitz, Peter. Interview with Felix Klieser, "Aber ich wollte eben unbedingt..." *Lausitzer Rundschau*. March 20, 2017.

Bocelli, Andrea. *The Music of Silence*. Virgin Publishing. London. 2000.

Bodley, Lorraine Byrne. *Goethe and Zelter: Musical Dialogues*. Ashgate Publishing Company. Burlington, VT. 2009.

Brown, Christy. *My Left Foot*. BBC Audiobooks Ltd. Bath, England. 2003.

Brown, Christy. *Down All the Days*. Minerva. London, England. 1990.

Buhre, Jakob. "Andrea Bocelli, Das Publikum spürt, ob ein Künstler echt ist." *Planet Interview*, January 4, 2009. https://www.planet-interview.de/interviews/andrea-bocelli/34806/

Cabruja, Miquel. Interview with Felix Klieser. "Klang hat sehr viel mit Vorstellung zu tun." *Klassik.com*. September 2013. https://por-traits.klassik.com/people/interview.cfm?KID=17036

Caeyers, Jan. *Beethoven. A Life.* University of California Press. Oak-land, CA. 2020.

Charles, Ray; Ritz, David. *Brother Ray. Ray Charles' Own Story.* Da Capo Press. Cambridge, MA. 2004.

Clemenz, Manfred, *Van Gogh. Manie und Melancholie. Ein Porträt.* Böhlau Verlag. Vienna, Cologne, Weimar. 2020.

Colvin, Geoff. *Talent is Overrated. What Really Separates World-Class Performers from Everybody Else. Revised Edition.* Portfolio/Penguin. New York, NY. 2018.

Davies, Peter J. *Beethoven in Person. His Deafness, Illnesses, and Death.* Greenwood Press. Westport, CT. 2001.

Davis, Sharon. *Stevie Wonder. Rhythms of Wonder.* Robson Books. London. 2003.

Felix, Antonia. *Andrea Bocelli. A Celebration.* St. Martin's Press. New York, NY. 2000.

Fox, Michael J. *Lucky Man. A Memoir.* Ebury Press. London. 2003.

Fox, Michael J. *Always Looking Up. The Adventures of an Incurable Optimist.* Hyperion. New York, NY. 2010.

Fox, Michael J. *No Time Like the Future. An Optimist Considers Mor-tality.* Flatiron Books. New York, NY. 2020.

Genschow, Karen. *Frida Kahlo. Leben, Werk, Wirkung.* Second Edi-tion. Suhrkamp Verlag. Frankfurt/Main. 2018.

Halbe-Bauer, Ulrike. *Margarete Steiff. "Ich gebe was ich kann."* Brunnen Verlag. Gießen. 2007.

Hambleton, Georgina Louise. *Christy Brown. The Life that Inspired My Left Foot.* Mainstream Publishing Company. Edinburgh. 2007.

Harrity, Richard; Martin, Ralph G. *The Three Lives of Helen Keller.* Doubleday & Company, Inc. Garden City, NY. 1962.

Hasselbeck, Kathrin. Interview mit Felix Klieser. "Musik soll das Leben verschönern." *Bayerischer Rundfunk Klassik.* December 15, 2017. https://www.br-klassik.de/aktuell/news-kritik/felix-klieser-hornist-sternstunden-gala-interview-100.html

Hawking, Stephen. *Brief Answers to the Big Questions.* John Murray. London. 2018.

Hawking, Stephen. *My Brief History.* Bantam Books. New York, NY. 2013.

Hawking, Jane. *Travelling to Infinity: My Life with Stephen.* Alma Books. Richmond, UK. 2014.

Henke, Matthias. *Beethoven. Akkord der Welt. Biografie.* Carl Hanser Verlag. Munich. 2020.

Heringlehner, Ralph. "Thomas Quasthoff über Bildungsbürger, Kritiker und Behinderungen." *Mainpost.* March 10, 2015. https://www.mainpost.de/ueberregional/kulturwelt/kultur/thomas-quasthoff-ueber-bildungsbuerger-kritiker-und-behinderungen-art-8616066

Herpell, Werner. "Jazz statt Klassik: Thomas Quasthoff will konsequent bleiben." *Neue Musikzeitung.* May 15, 2018. https://www.nmz.de/kiz/nachrichten/jazz-statt-klassik-saenger-quasthoff-will-konsequent-bleiben

Herrera, Hayden. *Frida. A Biography of Frida Kahlo.* Harper Collins. New York, NY. 2002.

Hill, Napoleon. *Think and Grow Rich: Instant Aid to Riches—New and Revised Edition.* Wilshire Book Co. New York, NY. 1966.

Holman, James. *The Narrative of a Journey Undertaken in the Years 1819, 1820 and 1821 Through France, Italy, Savoy, Switzerland, Parts of Germany Bordering on the Rhine, Holland and the Netherlands.* G. B. Whitaker. London. 1825.

Holman, James. *Travels Through Russia, Siberia, Poland, Austria, Prussia. Undertaken During 1822, 1823, and 1824, While Suffering From Total Blindness, Volume 1.* London 1825.

Holman, James. *Voyage Round the World, Including Travels in Africa, Asia, Australasia, America, Etc. Etc. Volume I.* Smith, Elder, And Co. London. 1834.

Holman, James. *Voyage Round the World, Including Travels in Africa, Asia, Australasia, America, Etc. Etc. Volume IV.* Smith, Elder, And Co. London. 1834.

Holstein, Philipp. Interview with Thomas Quasthoff. "Ich kann nicht so gut singen wie Pink." *RP Online.* May 1, 2013. https://rp-online.de/nrw/staedte/duesseldorf/kultur/ich-kann-nicht-so-gut-singen-wie-pink_aid-15654667

Jerdan, William. *Men I Have Known.* George Routledge and Sons. London. 1866.

Kahawatte, Saliya. *Mein Blind Date mit dem Leben. Als Blinder unter Sehenden. Eine wahre Geschichte.* Bastei Lübbe. Cologne. 2017.

Kahlo, Frida. *Escrituras.* Plaza y Janés. Mexico City, Mexico. 2004.

Khan, Oliver. *Ich. Erfolg kommt von innen.* riva Verlag. Munich. 2008.

Kaminsky, Anna. "Beinahe blind machte Johann König seinen Weg als Galerist." *Neue Zürcher Zeitung am Sonntag.* October 16, 2020. https://nzzas.nzz.ch/magazin/johann-koenig-will-eine-architek-turikone-in-berlin-retten-ld.1581794?reduced=true

Katz, Gabriele. *Margarete Steiff. Die Biografie. New and Revised Edition.* Lauinger Verlag, Der Kleine Buch Verlag. Karlsruhe. 2018.

Keller, Helen. *Optimism: An Essay.* T. Y. Crowell and Company. New York, NY. 1903.

Keller, Helen. *The Story of My Life.* Grosset and Dunlap. New York, NY. 1905.

Keller, Helen. *The World I Live In.* The Century Co. New York, NY. 1908.

Keller, Helen, *Teacher: Anne Sullivan Macy; A Tribute by the Foster-Child of Her Mind.* Doubleday & Company, Inc. Garden City, NY. 1955.

Kikol, Larissa. "Der ungehorsame Galerist. Ein Interview mit Johann König über seine Biografie *Der blinde Galerist.*" *Kunstforum International Vol. 262.* https://www.kunstforum.de/artikel/der-un-gehorsame-galerist/

Kippenberger, Susanne; Lippitz, Ulf. Interview with Johann König. "Ich hatte vergessen, wie meine Eltern aussahen." *Tagesspiegel*. April 25, 2018. https://www.tagesspiegel.de/gesellschaft/interview-mit-johann-koenig-ich-hatte-vergessen-wie-meine-eltern-aussa-hen/21194796.html

Klieser, Felix (with Céline Lauer). *Fußnoten. Ein Hornist ohne Arme erobert die Welt*. Patmos Verlag der Schwabenverlag AG. Ostfildern. 2014.

Kobel, Stefan. Interview with Johann König. *Artmagazine*. June 15, 2020. https://www.artmagazine.cc/content112236.html

Koch, Peter O. *The Life and Letters of America's First Scientific Historian*. McFarland & Company Publishers. Jefferson, NC. 2016

König, Johann; Daniel Schreiber. *Blinder Galerist*. Propyläen Verlag. Berlin. 2019.

Korff, Malte. *Ludwig van Beethoven*. Suhrkamp Verlag. Berlin. 2010.

Lauer, Céline. "Felix Klieser, der Ausnahme-Hornist ohne Arme." *Die Welt*. December 25, 2011. https://www.welt.de/vermischtes/arti-cle13782411/Felix-Klieser-der-Ausnahme-Hornist-ohne-Arme.html

Levy, Joel. *Hawking: The Man, the Genius, and the Theory of Everything*. André Deutsch. London. 2018.

Limitless Pursuits, Marla Runyan: America's Inspirational Runner. June 11, 2015.

Locke, Edwin A.; Latham, Gary P. (eds.) A Theory of Goal-Setting & Task Performance. Prentice Hall. Englewood Cliffs, NJ. 1990.

Lubow, Arthur. *A Transcendent Voice. The New York Times Magazine.* October 1, 2006. https://www.nytimes.com/2006/10/01/magazine/01quasthoff.html

Lydon, Michael. *Ray Charles. Man and Music.* Riverhead Books. New York, NY. 1998.

Maddocks, Fiona. "Thomas Quasthoff Speaks Very Frankly." *London Evening Standard.* February 25, 2005.

Marnham, Patrick. *Dreaming with His Eyes Open: A Life of Diego Rivera.* Alfred A. Knopf, Inc. New York, NY.1998.

Naifeh, Steven; Smith, Gregory White. *Van Gogh: The Life.* Random House. London. 2012.

Nasar, Sylvia. *A Beautiful Mind. The Life of Mathematical Genius and Nobel Laureate John Nash.* Simon & Schuster. New York, NY. 2001.

Parsons, Paul; Dixon. Gail. *3-Minute Stephen Hawking: His Life, Theories and Influence in 3-Minute Particles.* Metro Books. New York, NY. 2012.

*PBS.* "A Brilliant Madness. An Interview with John Nash." April 28, 2002. https://www.pbs.org/wgbh/americanexperience/features/nash-interview/

Peck, Harry Thurston. *English Men of Letters. William Hickling Prescott.* Columbia University. New York, NY. 1905.

Pfeiffer, Günther. *125 Jahre Steiff Firmengeschichte.* Heel Verlag. Königswinter. 2005.

Plag, Celina. "Johann König. Deutschlands modischster Galerist." *FAZ,* October 13, 2018. https://www.faz.net/aktuell/stil/mode-design/johann-koenig-deutschlands-modischster-galerist-15836261.html

Prescott, William Hickling. *The Conquest of Mexico, The Seven Book History of Hernan Cortes, Mayan and Mexican Civilization Complete in One Volume*. Adansonia Press. First published in 1843.

Prescott, William Hickling. *Die Eroberung Perus. Mit 20 Indianischen Abbildungen*. Dietrich'sche Verlagsbuchhandlung. Leipzig. 1975.

Quasthoff, Michael. *Thomas Quasthoff. Der Bariton*. Henschel Verlag. Berlin. 2006.

Quasthoff, Thomas. *The Voice*. Pantheon Books. New York, NY. 2008.

Ribowsky, Mark. *Signed, Sealed, and Delivered: The Soulful Journey of Stevie Wonder*. John Wiley & Sons. Hoboken, NJ. 2010.

Rieck, Christian. *Spieltheorie. Eine Einführung*. Christian Roeck Verlag. Friedrichsdorf. 2019.

Roberts, Jason. *A Sense of the World. How a Blind Man Became History's Greatest Traveller*. Simon & Schuster. London. 2006.

Rüth, Steffen. Interview with Thomas Quasthoff. "Der Jazz ist jetzt meine Welt." *Augsburger Allgemeine*, May 8, 2018. https://www.augsburger-allgemeine.de/kultur/Thomas-Quasthoff-Der-Jazz-ist-jetzt-meine-Welt-id51053181.html

Runyan, Marla (with Sally Jenkins). *No Finish Line*. G. P. Putnam's Sons. New York, NY. 2001.

Schär, Florian. "Felix Klieser im Interview." *Classicpoint.net. Das Klassikportal*, June 1, 2019. https://www.classicpoint.net/de/felix-klieser

Scheu, Renè. An interview with John Forbes Nash, Jr. "Keynesianer lieben Inflation." in *Schweizer Monat 990*. October 2011. https://schweizermonat.ch/keynesianer-lieben-inflation/#

Schneede, Uwe M. *Vincent van Gogh, Third Edition*. C.H. Beck Verlag. Munich. 2020.

Schoeck, Helmut. Envy. *A Theory of Social Behaviour*. Liberty Fund. Indianapolis, IN. 1966.

Siegfried, Tom. *A Beautiful Math. John Nash, Game Theory and the Modern Quest for a Code of Nature*. Joseph Henry Press. Washington, D.C. 2006.

Skiena, Steven; Ward, Charles B. *Who's Bigger? Where Historical Figures Rank*. Cambridge University Press. New York, NY. 2014.

Solomon, Maynard. *Beethoven*. Schirmer Trade Books, New York, NY. 1998.

Sonnek, O. G. (ed.), *Beethoven: Impressions by His Contemporaries*, Dover Publications. New York, NY. 1967.

Sorge, Helmut. An interview with Erik Weihenmayer. "Ein Blinder auf dem Mount Everest." *Der Spiegel*. December 20, 2001. https://www.spiegel.de/jahreschronik/a-172949.html

Späth, Sebastian. Interview with Johann König. "Das ist scheinheilig." *Wirtschaftswoche*, January 10, 2020. https://www.wiwo.de/my/unternehmen/dienstleister/galerist-johann-koenig-das-ist-scheinheilig/25420472.html?ticket=ST-758813-fBOlaSQllvwyHBvaD-doY-ap2

Spohr, Louis. *Lebenserinnerungen in Zwei Bänden (1860)*. Vol. I. Hans Schneider. Tutzing. 1968.

Stuff, Britta. An interview with John Forbes Nash, Jr. "Manchmal hatte ich Glück." *Die Welt*, February 9, 2010. https://www.welt.de/welt_print/vermischtes/article6311871/Manchmal-hatte-ich-Glueck.html

Tackenberg, Marcus. "Felix Klieser spielt Horn ohne Arme. 'Mein Lehrer hat nicht an mich geglaubt.'" *Neue Osnabrücker Zeitung*, May 2, 2015. https://www.noz.de/deutschland-welt/medien/artikel/571206/mein-lehrer-hat-nicht-an-mich-geglaubt

Thayer, Alexander Wheelock. *Thayer's Life of Beethoven*. Princeton University Press. Princeton, NJ. 1970.

Tibol, Raquel (Hrsg.), Frida Kahlo. *Jetzt, wo du mich verlässt, liebe ich dich mehr denn je. Briefe und andere Schriften*, Schirmer/Mosel Verlag, München 2018.

Ticknor, George. *Life of William Hickling Prescott*. Ticknor and Fields. Boston, MA. 1864.

Timm, Tobias. "Johann König. Der Blick des Blinden." *Die Zeit*. June 6, 2019. https://www.zeit.de/2019/24/johann-koenig-galerist-erfolg-kunstmarkt?utm_referrer=https%3A%2F%2Fwww.google.com%2F

Ullrich, Corinne. "Gefühle sind ja in uns allen." *Die Welt*. February 17, 2006. https://www.welt.de/print-welt/article198607/Gefuehle-sind-ja-in-uns-allen.html

Van Gogh, Vincent, *The Complete Letters of Vincent van Gogh, Volume One*, New York Graphic Society, Greenwich, Connecticut, 1958.

Van Gogh, Vincent, *The Complete Letters of Vincent van Gogh, Volume Two*, New York Graphic Society, Greenwich, Connecticut, 1958.

Van Gogh, Vincent, *The Complete Letters of Vincent van Gogh, Volume Three*, New York Graphic Society, Greenwich, Connecticut, 1958.

Völker-Kraemer, Sabine. *Wie ich zur Teddymutter wurde. Das Leben der Margarete Steiff nach ihren eigenen Aufzeichnungen.* Quell Verlag. Stuttgart. 1996.

Vujicic, Boris. *Raising the Perfectly Imperfect Child.* WaterBrook. Colorado Springs, CO. 2016.

Vujicic, Nick. *Life Without Limits.* Doubleday. New York, NY. 2010.

Vujicic, Nick. *Unstoppable. The Incredible Power of Faith in Action.* WaterBrook. Colorado Springs, CO. 2012.

Vujicic, Nick; Vujicic, Kanae. *Love Without Limits. A Remarkable Story of Love Conquering All.* WaterBrook. 2014.

Vujicic, Nick. *Be the Hands and Feet. Living out God's Love for All His Children.* WaterBrook. Colorado Springs, CO. 2018.

Waite, Helen E. *Valiant Companions: Helen Keller and Anne Sullivan Macy.* Macrae Smith Company. Philadelphia, PA. 1959.

Walton, Sam. *Made in America. My Story.* Doubleday. New York, NY. 1993.

Wegeler, Franz Gerhard; Ries, Ferdinand. *Beethoven Remembered,* translated by Frederick Noonan. Great Ocean Publishers. Arlington, VA. 1987.

Weihenmayer, Erik. *Touch the Top of the World: A Blind Man's Journey to Climb Farther Than the Eye Can See.* Penguin Putnam Inc. New York, NY. 2003.

Weihenmayer, Erik. *No Barriers*. Thomas Dunne Books. New York, NY. 2017.

White, Michael, John Gribbin. *Stephen Hawking. A Life in Science*. Dutton. New York, NY. 1992.

Zitelmann, Rainer. *The Power of Capitalism*. LID Publishing. London. 2018.

Zitelmann, Rainer. *Dare to Be Different and Grow Rich. The Secrets of Self-Made People*. LID Publishing. London. 2020.

Zitelmann, Rainer. *How People Become Famous: Geniuses of Self-Marketing from Albert Einstein to Kim Kardashian*. Management Books 2000. Oxford. 2021.

# Endnotes

## Chapter 1—Beethoven

1 I would like to express my gratitude to the Beethoven biographer Professor Matthias Henke for this and other valuable details.

2 Caeyers, 486.

3 The violinist Joseph Michael Böhm, quoted in Korff, 63.

4 Caeyers, 486.

5 Caeyers, 487.

6 Caeyers, 488.

7 Christian Gottlob Neefe, quoted in Caeyers, 26.

8 Caeyers, 90–91.

9 Caeyers, 106.

10 Caeyers, 108.

11 Beethoven, quoted in Korff, 29.

12 Caeyers, 186.

13 Caeyers, 170.

14 Brandenburg, 6.

15 Wegeler/Ries, 86–87.

16 Helene von Breuning, quoted in Solomon, 58.

17 Goethe, quoted in Bodley, 156.

18 Aloys Weißenbach, quoted in Henke, 89.

19 Beethoven's Letters, 87.

20 Henke, 74

21 Beethoven, "Heiligenstadt Testament," quoted in Thayer, 304.

22 Beethoven, "Heiligenstadt Testament," quoted in Thayer, 305.

23 Zitelmann, Dare to Be Different, 100–105.

24 Caeyers, 176.

25 Caeyers, 170.

26 Caeyers, 171.

27 Hill, 39.

28 Caeyers, 176.

29 Caeyers, 177–178.

30  Rossini, quoted in Beethoven: Impressions, 117.
31  See Davies, Beethoven in Person.
32  Henke, 273.
33  Henke, 274.
34  Caeyers, 184.
35  Caeyers, 181.
36  Caeyers, 185.
37  Korff, 48.
38  Henke, 171.
39  See Caeyers, 331.
40  See Henke, 70.
41  Caeyers, 290.
42  Caeyers, 290.
43  Beethoven, quoted in Caeyers, 298.
44  From the "decree," quoted in Caeyers, 300.
45  Beethoven, quoted in Caeyers, 305.
46  Beethoven, quoted in Caeyers, 369.
47  Louis Spohr: Lebenserinnerungen, in 2 Volumes (1860), Volume I, 180.
48  Caeyers, 494.
49  Allgemeine musikalische Zeitung, quoted in Korff, 86.
50  Caeyers, 495.
51  Grillparzer, quoted in Beethoven: Impressions, 229.

## Chapter 2—Holman

52  Holman, Voyage Round the World, Volume 1, 1–2.
53  Holman, Voyage Round the World, Volume 1, 2.
54  Holman, Voyage Round the World, Volume 4, 515.
55  Jerdan, 262.
56  Roberts, 320.
57  Roberts, 320.
58  Roberts, 37.
59  Roberts, 51.
60  Roberts, 55.
61  Holman, quoted in Roberts, 57.
62  Holman, quoted in Roberts, 66.
63  Holman, quoted in Roberts, 74.
64  Holman, quoted in Roberts, 75.
65  Roberts, 87.
66  Quoted in Roberts, 88.

67    Quoted in Roberts, 108–109.
68    Holman, Travels Through Russia, Volume 1, 2–3.
69    Holman, The narrative of a journey, 45.
70    Holman, Travels Through Russia, 282.
71    Roberts, 151.
72    Quoted in Roberts, 153.
73    Holman, Travels Through Russia, 2.
74    Holman, Travels Through Russia, 3.
75    Holman, quoted in Roberts, 167.
76    Holman, Travels Through Russia, 279–280.
77    Holman, Travels Through Russia, 283.
78    Holman, Travels Through Russia, 330.
79    Holman, Travels Through Russia, 328–329.
80    Holman, Travels Through Russia, 327.
81    Roberts, 189.
82    Holman, Travels Through Russia, 332.
83    Holman, quoted in Roberts, 192.
84    Roberts, 202.
85    Roberts, 203.
86    Holman, quoted in Roberts, 255.
87    Holman, quoted in Roberts, 254.
88    Expert opinion by Peter Mark Roget, quoted in Roberts, 307.
89    Roberts, 307.
90    Roberts, 338.
91    Roberts, 338.
92    Holman, Voyage Round the World, Volume 4, 512.

## Chapter 3—Prescott

93    Ticknor, 335, 356–357.
94    For more on the Noctograph, see page 46.
95    Koch, 23.
96    William Howard Gardiner, quoted in Ticknor, 16.
97    Koch, 81.
98    William Howard Gardiner, quoted in Ticknor, 17–18.
99    Ticknor, 18.
100   Koch, 31.
101   Koch, 35.
102   William Hickling Prescott in a letter to his parents, March 15, 1816, in Ticknor, 38–39.
103   Ticknor, 164, 401

104   William Hickling Prescott, quoted in Koch, 57.
105   William Hickling Prescott, quoted in Koch, 61.
106   Koch, 58.
107   Koch, 58.
108   Koch, 66.
109   Ticknor, 140.
110   William Hickling Prescott, quoted in Ticknor, 140.
111   Ticknor, 142.
112   Koch, 25.
113   Ticknor, 118–119.
114   Koch, 72.
115   Ticknor, 119.
116   Koch, 73, 90.
117   Prescott's father, quoted in Koch, 89.
118   Koch, 100.
119   Prescott, Mexico, V.
120   Prescott, quoted in Koch, 148.
121   Koch, 9–10.
122   Prescott, quoted in Koch, 7.
123   Prescott, Mexico, VII.
124   Letter from Prescott to Irving, December 31, 1838, in Ticknor,
       157.
125   Letter from Irving to Prescott, January 18, 1839, in Ticknor,
       158–159.
126   Prescott, Mexico, VII.
127   Peter Neumann, Afterword in Prescott's Die Eroberung
       Perus, 391–392.
128   Prescott, quoted in Koch, 83.
129   Ticknor, 214–215.
130   Ticknor, 142
131   Ticknor, 235.
132   Koch, 145.
133   Koch, 144.
134   Koch, 145.
135   Koch, 11.
136   Prescott, quoted in Koch, 159.
137   Koch, 120, 149–150.
138   Koch, 150.
139   Koch, 149.
140   Ticknor, 414.
141   Prescott, quoted in Ticknor, 240.

142    Prescott, quoted in Ticknor, 236.
143    Prescott, quoted in Koch, 175.

## Chapter 4—Steiff

144    Quoted in Katz, 58.
145    Diary of Margarete Steiff, quoted in Katz, 32.
146    Katz, 34.
147    Diary of Margarete Steiff, quoted in Katz, 38.
148    Diary of Margarete Steiff, quoted in Katz, 42.
149    Katz, 42.
150    Diary of Margarete Steiff, quoted in Katz, 50.
151    Diary of Margarete Steiff quoted in Katz, 57.
152    Katz, 70.
153    Völcker-Kraemer, 41.
154    Völcker-Kraemer, 50–51.
155    Diary of Margarete Steiff, quoted in Katz, 87.
156    Diary of Margarete Steiff, quoted in Katz, 74.
157    Diary of Margarete Steiff, quoted in Katz, 94.
158    Diary of Margarete Steiff, quoted in Katz, 108.
159    Dairy of Margarete Steiff, quoted in Völcker-Kraemer, 18.
160    Diary of Margarete Steiff, quoted in Katz, 96.
161    Katz, 122.
162    Quoted in Völcker-Kraemer, 52.
163    Völcker-Kraemer, 63.
164    Katz, 137.
165    Pfeiffer, 52–53.
166    Pfeiffer, 60.
167    Katz, 197.
168    Katz, 211.
169    Völcker-Kraemer, 92.
170    Paul Steiff, quoted in Katz, 238.
171    Völcker-Kraemer, 95.
172    Völcker-Kraemer, 96–97.
173    Quoted in Pfeiffer, 80.
174    Pfeiffer, 180–181.
175    Völcker-Kraemer, 89.
176    Quoted in Katz, 249–250.
177    Quoted in Katz, 259–260.
178    Katz, 290–291.
179    Quoted in Katz, 311–312.

## Chapter 5—Van Gogh

180    Van Gogh biographer Manfred Clemenz in a letter to the author, March 3, 2021.
181    Clemenz, 12.
182    Clemenz, 11.
183    Naifeh / Smith, 16.
184    Van Gogh's mother, Dorus, describing her 24-year-old son in a letter, quoted in Naifeh / Smith, 141.
185    Naifeh / Smith, 167.
186    Based on a comprehensive analysis performed by the Google Ranking Team, Skiena / Ward, 294.
187    Quoted in Naifeh / Smith, 37.
188    Quoted in Naifeh / Smith, 38.
189    Naifeh / Smith, 44.
190    Naifeh / Smith, 112.
191    Naifeh / Smith, 108.
192    Naifeh / Smith, 109.
193    Naifeh / Smith, 109.
194    Quoted in Naifeh / Smith, 115.
195    Naifeh / Smith, 122.
196    Naifeh / Smith, 132.
197    Quoted in Naifeh / Smith, 141.
198    Quoted in Naifeh / Smith, 142.
199    Quoted in Naifeh / Smith, 145.
200    Quoted in The Complete Letters, Volume One, 167.
201    Quoted in Naifeh / Smith, 184.
202    Quoted in Naifeh / Smith, 167–168.
203    Quoted in Naifeh / Smith, 207.
204    Letter to Theo, July 1880, The Complete Letters, Volume One, 195.
205    Letter to Theo, July 1880, The Complete Letters, Volume One, 195.
206    Quoted in Naifeh / Smith, 211.
207    Letter to Theo, December 1881, The Complete Letters, Volume One, 290.
208    Letter to Theo, November 1881, The Complete Letters, Volume One, 261.
209    Quoted in Naifeh / Smith, 228.
210    Letter to Theo, July 1880, The Complete Letters, Volume One, 195.

211    Naifeh / Smith, 271.
212    Quoted in Naifeh / Smith, 271.
213    Naifeh / Smith, 271.
214    Quoted in Naifeh / Smith, 265.
215    Letter to Theo, March 3, 1882, The Complete Letters, Volume
       One, 318.
216    Quoted in Naifeh / Smith, 334.
217    Quoted in Naifeh / Smith, 334.
218    Quoted in Naifeh / Smith, 388.
219    Naifeh / Smith, 390.
220    Letter to Theo, The Complete Letters, Volume Two, 372.
221    Letter to his sister, Wilhelmina, Summer or autumn 1887,
       The Complete Letters, Volume Three, 427.
222    Letter to the English painter Levens, August–October 1887,
       The Complete Letters, Volume Two, 513.
223    Schneede, 44.
224    Naifeh / Smith, 617.
225    Naifeh / Smith, 615.
226    Letter to Theo, The Complete Letters, Volume Three, 15.
227    Schneede, 81.
228    Naifeh / Smith, 704.
229    Naifeh / Smith, 708.
230    Quoted in Naifeh / Smith, 712.
231    Letter to Theo, May 3, 1889, The Complete Letters, Volume
       Three, 163.
232    Letter to Theo, May 3, 1889, The Complete Letters, Volume
       Three, 164.
233    Letter to Theo, May 3, 1889, The Complete Letters, Volume
       Three, 166.
234    Letter to Theo and Jo, May 9, 1889, The Complete Letters,
       Volume Three, 170.
235    Letter to Theo, May 22, 1889, The Complete Letters, Volume
       Three, 174.
236    Letter to Theo, September 10, 1889, The Complete Letters,
       Volume Three, 208.
237    Letter to his sister Wilhelmina, late September–early October
       1889, The Complete Letters, Volume Three, 458.
238    Naifeh / Smith, 169–179.
239    Clemenz, 386–391.
240    Quoted in Naifeh / Smith, 858.

241    Letter to Theo, May 20, 1888, The Complete Letters, Volume Two, 570.

242    Letter to Theo, September 20, 1889, The Complete Letters, Volume Three, 218.

243    Schneede, 118.

244    Pablo Picasso, quoted in Gilot / Lake, Life with Picasso, 66–67.

## Chapter 6—Keller

245    Keller, Teacher, 8.

246    Keller, The World I Live In, 113.

247    Keller, Story, 9.

248    Sullivan, quoted in Keller, Story, 389.

249    Keller, Story, 13.

250    Keller, Story, 16.

251    Keller, Story, 21.

252    Sullivan, quoted in Keller, Story, 308.

253    Sullivan, quoted in Keller, Story, 309.

254    Keller, Story, 62.

255    Sullivan, quoted in Keller, Story, 317.

256    Sullivan, quoted in Keller, Story, 316.

257    Sullivan, quoted in Keller, Story, 323.

258    Sullivan, quoted in Keller, Story, 351–352.

259    Keller, Teacher, 83.

260    Keller, Teacher, 112.

261    Sullivan, quoted in Keller, Story, 299.

262    Keller, Story, 83.

263    Keller, Story, 93.

264    Keller, The Three Lives of Helen Keller, 49.

265    Keller, Story, 96.

266    Keller, Teacher, 170.

267    Keller, Story, 101.

268    Keller, Story, 101.

269    John Macy, quoted in Keller, Story, 287–288.

270    Keller, The World I Live In, 92.

271    Keller, Teacher, 156.

272    Keller, Optimism, 47.

273    Keller, Optimism, 37.

274    Waite, Valiant Companions, 197–198.

275    Keller, Story, 140.

276     Keller, Teacher, 129.
277     Keller, Teacher, 169–170.
278     Keller, Teacher, 175.
279     Keller, Teacher, 158.
280     Keller, Teacher, 200.
281     Sullivan, quoted in Keller, Story, 364.

## Chapter 7—Kahlo

282     Genschow, 120.
283     Genschow, 7.
284     Genschow, 16.
285     Kahlo, quoted in Herrera, 48–49.
286     Herrera, 49.
287     Frida in a letter to Alejandro, quoted in Herrera, 51.
288     Henestrosa, quoted in Herrera, 62.
289     Frida in a letter to Alejandro, quoted in Herrera, 69.
290     Genschow, 64.
291     Frida Kahlo, Escrituras, 333.
292     Frida Kahlo, Escrituras, 333.
293     Herrera, 74.
294     Herrera, 199.
295     Frida, quoted in Herrera, 87.
296     Jesús Ríos y Valles, quoted in Herrera, 98.
297     Marnham, 251.
298     Marnham, 253.
299     Marnham, 254.
300     Frida Kahlo in a letter to Leo Eloesser, quoted in Herrera, 131.
301     Rivera, quoted in Herrera, 144.
302     Frida Kahlo in a letter to Abby Aldrich Rockefeller, Escrituras, 148.
303     Frida Kahlo in a letter to her husband, quoted in Herrera, 186.
304     Frida, quoted in Herrera, 396.
305     Frida in a letter to Lucienne Bloch, Escrituras, 206.
306     Frida, quoted in Herrera, 226.
307     Frida in a letter to Carlos Chávez, quoted in Herrera, 288.
308     Frida, quoted in Herrera, 245–246.
309     Frida, quoted in Herrera, 287.
310     Genschow, 50.
311     Picasso, quoted in Herrera, xiii.

312    Frida, quoted in Herrera, 254.
313    Frida in a letter to Sigmund Firestone, Escrituras, 260–261.
314    Frida in a letter to Dr. Leo Eloesser, quoted in Herrera, 309–310.
315    Herrera, 345–346.
316    Frida (2002) starred Salma Hayek in the title role and won two Oscars.
317    Genschow, 125.
318    Genschow, 60.
319    Frida, quoted in Herrera, 395.
320    Marnham, S. 421,
321    Frida, quoted in Herrera, 431.
322    Marnham, 373.

## Chapter 8—Nash

323    Nasar, 39.
324    Nasar, 41.
325    Nasar, 42.
326    Nasar, 45
327    Bott, quoted in Nasar, 45.
328    Quoted in Nasar, 64.
329    Nasar, 68.
330    Nasar, 70.
331    Nasar, 73.
332    Nasar, 73.
333    Nasar, 73.
334    Patrick Bernau, an interview with John Nash: "Die Menschen sind nicht immer rational" in FAZ, May 25, 2015 (Reprint of a 2010 interview).
335    Siegfried, 55.
336    Nasar, 80.
337    Nasar, 86.
338    Rieck, 21.
339    Nasar, 93.
340    Nasar, 15.
341    Nasar, 113.
342    Nasar, 114.
343    Nasar, 124.
344    Nasar, 128.
345    Nasar, 145.

346     Nasar, 156–157.

347     Nasar, 161.

348     Nasar, 242.

349     Nasar, 258.

350     Interview with John Nash, PBS, https://www.pbs.org/wgbh/americanexperience/features/nash-interview/

351     Stuff, Britta, "Manchmal hatte ich Glück," interview with John Nash, in Die Welt, February 9, 2010. https://www.welt.de/welt_print/vermischtes/article6311871/Manchmal-hatte-ich-Glueck.html

352     Nasar, 274. (SEATO is the South East Treaty Organization defense alliance that existed from 1954 to 1977.)

353     Patrick Bernau, interview with John Nash: "Die Menschen sind nicht immer rational," in FAZ, May 25, 2015 (Reprint of a 2010 interview).

354     Nasar, 349.

355     Nasar, 318.

356     Nasar, 332.

357     Nasar, 332.

358     Nasar, 333.

359     Daniel Feenberg, quoted in Nasar, 425.

360     Lloyd S. Shapley, quoted in Nasar, 350.

361     Nash, quoted in Nasar, 353.

362     Nash, quoted in Nasar, 354.

363     Nash, quoted in Nasar, 354.

364     Patrick Bernau, interview with John Nash, "Die Menschen sind nicht immer rational," in FAZ, May 25, 2015 (Reprint of a 2010 interview).

365     Stuff, Britta, "Manchmal hatte ich Glück," interview with John Nash in Die Welt, February 9, 2010. https://www.welt.de/welt_print/vermischtes/article6311871/Manchmal-hatte-ich-Glueck.html

366     Nasar, 379.

367     Scheu, René, interview with Nash in Der Monat https://schweizermonat.ch/keynesianer-lieben-inflation/

368     Siegfried, 52.

369     Siegfried, 52.

## Chapter 9—Charles

370     https://www.therichest.com/celebnetworth/celeb/musician/ray-charles-net-worth/

371     Lydon, 7.

372     Charles / Ritz, 3–4.

373     Charles / Ritz, 11.

374     Charles / Ritz, 15.

375     Charles / Ritz, 15.

376     Charles / Ritz, 25–26.

377     Charles / Ritz, 17.

378     Charles / Ritz, 17.

379     Charles / Ritz, 31.

380     Lydon, 20.

381     Charles / Ritz, 49.

382     Charles / Ritz, 31–32.

383     Charles / Ritz, 5.

384     Charles / Ritz, 31.

385     Lydon, 15.

386     Lydon, 24.

387     Lydon, 25.

388     Charles / Ritz, 41–42.

389     Charles / Ritz, 42.

390     Charles / Ritz, 42.

391     Charles / Ritz, 42.

392     Charles / Ritz, 88.

393     Charles / Ritz, 99.

394     Charles / Ritz, 110.

395     Charles / Ritz, 134.

396     Lydon, 40.

397     Charles / Ritz, 65.

398     Charles / Ritz, 68.

399     Charles / Ritz, 68.

400     Lydon, 34.

401     Charles / Ritz, 74.

402     Charles / Ritz, 75.

403     Charles / Ritz, 76.

404     Lydon, 43.

405     Lydon, 43.

406     Lydon, 43.

407     Charles / Ritz, 44.

408    Lydon, 60.
409    Charles / Ritz, 149.
410    Charles / Ritz, 178.
411    Charles / Ritz, 100.
412    Charles / Ritz, 226.
413    Charles / Ritz, 173.
414    Charles / Ritz, 148.
415    Lydon, 100.
416    Charles / Ritz, 153.
417    Lydon, 115.
418    Ahmet Ertegun, quoted in Lydon, 115.
419    Charles / Ritz, 77.
420    Charles / Ritz, 200.
421    Charles / Ritz, 108–109.
422    Charles / Ritz, 253.
423    Charles / Ritz, 110.
424    Charles / Ritz, 260.
425    Charles / Ritz, 284.
426    Charles / Ritz, 68.
427    Charles / Ritz, 73.
428    Charles / Ritz, 73.
429    Charles / Ritz, 251.
430    Lydon, 165.
431    Lydon, 168.
432    Lydon, 168.
433    Lydon, 168.
434    Lydon, 169.
435    Lydon, 170.
436    Lydon, 192,
437    Billboard, quoted in Lydon, 187.
438    Lydon, 319.
439    Charles / Ritz, 170–171.
440    Lydon, 145.
441    Charles / Ritz, 129.
442    Charles / Ritz, 170.
443    Ruth, quoted in Lydon, 301.
444    Lydon, 299.
445    Lydon, 300.
446    Charles / Ritz, 244–245.
447    Lydon, 151.
448    Charles / Ritz, 229.

449   Charles / Ritz, 206.
450   Charles / Ritz, 246–247.
451   Charles / Ritz, 251.
452   Lydon, 213.
453   Lydon, 213.
454   Lydon, 228.
455   Lydon, 180.
456   Lydon, 214.
457   Charles / Ritz, 210.
458   Charles / Ritz, 209.
459   Lydon, 309.
460   Lydon, 309, 317.
461   Charles / Ritz, 211.
462   Lydon, 346.
463   Ray, quoted in Lydon, 346.
464   Charles / Ritz, 300.
465   Charles / Ritz, 301.
466   Lydon, 333.
467   Lydon, 373–378.
468   Lydon, 384.
469   Charles / Ritz, 321.
470   Charles / Ritz, 188.

## Chapter 10—Brown

471   Hambleton, 214.
472   Brown, 2.
473   Bridget Brown, quoted in Hambleton, 23–24.
474   Hambleton, 23.
475   Brown, 4–5.
476   Brown, 10.
477   Brown, 10–11.
478   Brown, 14.
479   Brown, 15.
480   Brown, 41.
481   Brown, 46.
482   Brown, 46.
483   Brown, 51.
484   Brown, 53–54.
485   Brown, 59.
486   Brown, 86.

487    Brown, 102–103.
488    Brown, 103.
489    Brown, 128.
490    Hambleton, 65.
491    Brown in a letter to Katriona Maguire, quoted in Hambleton, 65–66.
492    Brown, 149.
493    Brown, 136.
494    Brown, 145.
495    Brown, 152–153.
496    Brown, 155.
497    Collis, quoted in Brown, 158–159.
498    Brown, 179.
499    Brown, 180.
500    Hambleton, 75.
501    Hambleton, 75.
502    Hambleton, 78.
503    Hambleton, 79.
504    Brown quoted in Hambleton, 80.
505    Hambleton, 81.
506    Brown quoted in Hambleton, 90.
507    Hambleton, 90.
508    Brown in a letter to Katriona Maguire, quoted in Hambleton, 103.
509    Hambleton, 106.
510    Hambleton, 183.
511    Hambleton, 133.
512    Brown to his brother Seán, quoted in Hambleton, 143.
513    Reviews quoted in Hambleton, 147.
514    Hambleton, 161.
515    Hambleton, 179.
516    Hambleton, 180.
517    Hambleton, 180.
518    Brown to Bill O'Donnell, quoted in Hambleton, 181–182.
519    Hambleton, 190–191.
520    Hambleton, 191–192.

## Chapter 11—Hawking

521    Levy, 6.

522     Hawking, My Brief History, 6. Parts of this chapter also appear in one of my other books The Art of Becoming Famous. Geniuses of Self-Marketing from Albert Einstein to Kim Kardashian.

523     Hawking, My Brief History, 13.

524     Hawking, My Brief History, 24.

525     Hawking, My Brief History, 36.

526     Hawking, My Brief History, 36.

527     Hawking, My Brief History, 46.

528     Levy, 25.

529     Levy, 25.

530     Hawking, My Brief History, 48.

531     Hawking, My Brief History, 49.

532     Hawking, My Brief History, 37.

533     Hawking, My Brief History, 122.

534     Hawking, My Brief History, 123.

535     White / Gribbin, 164–165.

536     Hawking, Brief Answers, 15.

537     Hawking, Brief Answers, 19.

538     Levy, 152.

539     Hawking, My Brief History, 122.

540     Hawking, My Brief History, 42.

541     White / Gribbin, 132–133.

542     Hawking, Brief Answers, 17.

543     Levy, 93.

544     Levy, 93.

545     White / Gribbin, 161.

546     White / Gribbin, 203.

547     White / Gribbin, 204.

548     White / Gribbin, 206.

549     Hawking, My Brief History, 92.

550     Hawking, My Brief History, 93.

551     White / Gribbin, 227.

552     White / Gribbin, S. 259.

553     Hawking, My Brief History, 93.

554     White / Gribbin, 240.

555     Hawking, My Brief History, 97.

556     Hawking, My Brief History, 97–98.

557     Hawking, My Brief History, 98.

558     Hawking, My Brief History, 99.

559     Peter Guzzardi, quoted in White/Gribbin, 243.

560   Hawking, My Brief History, 99.

561   White / Gribbin, 244.

562   White / Gribbin, 245.

563   Hawking, quoted in White/Gribbin, 245.

564   Levy, 136.

565   White / Gribbin, 250.

566   Hawking, Brief Answers, 81.

567   Hawking, Brief Answers, 147.

568   Levy, 123.

569   Hawking, Brief Answers, 141.

570   Hawking, My Brief History, 98.

571   Levy, 114–115.

572   Levy, 115.

573   Hawking, My Brief History, 125–126.

## Chapter 12—Wonder

574   Elton John, quoted in *Rolling Stone,* "100 Greatest Artists"
      *(December 3, 2010).*

575   Ribowsky, 10.

576   Ribowsky, 13–14.

577   Ribowsky, 13.

578   Ribowsky, 15.

579   Wonder, quoted in Davis, 16.

580   Bobby Rogers, quoted in Ribowsky, 41–42.

581   Ribowsky, 45.

582   Berry Gordy, quoted in Ribowsky, 46.

583   Ribowsky, 47–48.

584   Wonder, quoted in Ribowsky, 111.

585   Davis, 38.

586   Ribowsky, 126–127.

587   Davis, 46.

588   Gordi, quoted in Ribowsky, 131.

589   Ribowsky, 171.

590   Davis, 68.

591   Wonder, quoted in Davis, 70.

592   Ribowsky, 195.

593   Ribowsky, 208–209.

594   Ribowsky, 257.

595   Interview with *The Guardian,* 1972 https://www.theguardian.
      com/music/2013/oct/30/stevie-wonder-rocks-backpages-

interview-1972.

596    Ribowsky, 252.

597    Orth, "Stevie, the Wonder Man" in Newsweek, October 28, 1974, 59–62.

598    "Black, Blind and on Top of Pop." Time, April 8, 1974, 51–52.

599    Wonder, quoted in Davies, 128.

600    Ribowsky, 269.

601    Davis, 100.

602    Davis, 190.

603    Davis, 204.

604    Davis, 176.

605    Syreeta Wright, quoted in Davis, 124.

606    Jean Carn, quoted in Davis, 177.

607    Ribowsky, 262.

608    Quoted in Davies, 192.

609    Wonder quoted in Ribowsky, 247.

610    Wonder, quoted in Davies, 120.

## Chapter 13—Bocelli

611    Felix, 14.

612    Felix, 17.

613    Bocelli's mother, quoted in Felix, 15–17.

614    Bocelli's mother, quoted in Felix, 17.

615    Bocelli, 47.

616    Bocelli, 48.

617    Bocelli, 49.

618    Bocelli, quoted in Felix, 27.

619    Bocelli, 87. In his autobiography, Bocelli writes about himself in the third person and refers to himself as "Amos." He explains this by saying that in some respects he has changed a lot since then: "To speak of him as 'me' somehow feels false, something I'd be embarrassed to do." Bocelli, x.

620    Bocelli, 86.

621    Bocelli, quoted in Felix, 20.

622    Bocelli, quoted in Felix, 28.

623    Bocelli, 23–24.

624    Bocelli, quoted in Felix, 48–49.

625    Bocelli, quoted in Felix, 49.

626    Bocelli, 152.

627    Bocelli, 153.

628    Bocelli, 178.
629    Bocelli, 178.
630    Bocelli, 180.
631    Bettarini, quoted in Bocelli, 181.
632    Bocelli, 182.
633    Felix, 81.
634    Pavarotti, quoted in Felix, 83.
635    Bocelli, 185.
636    Bocelli, 189.
637    Bocelli, 193.
638    Torpedine, quoted in Bocelli, 203.
639    Bocelli, 205.
640    Bocelli, 209.
641    Bocelli, 211.
642    Corelli, quoted in Bocelli, 212.
643    Bocelli, 212.
644    Bocelli, 213.
645    Bocelli, 214.
646    Felix, 87.
647    Bocelli, 228.
648    Felix, 80.
649    Bocelli, 235.
650    Bocelli, quoted in Felix, 145–146.
651    Felix, 146.
652    Felix, 145.
653    Bocelli, quoted in Felix, 146.
654    Felix, 147.
655    Bocelli, quoted in Felix, 157.
656    https://ssd.jpl.nasa.gov/sbdb.cgi?sstr=Andreabocelli
657    Bocelli, quoted in Felix, 188.
658    http://www.planet-interview.de/interviews/andrea-bocelli/34806/
659    Ana Maria Martinez, quoted in Felix, 189.

## Chapter 14—Quasthoff

660    Quasthoff, 39.
661    Quasthoff, 39.
662    Quasthoff, 42.
663    Quasthoff, 43.
664    Quasthoff, 55.

665     Michael Quasthoff, 30.

666     Quasthoff, 57.

667     Quasthoff, 60.

668     Quasthoff, 65.

669     Quasthoff, quoted in Lubow, A Transcendent Voice.

670     Quasthoff, 79.

671     Quasthoff, 90.

672     Corinne Ullrich, "Gefühle sind ja in uns allen," in Die Welt, February 17, 2006.

673     Michael Quasthoff, 56.

674     Michael Quasthoff, 56.

675     Süddeutsche Zeitung, quoted in Quasthoff, 96–97.

676     Bunte, quoted in Quasthoff, 97–98.

677     Michael Quasthoff, 71.

678     Quasthoff, 101.

679     Quasthoff, 103.

680     Quasthoff, 104.

681     Quasthoff, 105.

682     Lubow, A Transcendent Voice.

683     Quasthoff, quoted in Lubow, A Transcendent Voice.

684     Quasthoff, 108.

685     Quasthoff, 110.

686     Quasthoff, 119.

687     Quasthoff, 117.

688     Quasthoff, quoted in Lubow, A Transcendent Voice.

689     Quasthoff, 143.

690     Simon Rattle, quoted in Michael Quasthoff, 89.

691     FAZ, quoted in Quasthoff, 140.

692     Fiona Maddocks, "Thomas Quasthoff Speaks Very Frankly," Adante. Everything classical, February 25, 2005, archived at http://web.archive.org/web/20050305114834/http://www.andante.com/article/article.cfm?id=25239

693     Quasthoff, 147.

694     Thomas Quasthoff, "Der Jazz ist jetzt meine Welt," in Augsburger Allgemeine, May 8, 2018.

695     Quasthoff, 148.

696     Corinne Ullrich, "Gefühle sind ja in uns allen," in Die Welt, February 17, 2006

697     Michael Quasthoff, 160.

698     Corinne Ullrich, "Gefühle sind ja in uns allen," in Die Welt, February 17, 2006.

699    Thomas Quasthoff, "Der Jazz ist jetzt meine Welt," in Augsburger Allgemeine, May 8, 2018.

700    An interview with Thomas Quasthoff, "Meine Seele war verletzt," in Tagesspiegel, January 5, 2020.

701    Quasthoff, quoted in "Thomas Quasthoff Leaves The Stage," npr, January 12, 2012, archived at https://www.npr.org/sections/deceptivecadence/2012/01/11/145049483/thomas-quasthoff-leaves-the-stage?t=1616066775441.

702    "Quasthoff nimmt Abschied," in Deutsche Welle, January 27, 2012.

703    "Jazz statt Klassik: Thomas Quasthoff will konsequent bleiben," in Neue Musikzeitung, May 15, 2018.

704    An interview with Thomas Quasthoff, "Meine Seele war verletzt," in Tagesspiegel, January 5, 2020.

705    "Jazz statt Klassik: Thomas Quasthoff will konsequent bleiben," Neue Musikzeitung, May 15, 2018.

706    Quasthoff, 204.

707    Quasthoff, 205.

708    Schoeck, 285.

709    Schoeck, 285.

710    Schoeck, 285.

711    Quasthoff, 33.

712    Ralph Heringlehner, "Thomas Quasthoff über Bildungsbürger, Kritiker und Behinderungen," Mainpost, March 10, 2015.

713    Quasthoff, quoted in Lubow, A Transcendent Voice.

## Chapter 15—Fox

714    Fox, Lucky Man, 38.

715    Fox, Lucky Man, 48.

716    Fox, Lucky Man, 45.

717    Fox, Lucky Man, 67.

718    Fox, Lucky Man, 59.

719    Fox, Lucky Man, 62.

720    Fox, Lucky Man, 62.

721    Fox, Lucky Man, 63.

722    Fox, No Time, 110.

723    Fox, No Time, 110.

724    Fox, Lucky Man, 84–85.

725    Fox, Lucky Man, 109–110.

726   Fox, Lucky Man, 110.
727   Fox, Lucky Man, 113.
728   Fox, Lucky Man, 120.
729   Fox, Lucky Man, 178.
730   Fox, Lucky Man, 179.
731   Fox, Lucky Man, 189.
732   Fox, Lucky Man, 193.
733   Fox, Lucky Man, 194.
734   Fox, Lucky Man, 256.
735   Fox, Lucky Man, 266.
736   Fox, Lucky Man, 267.
737   Ali, quoted in Fox, Lucky Man, 285.
738   Fox, Lucky Man, 297.
739   Fox, Always Looking Up, 15.
740   Fox, Always Looking Up, 17.
741   Fox, Always Looking Up, 30–31.
742   Fox, Always Looking Up, 56.
743   Fox, Always Looking Up, 89.
744   Fox, Always Looking Up, 27.
745   Fox, Always Looking Up, 137.
746   Fox, Always Looking Up, 148.
747   Fox, Always Looking Up, 150.
748   Fox, No Time Like the Future, 33.
749   Fox, No Time Like the Future, 27.
750   Fox, No Time Like the Future, 227.
751   Fox, No Time Like the Future, 231.

## Chapter 16—Weihenmayer

752   Quoted in Weihenmayer, Touch the Top, 312.
753   Weihenmayer in an interview with the author, December 21, 2020.
754   Time, June 18, 2001.
755   Weihenmayer, No Barriers, 16.
756   Weihenmayer, No Barriers, 15.
757   Weihenmayer in an interview with the author, December 21, 2020.
758   Weihenmayer, Touch the Top, 10.
759   Weihenmayer, Touch the Top, 11.
760   Quoted in Weihenmayer, Touch the Top, 17.
761   Quoted in Weihenmayer, Touch the Top, 19–20.

762    Weihenmayer, Touch the Top, 45.
763    Weihenmayer, Touch the Top, 47.
764    Quoted in Weihenmayer, Touch the Top, 64.
765    Weihenmayer, Touch the Top, 96–97.
766    Weihenmayer, Touch the Top, 155.
767    Weihenmayer, Touch the Top, 159.
768    Weihenmayer, Touch the Top, 186.
769    Weihenmayer, Touch the Top, 205.
770    Interview with Erik Weihenmayer, "Ein Blinder auf dem Mount Everest" in Der Spiegel, December 20, 2001.
771    Weihenmayer, Touch the Top, 272.
772    Weihenmayer in an interview with the author, December 21, 2020.
773    Weihenmayer, Touch the Top, 289.
774    Weihenmayer, Touch the Top, 289.
775    Weihenmayer, Touch the Top, 293.
776    Weihenmayer, Touch the Top, 297.
777    Weihenmayer, Touch the Top, 309.
778    Weihenmayer in an interview with the author, December 21, 2020.
779    Interview with Erik Weihenmayer, "Ein Blinder auf dem Mount Everest" in Der Spiegel, December 20, 2001.
780    Interview with Erik Weihenmayer, "Ein Blinder auf dem Mount Everest" in Der Spiegel, December 20, 2001.
781    Blindsight, 2006.
782    Weihenmayer, No Barriers, 394.
783    Weihenmayer, No Barriers, 432–433.
784    Weihenmayer, No Barriers, 434.
785    Weihenmayer, No Barriers, 435.
786    Weihenmayer, No Barriers, 437.
787    https://nobarriersusa.org/
788    Weihenmayer in an interview with the author, December 21, 2020.
789    Weihenmayer in an interview with the author, December 21, 2020.
790    Weihenmayer in an interview with the author, December 21, 2020.
791    Weihenmayer in an interview with the author, December 21, 2020.

## Chapter 17—Runyan

792    Runyan, 3.
793    Runyan, 7.
794    Runyan, 6.
795    Runyan, 32.
796    Runyan, 52.
797    Runyan, 57.
798    Runyan, 65.
799    Runyan, 72.
800    Runyan, 69.
801    https://limitlesspursuits.com/land/marathon-running/marla-runyan-americas-inspirational-runner/
802    Runyan, 69.
803    Runyan, 69.
804    Runyan, 107.
805    Runyan, 84.
806    Runyan, 80.
807    Runyan, 80.
808    Runyan, 80.
809    Runyan, 83.
810    Runyan, 83.
811    Runyan, 121.
812    Runyan, 121.
813    Runyan, 125.
814    Locke / Latham, Goal Setting Theory, 5.
815    Locke / Latham, Goal Setting Theory, 5.
816    https://limitlesspursuits.com/land/marathon-running/marla-runyan-americas-inspirational-runner/
817    Runyan, 130–131.
818    Runyan, 135.
819    Kahn, 219.
820    Runyan, 135.
821    Runyan, 194.
822    Runyan, 188.
823    Runyan, 209.

824    Runyan, 244.
825    Runyan, 261.
826    https://limitlesspursuits.com/land/marathon-running/marla-runyan-americas-inspirational-runner/

827    https://limitlesspursuits.com/land/marathon-running/
marla-runyan-americas-inspirational-runner/

828    https://limitlesspursuits.com/land/marathon-running/
marla-runyan-americas-inspirational-runner/

829    Runyan, 298.

## Chapter 18—König

830    Riebsamen, "Der Popstar unter den deutschen Galeristen,"
in FAZ, September 16, 2019.

831    Riebsamen, "Der Popstar unter den deutschen Galeristen,"
in FAZ, September 16, 2019.

832    Tuma, interview with Johann König, "Es ist einiges
schiefgegangen," in Handelsblatt, January 28, 2021.

833    Kikol, "Der ungehorsame Galerist," in Kunstforum
International, Vol. 262.

834    Plag, "Deutschlands modischster Galerist," in FAZ, October
13, 2018.

835    König / Schreiber, 88–89.

836    König in an interview with the author, January 31, 2021.

837    König / Schreiber, 139.

838    König in an interview with the author, January 31, 2021.

839    Tuma, interview with Johann König, "Es ist einiges
schiefgegangen," in Handelsblatt, January 28, 2021.

840    Tuma, interview with Johann König, "Es ist einiges
schiefgegangen," in Handelsblatt, January 28, 2021.

841    Späth, interview with galerist Johann König, "Das ist
scheinheilig," in Wirtschaftswoche, January 10, 2020.

842    Tuma, interview with Johann König, "Es ist einiges
schiefgegangen," in Handelsblatt, January 28, 2021.

843    As König revealed during an interview with the author,
January 31, 2021.

844    Interview with Johann König, "Ich hatte vergessen, wie
meine Eltern aussahen," in Tagesspiegel, April 25, 2018.

845    König / Schreiber, 46–47.

846    Interview with Johann König, "Ich hatte vergessen, wie
meine Eltern aussahen," in Tagesspiegel, April 25, 2018.

847    König / Schreiber, 55.

848    König / Schreiber, 68.

849    König / Schreiber, 82.

850    Walton, 47.

851     König / Schreiber, 83.

852     König in an interview with the author, January 31, 2021.

853     König / Schreiber, 94.

854     König / Schreiber, 84.

855     König / Schreiber, 85.

856     Stange, "An die Wand gefahren," in Tagesspiegel, October 19, 2002.

857     König / Schreiber, 110.

858     König / Schreiber, 110–111.

859     König in an interview with the author, January 31, 2021.

860     König / Schreiber, 127.

861     Timm, "Johann König. Der Blick des Blinden," in Zeit No. 24/2019, June 9, 2019.

862     Kikol, "Der ungehorsame Galerist," in Kunstforum International, Vol. 262.

863     Kobel, interview with Johann König in artmagazine, June 15, 2020.

864     Interview with Johann König, "Ich hatte vergessen, wie meine Eltern aussahen," in Tagesspiegel, April 25, 2018.

865     Plag, "Deutschlands modischster Galerist," in FAZ, October 13, 2018.

866     König / Schreiber, 112–113.

867     König in an interview with the author, January 31, 2021.

868     Interview with Johann König, "Ich hatte vergessen, wie meine Eltern aussahen," in Tagesspiegel, April 25, 2018.

## Chapter 19—Vujicic

869     Vujicic, Be the Hands and Feet, 165.

870     Vujicic, Life Without Limits, 52.

871     Vujicic, Be the Hands and Feet, 153.

872     Vujicic, Be the Hands and Feet, 165.

873     Vujicic, Be the Hands and Feet, 64.

874     Boris Vujicic, Raising the Perfectly Imperfect Child, 17,

875     Boris Vujicic, Raising the Perfectly Imperfect Child, 18.

876     Boris Vujicic, Raising the Perfectly Imperfect Child, 18–19.

877     Boris Vujicic, Raising the Perfectly Imperfect Child, 22.

878     Boris Vujicic, Raising the Perfectly Imperfect Child, 48.

879     Boris Vujicic, Raising the Perfectly Imperfect Child, 37.

880     Boris Vujicic, Raising the Perfectly Imperfect Child, 57.

881     Vujicic, Life Without Limits, 12.

882    Boris Vujicic, Raising the Perfectly Imperfect Child, 80.
883    Boris Vujicic, Raising the Perfectly Imperfect Child, 92.
884    Boris Vujicic, Raising the Perfectly Imperfect Child, 92.
885    Vujicic, Life Without Limits, 17.
886    Vujicic, Life Without Limits, 48–49.
887    Vujicic, Life Without Limits, 112–114.
888    Vujicic, Life Without Limits, 115.
889    Vujicic, Life Without Limits, 143–144.
890    Vujicic, Life Without Limits, 144.
891    Vujicic, Life Without Limits, 145.
892    Vujicic, Life Without Limits, 20–21.
893    Vujicic, Life Without Limits, 19.
894    Vujicic, Be the Hands and Feet, 13.
895    Vujicic, Life Without Limits, 131.
896    Vujicic, Life Without Limits, 131.
897    Vujicic, Life Without Limits, 188.
898    Vujicic, Unstoppable, 77.
899    Vujicic, Life Without Limits, 190.
900    Vujicic, Life Without Limits, 178.
901    Vujicic, Life Without Limits, 47.
902    Vujicic, Life Without Limits, 44.
903    Vujicic, Life Without Limits, 134.
904    Vujicic, Life Without Limits, 24.
905    Vujicic, Life Without Limits, 226–227.
906    Vujicic, Love Without Limits, 13.
907    Vujicic, Love Without Limits, 20–24.
908    He tells the story of how he met his dream woman in Chapter 3 (49) in Vujicic, Unstoppable.
909    Vujicic, Be the Hands and Feet, 77.
910    Vujicic, Love Without Limits, 67.
911    Boris Vujicic, Raising the Perfectly Imperfect Child, 195.
912    Boris Vujicic, Raising the Perfectly Imperfect Child, 197.
913    Vujicic, Be the Hands and Feet, 62.
914    Vujicic, Be the Hands and Feet, 25.
915    Vujicic, Be the Hands and Feet, 26.
916    Vujicic, Be the Hands and Feet, 26.
917    Vujicic, Unstoppable, 227.
918    Boris Vujicic, Raising the Perfectly Imperfect Child, 10.

## Chapter 20—Klieser

919     Klieser, 27.

920     Lauer, "Felix Klieser, der Ausnahme-Hornist ohne Arme," in Die Welt, December 25, 2011.

921     Klieser, 20.

922     Klieser, 25.

923     Klieser, 25.

924     An interview with Felix Klieser in Classicpoint.ne. Das Klassikportal, June 1, 2019.

925     Klieser, 46.

926     Klieser, 65.

927     Klieser, 72.

928     Klieser, 73.

929     Interview with Felix Klieser in Classicpoint.ne. Das Klassikportal, June 1, 2019.

930     Marcus Tackenberg, "Felix Klieser spielt Horn – ohne Arme. 'Mein Lehrer hat nicht an mich geglaubt'," in noz.de, May 2, 2015.

931     Klieser in an interview with the author, January 4, 2021.

932     Klieser, 107.

933     Klieser, 89.

934     Klieser, 81.

935     "Klang hat viel mit Vorstellung zu tun," in Klassik.com, September 20, 1993.

936     Klieser in an interview with the author, January 4, 2021.

937     Klieser, 10.

938     Interview with Felix Klieser, "Aber ich wollte eben unbedingt...," in Lausitzer Rundschau, March 20, 2017.

939     Interview with Felix Klieser, "Aber ich wollte eben unbedingt...," in Lausitzer Rundschau, March 20, 2017.

940     An interview with Felix Klieser in Classicpoint.ne. Das Klassikportal, June 1, 2019.

941     Marcus Tackenberg, "Felix Klieser spielt Horn – ohne Arme. 'Mein Lehrer hat nicht an mich geglaubt'," in noz.de, May 2, 2015.

942     Klieser, 10.

943     Klieser, 18.

944     Klieser, 38–39.

945     Klieser, 41.

946     Kathrin Hasselbeck, an interview with Felix Klieser, "Musik soll das Leben verschönern," Bayerischer Rundfunk Klassik, December 15, 2017.

947     Klieser, 154.
948     Klieser, 127.
949     Klieser, 163.
950     Klieser in an interview with the author, January 4, 2021.
951     Klieser, 106.
952     Klieser in an interview with the author, January 4, 2021.